To George,

WHAD'YA

Best wishes,

Michael Feldman

KNOW?

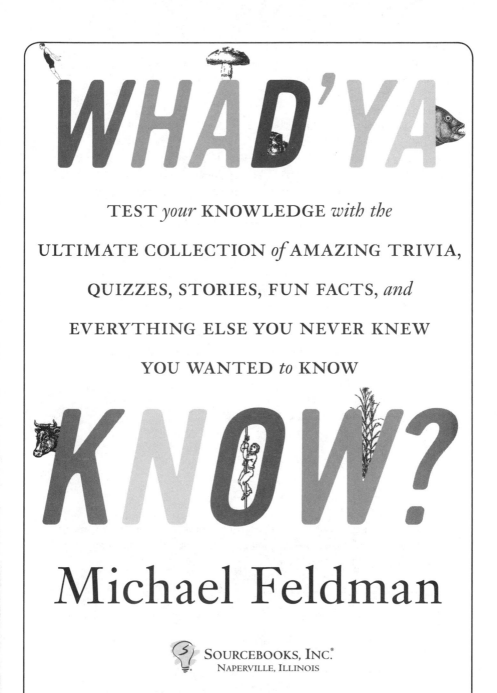

WHAD'YA

TEST *your* KNOWLEDGE *with the*

ULTIMATE COLLECTION *of* AMAZING TRIVIA,

QUIZZES, STORIES, FUN FACTS, *and*

EVERYTHING ELSE YOU NEVER KNEW

YOU WANTED *to* KNOW

KNOW?

Michael Feldman

SOURCEBOOKS, INC.®
NAPERVILLE, ILLINOIS

Cartoons © John Sieger
Image on page 6 © Michael Shaw
Photo on page 129 © Eat Door
Photo on page 165 © Andy Manis, *Washington Post*
Images on pages 247, 344, 361, 405 © Nora Feldman
Thanks to Lyle Anderson for assorted snapshots and refrigerator magnets.

Published by Sourcebooks, Inc.
P.O. Box 4410, Naperville, Illinois 60567-4410
(630) 961-3900
Fax: (630) 961-2168
www.sourcebooks.com

Library of Congress Cataloging-in-Publication Data
Feldman, Michael
  Whad'ya know? : test your knowledge with the ultimate collection of amazing trivia, quizzes, stories, fun facts, and everything else you never knew you
wanted to know / Michael Feldman.
     p. cm.
 1. American wit and humor. 2. Questions and answers. I. Title.
PN6162.F3915 2009
818'.5402—dc22
                              2009003935

Printed and bound in the United States of America
DR 10 9 8 7 6 5 4 3 2 1

For Ellie and Nora—

—lud!

CONTENTS

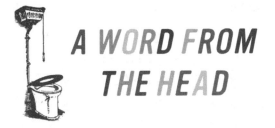

A WORD FROM
THE HEAD

It was the place you could drag the phone into—back when our number was still Custer 3-6909—to better hear Mary Lou Bromberg hint at the first of many psychological mysteries of the female I would encounter. Where asylum could be sought after taunting Arthur to the point of attack, recoiling behind the toilet as the solid old door with the only lock in the house flexed and heaved as if to splinter. Where, engrossed in "Lady Pearl Divers of Tahiti," the latest *National Geographic* soft porn, Dad would inevitably blow the mood entirely by trumpeting, "Did you fall in?" Reading matter always available tank top—Dad's *I, the Jury* or one Zane Grey or another; Clayton's *Gray's Anatomy*, which had some possibilities, albeit in cross section; Howard's completely useless torts, which disabused me of any notion of following him into law early on. The only bathroom (and the only room in the house remodeled semi-professionally, plumbing being beyond Dad's wide-ranging home repair instincts) was the Sanctum Santorum, the olly olly oxen free, phone booth, and lending library of 2718 N. 58th Street, Milwaukee. It was an historic site: Dad taught me how to pee in there by shredding and sinking his Winstons, and there my early childhood development was stunted, when, having to share a tub with Arthur, he told me the specks floating in the water were other people's poops and that if you sat in the tub while it was draining, you would be sucked through the pipes all the way to Jones Island, where, instead of donkeys, little Milwaukee boys became Milorganite, the rich and famous fertilizer...made of PEOPLE!

Our water closet in the twenty-first century doesn't have the same aura—certainly not the one Dad used to give ours to cries of "Bombs over Tokyo"—mainly because the girls are always in it, crimping, pressing, and blowing over Nas on the shower tunes. No-man's land. I'm not Jesus, and I can't throw the money changers out of the temple, so I slip in at odd hours, usually to, "Dad! Are you going to be in there long?" It's hard on a former boy who sang the Beach Boys song as "In My Bathroom" and who knew that when the Beatles said "There's a Place" this was it, because it's all there was. My bedroom was a cell I shared with Arthur, who used to come up from the basement in the middle of the night to go to bed, flip on the big light, and file his toes with his sweat socks on the edge of his bed, oblivious to my teeny cries and curses. The only other semiprivate room in the house was Howard's sports central in the basement, with his collections of cards, autographs, statistics, and collated *Sports Illustrateds*, and the mimeo machine which put out the "Sports Flash" for nobody in particular. Arthur ruled the shop, next door, with an iron hand, and after Jeffrey Dahmer, another Milwaukee boy who loved tools, I'm glad I never tried to slip in there between saw bursts.

And so, to the private place that all of us need and to all of us who need it, I dedicate the *Whad'Ya Know?* bathroom reader. May it help you rise above the pounding on the door and the chaos that passes for family life, even if for a few minutes, while you perform what Mom used to call your ablutions. Here's wishing you comic relief,

—*Michael Feldman*

WHAD'YA KNOW

ABOUT

PEOPLE?

STATISTICS DON'T LIE... OR DO THEY?

I know, we're people, not statistics—but can't we be both? Isn't it somehow reassuring to know that your every habit, behavior, and taste is smack dab in the middle of the mean of everybody else's in your demographic? We are, after all, information that walks, every man Jack and Lady Jane an Encyclopædia (Your Name Here)-ica. Comes a stiff breeze, the pages flip open to reveal:

53 percent of American workers feel they work "with a bunch of monkeys." What the monkeys think, we don't know.

77 million American workers say they are burned out. There are 100 million American workers.

Psychologists are much more satisfied with their jobs than roofers.

Over half of all office workers intentionally dress like their bosses.

Only 1 woman out of 100 wears 4-inch heels or better every day, but God bless her.

3 out of 4 cell phone users store texts they prefer others never see; about 1 in 3 have pictures that are even worse.

54 percent of Mexican workers are emotionally invested in their jobs; 29 percent of Americans and only 3 percent of Japanese workers are.

While 91 percent of adults pick their noses, only 1 in 12 eat it.

1 American in 3 says lack of intimacy is the reason for lack of intimacy.

85 percent of all men would not enjoy a nice manicure.

83 percent have steered with their knees.

Statistically, everyone but women are getting fatter.

2 out of 3 are with the man of their dreams.

Out of 117 small cities, La Crosse, WI, is 110th in stress.

Casual Fridays cause individual office workers to burn an additional 25 calories.

More Americans experience creative thinking in their cars than their beds.

In a crowd of 100 Americans, 7 can play the clarinet and 11 the organ.

The average American man's head is a 7¼.

1 in 3 women is traumatized buying a swimming suit.

65 percent of Americans make an effort to eat vegetables in the cabbage family.

CONFESSIONS OF A WORKAVOIDIC

I'm a workavoidic, the flip side of the workaholic coin. Homer Simpson is my patron saint. Work has always been a priority for me, just a low one. In order to work at all, I have to trick myself into thinking it's a game, which goes back to my first job at Auto Parts and Service, Inc., where I spent the best part of a working day hiding from the muffler moguls in the tailpipe bin. Needless to say, by the end of the day I was exhausted.

Workavoidics are the paranoids of physical effort. We think people are out to get us—to work. And what's worse, for them. Workavoidics are idealistic: the notion of working for "superiors" flies in the face of our democratic ideals. It's not that we're too good to work, it's that we're not good enough. Years ago a guidance counselor (who, I realize now, was a closet workavoidic) diagnosed me as a perfectionist unable to deal with the shoddy work I

produced. Torn with inner conflict, I feel compelled to take the afternoon off and go home to snake the toilet. Beehives of activity give me
hives. When I see a guy leaning on a shovel, I want to go over, prop
him up with a two-by-four, and shake his hand. George W. Bush had
the right idea: five hours a day in the saddle, tops—any more and you
end up being tied to it. I've thought about forming a support group
for workavoidics, but it hardly seems worth the effort. Instead I've
put together some tips for fence-sitters who really would like to be
sloughing off but haven't gotten around to it. I call these The Four
Shortcuts:

1. Delegate authority. All of it, if possible.

2. Avoid pressing concerns unless your pants are involved.

3. Use your time efficiently. Take a working lunch and eat as much
   paperwork as possible. Keep in mind the paperless workplace is
   a stepping-stone to the workless workplace.

4. If you must work, remember that work equals force times distance: take a little work and make it go a long way.

Remember, no one ever got rich through hard work. If you insist
on working hard, you do so at your own economic peril.

"Love the gravitas, Feldman."

ZIPPING POINTS

We may have reached the zipping point for **tipping point**, and it seems that nobody has **ramped up** for a while now, or **thought out of the box**, although far too many continue to **try to wrap their minds around things**. Here are some of the newest saws for your workplace tool chest:

1. **"Going forward"**: this never happened. Time to **"loop in"** and get back to where you once belonged, Loretta.

2. The BBC reports **"idea showers"** have replaced **"brain storming"** in the UK, to avoid defaming epileptics. **"Brain dump"** is still OK.

3. **"Incentivize"** is the latest **"-ize,"** in the line of **"prioritize,"** **"commoditize," "modularize," "operationalize,"** and **"Blackberryize."**

4. **"Low hanging fruit,"** an easily obtainable prize, has never hung lower.

5. **"Manage expectations"**: as in lower them.

6. **"Go Offline"**: to take out of earshot of the cubicles.

7. **"Game changer"**: everywhere this past political season, and hardly ever the case. **"Mission critical"** may have already replaced it.

8. "**JAMPoJ**": "Just another mediocre piece of junk," a.k.a. product.

9. To officially define reality is to **"disambiguate."** There doesn't seem to be an "ambiguate," but maybe there should be.

10. **"Eating your own dog food"** has **gained traction**, along with the Indiana Jones–inspired **"nuking the fridge,"** to introduce a gross improbability (e.g., surviving a nuclear blast in a fridge), replacing **"jump the shark."**

Honorable Mention: nudge, Wikinomics, long tails, econs, Homers, choice architecture, thin slicing, the locked door, delayering, knowledge acquisition, dark marketing, and Warren Harding errors.

Retired: siloing, outsourcing, tipping point, digitization, get your game on, ramping up, nanomanaging, re-architecture, and airball.

AGING DISCOUNTED

It should have dawned on me when Helen Mirren started looking really (I mean *really*) good. There are clues if we choose to see them, or if we can without remembering where we put our trifocals. After the Atlanta Bread incident, my Tara was forever gone with the wind: Ellie and I stopped for an après behind-the-wheel turkey on wheat and three-juice smoothie when she flipped the little "10% Senior Discount" counter sign toward me with an "Ask for it!" You can throw away the AARP mailings, but you can't evade Ellie's insistence on saving you 95 cents for the simple accomplishment of having lived this long (this break comes to 1.6666 cents per annual ring, and, like everything else, drops with time.) "You don't even look 50 to me," the girl said as she rang me up, after graciously shushing my attempt at a youthful-sounding expletive. But it does: **It bites**. "She didn't even ID you," Ellie said.

I've never flaunted my over-50 advantage—never taken an Early Bird special, and I could have, or an active Elder Hostel safari to Kenya or Shambala, never once the $2.00 off at SuperCuts, the 10 percent at the Johnson Creek Factory Outlets (including, oddly enough, the Motherhood Maternity shop—*Motherhood Maturity?*), or, sadly, 10 cents off the Dollar Shop. When I ask for the senior discount at the Dollar Shop, please have my daughter come and get me. Until such time, should I, in a whimsical senior moment, ship out on the Alaska Bay Glacier Cruise, I insist on paying full price *plus*; ditto, Carnival, Celebrity, Princess, Holland America, and/or Disney. Call it a right of passage.

A buck saved at Noah's Ark in the Dells is not worth the humiliation of asking for it, and moot, anyway, since my back is not up for the Great Tsunami; but some savings, like the 15 percent the first Wednesday of the month at the Shopko pharmacy, are worth keeping in mind. I have to say PetMeds is a disappointment with their 5 percent off figured in dog years, but that may be to discourage dog food consumption in my demographic. USA Florists sympathetically lops 20 percent off condolence bouquets each time a cohort bites the dust, which can add up. Should you at some point require an amplified phone, neck brace magnifier (I hear Dylan has one where his harmonica used to be), clock that projects the time on the ceiling like the Batman alert, hydraulic toilet ejection seat, or WanderGuard, SeniorShops.com will ease your bewilderment a measly 5 percent with coupon code SD506. You're better off squinting and peeing the bed with dignity.

☞ 20-somethings say life is good; 50-somethings say life is way good.

☞ 43 percent of 50+-year-olds are comfortable, second only to the 45 percent of 60+-year-olds who are.

☞ Of all workers, only those over 50 make enough.

☞ Half to three-quarters of those over 55 are sexually active; none can account for the variance.

☞ 60 percent of Americans over 60 hope for jury duty.

☞ At bingo games, women outnumber men 3 to 1.

YOU SHOULD LIVE SO LONG!

Longevity isn't what it used to be. The Bible says that before the flood man lived to an average age of 912 years, 910 if he smoked. After the flood, man's stock plummeted to 317, showing the degree to which the Creator had tired of His Creation. Secular investigation reveals that prehistoric man lived to age eighteen and died from a blow to the head. Today, thanks largely to improved nutrition, an eighteen-year-old is merely stunned by a blow to the head. Since that time, life spans have crept upward. Though they crammed in a lot of living, Vikings were pretty much plundered out by twenty-three. In the Middle Ages, ironically, very few people were, since thirty was pushing it. Life expectancy in New England in 1789 was 35.5 years, a fact not lost on the Founding Fathers, who set the minimum age for the presidency at thirty-five to promote turnover.

Statistically, Scandinavians live longer than anyone except Frenchwomen. Americans live longest in the states with the fewest distractions: South Dakota, Minnesota, Iowa, Kansas, and, the winner in the long run, Nebraska, where a woman who isn't seventy-four isn't trying. On the other hand, a man in Arkansas is as good as dead.

Americans, it turns out, could live a year longer if they moved to Canada, but would find magazines slightly higher. Clergymen outlive athletes, but college graduates die like everybody else. The average married man lives 2,005 days longer than his unmarried counterpart, and would trade them all to be single again. According to Metropolitan Life, life insurance policyholders live two-and-a-half years longer than the uninsured, or, as fate would have it, nearly exactly the time it takes to earn the premiums.

Curiously, the best source for finding out who lives how long where is the CIA *World Factbook*, which reveals an Andorran woman can count on 86.23 years in the happy little tax haven of the Pyrenees, with a woman from Macao nipping at her heels at 85¼. Women tend to bunch up at 85-ish in Japan, San Marino, Singapore, and Hong Kong, while their husbands tend to check out seven to ten years earlier, like everywhere else. Canadians are rewarded with two extra years for toughing it out north of North Dakota, but there is a three-year life penalty to insure turnover in Acapulco. People in the United Arab Emirates live four years longer than Egyptians and have a lot more money. Serbs have one year on Croats, Ukrainians two years on the Russians, and Indians have five years over Pakistanis. Men fare worse than women everywhere, but nowhere more so than in Swaziland, where thirty-two qualifies you for elder.

THANKS FOR THE MEMOS:
ONE MEATBALL

Question:

I find our cafeteria prices difficult to understand. For example, I bought 1 meatball and was charged $1.61. How do they come up with their pricing?

Answer:

The price of most items is plainly posted. In the case of the meatball you referenced, that cost was determined by breaking down the cost of the meatball hoagie platter that was featured that day for $4.25: Two 5-ounce meatballs at $1.50 each, hoagie roll at $0.25, and french fries at $1.00. The cost of one meatball was $1.50 plus tax, totaling $1.61. To avoid surprises in the future, don't hesitate to ask the price of an item before ordering it.

WHAD'YA KNOW ABOUT PEOPLE? ROUND 1

1. Honors for the lowest job satisfaction in the federal government go to:

   (a) Homeland Security

   (b) Small Business Administration

   (c) Public Information

2. Percentage of office workers who sometimes forward jokes, clips, jpegs, and funny news via office email:

   (a) 29 percent

   (b) 59 percent

   (c) 72 percent

3. Which do office workers hate the most?

   (a) A condescending boss

   (b) Perfume or other odors

   (c) Loud cubicle neighbors

4. Most stressed out?

   (a) Librarian

   (b) Air traffic controller

   (c) School crossing guard

5. How many unpaid hours go into raising two children to age eighteen?

   (a) 57,661

   (b) 116,516

   (c) 157,680

6. A majority of men spend _____ picking out their clothes in the morning.

   (a) no time

   (b) practically no time

   (c) less than two minutes

7. Look to your left, look to your right, peek over the partition: How many of your coworkers out of the 12 in the vending area are having/have had an office romance?

   (a) 1

   (b) 3

   (c) 5

8. Of the seriously underestimated two wasted hours of the average worker's day, the largest part goes to:

   (a) personal business

   (b) socializing

   (c) the Internets

9. Due to clutter, 1 in ___ office workers cannot see their desks.

    (a) 4

    (b) 9

    (c) 12

10. Non-athletic, well-educated, professional men in their thirties make up the majority of _____ users.

    (a) ED medication

    (b) crack

    (c) steroid

☞ 59 percent of women think their mates need a makeover.

☞ The University of Pennsylvania found that people who bowl with strangers are happier.

☞ 1 in 5 people have been dumped by text.

☞ 8 percent of adults clean when they have the flu.

☞ 56 percent of women would rather be thinner than smarter.

☞ 15 percent of obese people think they are.

WHAD'YA KNOW ABOUT PEOPLE? (ROUND 1 ANSWERS)

1. (b) Small Business Administration. Half of all small business administrators fail within the first year.

2. (c) 72 percent. This has gotta be low. So if they find it on your work station, who's fault is it?

3. (a) A condescending boss. If they wanted condescension, they could stay home. Half say condescension's what they hate about work; 37 percent also hate public reprimands, 34 percent hate being micromanaged, and 32 percent hate loud cubicle neighbors.

4. (a) Librarians. Not only are they stressed out, they have to express it in a very low voice. Due to people not respecting the Dewey decimal system, librarians are more stressed than EMRs. Patrons can be so patronizing.

5. (a) 57,661 hours—which, with minimum wage at $6.55, comes to $377,679.55 the little suckers owe you…cash, no savings bonds, please. Would be a lot more if parenting weren't regarded as unskilled labor.

6. (c) (Much) less than two minutes. In fact, I wouldn't call it picking out at all, I'd call it "what's clean?" Or what's cleanest, maybe. The average man spends 852 hours of his life picking out his clothes, which sounds like a lot until you figure that a

woman spends 27,010. A guy's lucky to have that many hours in his life.

7. (c) 5. No wonder they're thirsty. When you think of the people you work with, how scary is it to realize that 40 percent are… ohmygod. Cracking the copier glass with their butts is one thing. But that's what Harris found, so it must be true.

8. (c) 42 on the Internets, the Googles, the social networking, the Twitters, the YouTubes, the MySpaces, the always with the blogging, the Twitters, the Facebooks, the eBays, the what-have-Youporns. But at least it keeps them out of trouble.

9. (b) 1 in 9 workers don't know what field they're in, it's so cluttered. Most will tell you it's highly organized until you ask them for something.

10. (c) Steroids. Most steroid users are not athletes but professional men in competitive occupations looking for a competitive edge in the gym, according to the International Sports Nutrition Journal.

69 REASONS TO HAVE SEX

Cindy M. Meston and David M. Buss, psychologists at the University of Texas–Austin, asked nearly two thousand people why they had sex and assembled a list of 237 reasons.
—*New York Times*, July 31, 2007

Only thing works for the migraines.
Squeaky wheel gets the grease.
Not against my better judgment.
Finals.
Daylight savings.
Aerobic.
Do a world of good.
Win-win.
Both adults.
Moving to non-adjacent state.
Dog park meetings no coincidence.
Never done my type.
Allure said to.

If not now, when (if not me, who)?

Not fond of abstinence.

Or get off the pot.

Miles to go before I sleep.

Get back at your sister.

No harm, no foul.

No dryers free.

Kundalini.

I'm a giver.

Biopsy negative.

Wouldn't look at me in high school.

Ringer for Joey Heatherton.

Peer pressure.

Venus in Aquarius.

Beats texting.

Cool, clear eyes of a seeker of wisdom and truth.

It was 11:11.

I did not have sexual relations.

Glue needs to set.

Tired of the lesbian scene.

Polls not yet closed in CA.

Biology.

Coupon.

Just the one bed.

She was locked out.

300-mile rule.

Can't play tennis due to shoulder.

Keeping abreast.

Forgot reading glasses.

This far apart.

Too much Animal Planet.

Dat old debbil moon.

No particular place to go.

Viagra window of opportunity.

Revenge.

Pity.

Charity beginning at home.

"Pressure? What pressure?"

For the good times.

What happens in Oskaloosa, stays in Oskaloosa.

Guy Fawkes Day.

Rebounding.

Ricochet.

Natural order.

Pressure at work.

Relaxation technique.

To not go gently into that good night.

For auld lang syne.

Date's circled.

Depends what you mean by "having."

Last crack at Mile High Club.

Thirty minutes on the meter.

Trading deadline.

So as not to appear rude.

Couldn't sleep.

No reason.

Did I mention the migraine?

JOKES, BY
PROFESSION

INSURANCE SALESMAN

A man walked into an insurance office and asked for a job.

"We don't need anyone," the agent replied.

"You can't afford not to hire me. I can sell anyone anything."

"We have two prospects that no one has been able to sell to. If you can sell just one, you have a job."

He was gone for about two hours and returned, handing the agent two checks, one for an $80,000 policy and another for a $50,000 policy.

"How in the world did you do that?" the agent asked.

"I told you, I'm the world's best salesman; I can sell anything, anywhere, anytime."

"Did you get a urine sample?" he asked him.

"What's that?" he asked.

"Well, if you sell a policy worth over $40,000, the company requires a urine sample. Take these two bottles and go back and get urine samples."

The man was gone for about eight hours before he walked back in with two five-gallon buckets, one in each hand. He set the buckets down, reached in his shirt pocket, and produced two bottles of urine. He set them on the desk and said, "Here's Brown's and here's Smith's."

"That's good," the agent said, "but what's in the buckets?"

"Well, I passed by the firehouse and sold them a group policy."

CATTLE BUYER

Two cattle buyers from Oklahoma were on a trip to Central Texas to look at a set of cows when they were pulled over by a state trooper. The trooper walked up and tapped on the driver's-side window with his nightstick. The cattle buyer rolled down the window and WHACK, the trooper smacked him in the head with his nightstick.

"What the hell was that for?" the cattle buyer asked.

"You're in Texas," the trooper answered. "When we pull you over in Texas, you better have your license ready by the time we get to your car."

The trooper ran a check on the license and the cattle buyer was clean, so he gave him his license back. The trooper then walked around to the passenger side and tapped on the window. The other cattle buyer rolled down his window and WHACK, the trooper smacked him on the head with the nightstick.

"What'd you do that for?" the cattle buyer demanded.

"Making your wish come true," replied the trooper.

"Making *what* wish come true?" the cattle buyer asked.

"I know you cattle buyer types," the trooper said. "A hundred feet down the road, you would've turned to your buddy and said, 'I wish that s-o-b would've tried that on me!'"

—*Joel Achenbach*

GEOPHYSICIST

What's 2+2?

The engineer pulls out a calculator and says, "To three decimal places, it's 4.000, but beyond that, I don't know."

The hydrologist runs the program MOD-FLOW and says, "Something between 3.9 and 4.1."

The geophysicist, looking both ways to be sure no one is listening, whispers, "What do you *want* it to be?"

CHEMIST

A physicist, biologist and a chemist go to the ocean for the first time.

The physicist sees the ocean and is fascinated by the waves. Saying he wants to do some research on the fluid dynamics of the waves, he walks in and drowns.

The biologist wants to research the flora and fauna in the ocean; she walks in and drowns.

The chemist waits on the shore for a long time, then writes the observation, "Physicists and biologists are soluble in water."

Q: What do chemists call a benzene ring with iron atoms replacing the carbon atoms?

A: A ferrous wheel:

```
  Fe – Fe
  /      \
Fe        Fe
  \      /
  Fe – Fe
```

Q: Why do chemists like nitrates so much?
A: They're cheaper than day rates.

Outside his Buckyball home, a molecule overheard another molecule saying, "I'm positive that a free electron once stripped me of an electron after he lepton me. You gotta keep your ion them."

—*Jupiter Scientific*

ENGINEER

Three men—a project manager, a software engineer, and a hardware engineer—are helping out on a project. About midweek they decide to walk up and down the beach during their lunch hour. Halfway up the beach, they stumble upon a lamp. As they rub the lamp, a genie appears and says, "Normally I would grant you three wishes, but since there are three of you, I will grant you each one wish."

The hardware engineer went first. "I would like to spend the rest of my life living in a huge house in St. Thomas with no money worries." The genie granted him his wish and sent him off to St. Thomas.

The software engineer went next. "I would like to spend the rest of my life living on a huge yacht cruising the Mediterranean with no money worries." The genie granted him his wish and sent him off to the Mediterranean.

Last, but not least, it was the project manager's turn. "And what would your wish be?" asked the genie.

"I want them both back after lunch."

Three Metal Spheres

The board of trustees of a well-known university decides to test the professors, to see if they know their stuff. First they take a math prof and put him in a room containing a table and three metal spheres about the size of softballs. They tell him to do whatever he wants with the balls and table for one hour. After he comes out, the trustees look in and find the balls arranged in a triangle at the center of the table. They give the same test to a physics prof and, after an hour, find the balls stacked one on top of the other in the center of the table. Finally, they give the test to an engineering prof. After an hour, they look in and find one of the balls is broken, one is missing, and he's carrying the third out in his lunchbox.

—*Inflection Point, Inc.*

Q: What is the difference between mechanical engineers and civil engineers?

A: Mechanical engineers build weapons, civil engineers build targets.

Q: What do engineers use for birth control?

A: Their personalities.

Q: How can you tell an extroverted engineer?

A: When he talks to you, he looks at your shoes instead of his.

Q: Why did the engineers cross the road?

A: Because they looked in the file, and that's what they did last year.

—*Baylor*

BANKER

Einstein dies and goes to heaven only to be informed that his room is not yet ready. St. Peter tells him, "I hope you will not mind waiting in a dormitory. We're very sorry, but you'll have to share the room." Einstein says that this is no problem at all and no need to make such a great fuss. So St. Peter leads him to the dorm where Einstein is introduced to the inhabitants.

"Here's your first roommate. He has an IQ of 180!"

"Why, that's wonderful!" says Einstein. "We can discuss literature!"

"And here is your second roommate. His IQ is 150!"

"Excellent!" says Einstein. "We can discuss mathematics!"

"And here's your third roommate. His IQ is 100!"

"Fine! We can discuss the latest plays at the theater!"

Just then another man comes out to shake Einstein's hand. "I'm your last roommate, and I'm sorry to say my IQ is only 80." Einstein smiles and says, "So, where do you think interest rates are headed?"

Interviewing the young Swede for a job as teller, the bank president is amazed with the skill the applicant exhibits at handling money.

"So," the president says, "where did you get your training?"

"Yale," the fair-haired youth replies.

"I see. And what did you say your name was?"

He answers, "Yackson."

LIFER

A twenty-two-year-old kid is sent to a maximum security prison for larceny. He gets an older, veteran cellmate who takes a liking to him and helps him get acclimated to prison life.

The first night in the cell block, the kid hears something strange. Other prisoners are calling out numbers in the darkness.

"Sixteen!"

All the prisoners laugh, except for the new kid.

"Twenty-five!"

More laughter.

And so on. The kid asks his cellmate to explain what everyone's laughing at.

"Well, at night, we've got nothing better to do than to tell jokes."

"But they're not jokes. They're just numbers."

"That's all you know. Thing is, we've all been here so long that we've heard each other's jokes so often that we've memorized them. So rather than tell the whole joke again, we've numbered 'em all. Now we just remind each other of the joke by calling out the number."

"Huh. Can I try it?"

"Knock yourself out, kid."

So the kid calls out, "Eleven!"

Silence.

He tries again. "Twenty-two!"

There's just one half-hearted chuckle, and it dies quickly.

The kid turns to his cellmate and says, "I don't get it. What's going wrong?"

The cellmate shakes his head. "Some people can tell a joke, and some can't."

—*Karen Blocher*

Two convicts were about to be executed. The warden says to the first one, "Do you have a last request?"

The convict says, "Yes. I'd like to hear 'Achy Breaky Heart' one last time."

The warden says, "OK, I think we can arrange that." Then he says to the second convict, "How about you? Last request?"

The second convict says, "Yeah. Kill me first."

CONSULTANT

The World's Oldest Profession

A physician, a civil engineer, and a consultant are arguing about what is the oldest profession in the world.

The physician says, "Well, in the Bible, it says that God created Eve from a rib taken out of Adam. This clearly required surgery, and so I can rightly claim that mine is the oldest profession in the world."

The civil engineer replies, "Even earlier in the book of Genesis, God created the order of the heavens and the Earth from out of the chaos. This was the first and certainly the most spectacular application of civil engineering. Therefore, mine is the oldest profession in the world."

The consultant leans back in her chair, smiles, and says confidently, "Ah, but who do you think created the chaos?"

DOCTOR

According to Henny Youngman...

A doctor gave a man six months to live. The man couldn't pay his bill, so he gave him another six months.

My doctor grabbed me by the wallet and said, "Cough!"

The doctor called Mrs. Cohen, saying, "Mrs. Cohen, your check came back."

Mrs. Cohen answered, "So did my arthritis!"

The doctor says, "You'll live to be sixty!"

"I *am* sixty!"

"See, what did I tell you?"

A doctor says to a man, "You want to improve your love life? You need to get some exercise. Run ten miles a day."

Two weeks later, the man called the doctor. The doctor says, "How is your love life since you have been running?"

"I don't know, I'm 140 miles away!"

The patient says, "Doctor, it hurts when I do this."

"Then don't do that!"

A man goes to a psychiatrist—"Nobody listen to me!"

The doctor says, "Next!"

The doctor says to the patient, "Take your clothes off and stick your tongue out the window."

"What will that do?" asks the patient.

The doctor says, "Nothing, but I'm mad at my neighbor!"

"I KNOW A GOOD, CHEAP PLASTIC SURGEON!"

A doctor has a stethoscope up to a man's chest. The man asks, "Doc, how do I stand?"

The doctor says, "That's what puzzles me!"

"Doctor, my leg hurts. What can I do?"

The doctor says, "Limp!"

The doctor says to a man, "You're pregnant!"

The man says, "How does a man get pregnant?"

The doctor says, "The usual way: a little wine, a little dinner…"

A man goes to a psychiatrist. The doctor says, "You're crazy."

The man says, "I want a second opinion!"

"OK, you're ugly too!"

"Doctor, I have a ringing in my ears."

"Don't answer!"

Nurse: "Doctor, the man you just gave a clean bill of health to dropped dead right as he was leaving the office."

Doctor: "Turn him around and make it look like he was walking in."

According to Rodney Dangerfield...

I tell you, with my doctor, I don't get no respect. I told him, "I've swallowed a bottle of sleeping pills." He told me to have a few drinks and get some rest.

Last week I told my psychiatrist, "I keep thinking about suicide." He told me from now on I have to pay in advance.

My doctor told me to watch my drinking. Now I drink in front of a mirror. I drink too much. Way too much. My doctor drew blood. He ran a tab.

When I was born, the doctor came out to the waiting room and said to my father, "I'm very sorry. We did everything we could...but he pulled through."

I went to see my doctor...Doctor Vidi-boom-ba. Yeah...I told him once, "Doctor, every morning when I get up and look in the mirror I feel like throwing up. What's wrong with me?

He said, "I don't know, but your eyesight is perfect."

I told my dentist my teeth are going yellow. He told me to wear a brown necktie.

MOHEL

(*Note: the* mohel *is the man who circumcises male babies*)

A man passed a store window with nothing in it but a clock; he stepped inside and asked, "How long would it take to fix my watch?"

"How should I know?" the man shrugged. "I don't fix watches. I'm a mohel."

"But—in your window—you have a clock!"

"So what would you put in the window?"

—*Leo Rosten*

CLERGY

A Minister, a Priest, and a Rabbi

A minister, a priest, and a rabbi go for a hike on a very hot day.

Sweating and exhausted, they come to a small lake. Since it is fairly secluded, they take off all their clothes and jump in the water. Feeling refreshed, the trio decides to pick a few berries while enjoying their "freedom." As they cross a field, who should come along but a group of ladies from town. Unable to get to their clothes in time, the minister and the priest cover their privates and the rabbi covers his face while they run for cover.

After the ladies leave and the three get their clothes back on, the minister and the priest ask the rabbi why he covered his face instead of his privates. The rabbi replies, "I don't know about you, but in my congregation it's my face they would recognize."

A Baptist minister was completing a temperance sermon. With great expression, he said, "If I had all the beer in the world, I'd take it and pour it into the river."

With even greater emphasis, he said, "And if I had all the wine in the world, I'd take that and pour it in the river."

Finally, he cried, "And if I had all the whiskey in the world, I'd take it and pour it into the river." Sermon complete, he then sat down.

After a few moments, the song leader stood very cautiously and announced with a smile, "For our closing song, let us sing hymn #365: 'Shall We Gather at the River.'"

LAWYER

A dying curmudgeon calls in his three sons, from whom he was distant for most of his life. One is a mathematician, another an engineer, and the third a lawyer. He tells the three that he will give his entire estate to the one who answers his question correctly.

Alone with the mathematician, he asks him, "How much is one and one?" Dumbfounded by the simplicity of the question, the son replies, "Why two, father. You know I learned that watching *Sesame Street*."

Alone with the engineer, he poses the same question. Thinking it some kind of joke, the son replies, "Two," and waits for a punchline.

Alone with the lawyer, he asks the question yet again. The son walks over to the door, closes it, then turns to each window and closes the blinds. He leans over his father and whispers, "How much would you like it to be?"

—*Stephen Hurley*

Curiously, this joke is nearly identical to the geophysicist, engineer, and chemist "How much would you like it to be?" joke. Attorney Hurley apparently represents a geophysicist...

A barber gave a haircut to a priest one day. The priest tried to pay for the haircut, but the barber refused, saying, "You do God's work." The next morning, the barber found a dozen bibles at the door to his shop.

A policeman came to the barber for a haircut, and again the barber refused payment, saying, "You protect the public." The next morning, the barber found a dozen doughnuts at the door to his shop.

A lawyer came to the barber for a haircut, and again the barber refused payment, saying, "You serve the justice system." The next morning, the barber found a dozen lawyers waiting for a free haircut.

Closing Arguments

What is a criminal lawyer?

Redundant.

Did you hear they just released a new Barbie doll called "Divorced Barbie"?

Yeah, it comes with half of Ken's things and alimony.

THANKS FOR THE MEMOS:
VIOLENT STOOL SHIFTERS ARISE!

INTRA-OFFICE COMMUNICATION

DATE: February 7
TO: Coordinator, Development
FROM: BJ, Director—Physical Plant
SUBJ: LADIES ROOM 2ND FLOOR LAV.—WATER ON FLOOR

Thank you for your memo bringing to our attention this water problem. We would prefer that when you have an immediate problem that indicates a water leak, you call the Physical Plant office immediately rather than putting a memo through the campus mail. The memo you wrote on February 3 was not received in our office until February 5 in the p.m. We had our plumber work on the problem February 6. Had you called this problem to our attention on the 3rd, we could have immediately had the problem fixed.

The cause of this water leak was not readily apparent. In fact, by just flushing the stool, our shop personnel could find no leaking water at all. This is probably why our custodians did not report the problem. One of our shop persons had to actually sit on the stool and shift weight fairly violently while the stool was being flushed in order to cause the problem to occur. It was discovered that a seal was not holding properly when there was a fairly active shifting of weight on the stool.

It is impossible to anticipate this type of problem and to make any modifications that would permanently solve the problem. The main cause of malfunctions in this area is the extremely heavy use this restroom receives.

BJ

WHAD'YA KNOW ABOUT
PEOPLE?
ROUND 2

1. ____ percent of soap opera people in a coma recover fully.
   - (a) 67
   - (b) 75
   - (c) 89

2. Republicans are ____ percent more likely to water ski than Democrats.
   - (a) 5
   - (b) 50
   - (c) 67

3. 1 in 2 boys trash talks; 1 in ____ girls does.
   - (a) 2
   - (b) 5
   - (c) 10

4. Out of 12 people boarding a flight, how many secretly hope to find a spouse in the next seat?

   (a) 1

   (b) 2

   (c) 3

5. The percentage of men who completely miss not-so-subtle cues of interest from women?

   (a) 87

   (b) 93

   (c) 99

6. *GQ* has discovered that _____ men would wear makeup for a 25 percent salary increase.

   (a) 1 in 100

   (b) 1 in 7

   (c) 1 in 30

7. Do men like men more than women like women?

8. Is marriage more fattening for husband or wife?

9. The width of the average woman's foot is 3.6 inches. What is the width of the average woman's shoe?

   (a) 3.5 inches

   (b) 3.2 inches

   (c) 3 inches

10. _____ American women take their dog's opinion into consideration when choosing a mate.

(a) 1 in 7

(b) 1 in 20

(c) 1 in 50

"ACTUALLY NO, NOT ALL THAT FRIENDLY"

☞ If you held the average American upside-down and shook, it should rain $27.00.

☞ Out of 100 fathers, 4 have good reason to wonder why their kids don't look like them.

☞ Boyfriends do more housework than husbands.

☞ Husbands sleep better next to their wives than wives do next to husbands.

WHAD'YA KNOW ABOUT PEOPLE? (ROUND 2 ANSWERS)

1. (c) 89 percent recover to commit infidelity again; 11 percent are killed off. Comas and general amnesia are much more common and are more likely to end well in soap operas than in life.

2. (c) 67 percent. There is a fun element to Republicans that has never been fully appreciated, if the water skiing results are any indication. Democrats are more likely to go to an art museum.

3. (b) 1 in 5 girls trash talks, most likely something about their fathers.

4. (c) 3 out of 12. There are eighteen passengers in coach on any given flight who are disappointed in their seatmates for mating reasons.

5. (a) 87 percent of men can't tell when a woman is interested; a similar number can't tell when they're not. Women just need to be a lot more overt.

6. (b) 1 in 7 men would wear makeup for a good-sized raise; chances of it happening, one in a billion. But it's the idea of it. Male grooming products are now a $5 million market in the U.S., alarmingly small compared to the billion dollars spent on deodorants.

7. No; everybody likes women more. Maybe because women are
    four times more likely to say nice things about other women
    than men are about men, a study at Purdue found.

8. Husband. Should be "until pants do we split": 71 percent of
    husbands are overweight, compared to 49 percent of wives, ac-
    cording to the Center for Health Statistics.

9. (c) 3 inches. Some serious overlap issues here, on top of having
    to curl up your toes. The two articles of clothing having least
    in common with the woman's actual size are her shoes and
    her bra.

10. (a) 1 in 7. If you want to love her, you better love her dog, ac-
    cording to *Pedigree*. And that's no guarantee the Afghan Hound
    will feel the same way.

THE MORE,
THE MARRIAGER

I'm glad to see the marriage franchise expanding—personally, I'd hoped to see some-sex marriage in my lifetime, but, that disclaimer aside, here's to gay unions, triathlons, bisexual tag teams, marriage between interlocking directorates, marriages of convenience and in-; the more, the marriager. All benefiting from the full sword of Damocles we, the conventional, have swinging over us—dubious tax advantages, tandem health club memberships, visiting hours, and a marginally enhanced probability of somebody doing the laundry or cleaning the gutters. You will want to be careful about having the long-term relationship between you and your roommate being unintentionally solemnized when the only piece of paper you need is the rent check. Otherwise, anything goes, including those little radios.

Never a poster boy for marriage, my two feeble attempts have been long-term bad relationships that ripened on the bramble, advantaged only by a tax break for weather stripping, and my attachment to her AARP card, disadvantaged by the equivalent of having to live with your brother for the rest of your natural life. My first was a starter wife, and my second a closer—what I've lacked all these years is middle relief. One was all youth and high hopes; two, well, I should have known something was out of whack when she wanted us to write our own vendettas for the ceremony, performed by an ordained abnormal psychologist. No one ever explained the concept of marriage to me—no priest way in over his collar (maybe it is like placating the Rector), no sage Talmudic scholar who understood that Rashi's commentaries were nothing compared to his wife's. The only examples we have from the Old Testament—Lot's wife turning to salt, King David's Bathsheba tolerating a small city of concubines, Eve waiting for the right guy to come along even when there was nobody else—are not particularly helpful in our day and age, or the one just past. The New Testament shows us Jesus never married because she would have had him hanging doors full time; besides, who would have been good enough for Mother Mary?

A doctor at the Quisling Clinic once told me to forget about fluids or irrigating my canals and get married. Marriage, he said, was a good health practice for the male, extending his life a good eighteen months—if good is the word, or life. May this man be alone and blowing smoke out the cracked window of his room at the Y today, if he was lying. Marriage has made me the man you see today, or would, were anybody still looking. You need a Ouija board to communicate with me in this lifetime. Realistically, once you reach the Great Divide in the long-term bad relationship, it doesn't much matter whether you go on or go back, except that you can't go back, so you go on. Communication, the euphemism all couples share, comes down to body language and messages trance-channeled through the kids: "Tell your mother her car is still running in the garage" kind of thing. I'm not saying it's ideal, but it's workable, until the real thing comes along, with its hood and scythe, and you do part.

THE IT GUY

Hard to believe I am now the IT guy of my little domain, even with one daughter Mac and one PC. Me, the same technophobe who once typed over the phone to demonstrate what a step backward email was. Me, the guy who was amazed you could double-click on a TV screen and get the picture to change. Who associated icons with the Greek Orthodox Church. To date, I have wiped out all my information maybe a dozen times (remember when we didn't used to have information?), slain entire operating systems, ground hard drives under my boot, and built my own barebones with only third-degree burns over 10 percent of my body—not bad.

I never thought I'd say this, but I have seated a quad core. I don't expect it to end there. The more cores, the better, right? I forget how much memory I have, but it's a lot. More than you can shake a memory stick at. Not to mention online storage in case the Earth is destroyed. No brag, just fact, but I have stared straight into the graphic interface of Vista and fingered its cabinets, before yanking it out entirely with the Microsoft $59 all-you-can-eat help. (I had castrated the UAC and pre-empted any updates, but, like HAL, my drunk-with-Vista machine would not power down and only half-slept, lurking blue-eyed and blinking at the foot of my bed.) Just one of scores of encounters of the total waste-of-time kind. After turning Vista into Shmista, I put XP on a Mac, tried and failed to put Mac on a PC, got in and out of Linux (Ubuntu, you?), and forged an ethernet of five computers at the home office that will not speak to one another (just like home), all of which are used only by me for whatever computing mood I may be in. One's just got Donkey Kong on it. It's great, like having five sinks to pee in and no female around to inhibit your doing it. A very nice man in Bangalore helped me with some problems I was having cloud computing, because as an IT you have to think globally and screw up everything locally.

COMING OF
AGE IN IOWA

Americans are the lab rats of the world, studied to within an inch of our whiskers. Closer. What Margaret Mead did for Samoa, AC Neilson did for Iowa—ferreting out preferences and habits Iowans didn't know they had since 1923. The Harris Poll has canvassed American public opinion since 1963; before then, we had it but didn't offer it to strangers. The upside is we know a lot about each other, more than we ever thought we would know, in fact. NPR listeners, for example, are two-and-a-half times more likely to drink Scotch than non-members, but only half as likely to do it in panty hose. 55 percent of Americans buy books solely for decoration. Shoppers are more annoyed by too much attention than too little. In lieu of prayers, a majority of Americans plug in their cell phones to charge last thing. Three-quarters of young women have looked through the call logs of their boyfriends' cell phones. 1 out of 9 Canadians separate the layers of their candy bars (surprisingly, only 1 in 100 eats a Snickers with a knife and fork, eh). Bratwurst garnishes, in order of importance, are mustard, onions, and ketchup/kraut (dead heat). 56 percent of American men are convinced they could carry off a banana hammock swimsuit. You can find the password on a Post-it on 1 in 5 office monitors. While dead for some time now, Lucille Ball remains America's most popular star (*I Love Lucy: Dead or Alive*). Women want Jessica Simpson's hair. In the order of their shoplifting: Advil, Preparation H, Primatine, EPT Pregnancy Test. Men are impressed by risk-taking men; women are not. The good-looking receive a 5 percent pay bonus. In a half-hour, the average male will make thirteen glances at the average female in a bar. Only 23 out of 100 Americans will eat the recommended five fruits and vegetables today. As an Iowan, you are much more likely to bunch your toilet paper than fold it over a few times and hope for the best.

FOR YOUR REAR ONLY

40 percent of toilet paper users fold or stack;

40 percent wad or crumple;

20 percent wrap it around their hand;

52 percent of men are folders, while 38 percent of women are;

38 percent of men and 52 percent of women are wadders;

6 percent of both women and men have no preference;

While 4 percent of men and 3 percent of women don't know how they wipe their butts.

—Kimberly-Clark

THANKS FOR THE MEMOS:
KEEP ON TRUCKIN'

Dear Mrs. DeLouise,

Enclosed is a copy of the contract which we mishandled greatly and for which we offer our apologies. There was no excuse except to relate what happened as follows.

On Thursday, September 14th, we sent our tractor-trailer with two experienced men and $850 in cash to Chicago via Cleveland. They completed work on a tent outside Cleveland at 4:30 p.m. Saturday and left for Chicago. At 11:00 p.m., they arrived in Indiana and ate supper at a Truckstop, which we have verified. At this point the Foreman was to go to a motel and be at the Restaurant the next morning at 8:00 o'clock. After supper at the Truckstop, the Foreman (without any company authorization) drove to Milwaukee to visit relatives. The Assistant went to his own relatives and the next morning could not locate the Foreman, nor did he have the keys to the tractor.

At approximately noon Sunday, your company contacted our Operations Manager. He was at a complete loss, since we knew the men should have been in the area Saturday. He contacted local relatives and was told by the Asst. Foreman's Mother that her son called at 9 o'clock Sunday and said they were outside Chicago and on the way to the city. When they were not there by 2:00 p.m., he called the company which handles our vehicles nationwide to see if they had a mechanical breakdown. They reported no calls.

At this point the Operations Manager called me and I contacted another tent company. They had a crew working Sunday and would send two experienced men out at 4:00 p.m. They gave each man $300 expense money and instructed them to call immediately on arrival in Chicago.

The men never arrived, and the General Manager of the tent company talked to the Police about an all points bulletin to see if anything happened.

At 3:00 a.m., with two crews disappearing and after at least ten (10) phone calls, the Operations Manager left by car for Chicago. He arrived about 8:00 a.m., and the tent was removed.

Subsequently, we learned that the Foreman returned the tractor-trailer to Indiana late Sunday night and abandoned it. Monday, the Assistant called to relate his story and we immediately sent him by taxi to the Restaurant to help the Manager. We also found out that one of the men spent his $300 when they arrived in Chicago on an illegal purpose and arrived about noon.

All of these men have been terminated.

WHAD'YA KNOW ABOUT
PEOPLE?
ROUND 3

1. _____ out of 10 children playing organized sports say their parents yell at the officials.

   (a) 3

   (b) 4

   (c) 9

2. Alternative therapies— acupuncture, herbal, aroma, chiropractic, hypnosis, colonic irrigation, reflexology, etc.— are least likely to appeal to people from the:

   (a) Northeast

   (b) South

   (c) Midwest

3. Do women spend more time looking for a present for their husbands or their pets?

55

4. _____ office workers say their office needs work.

   (a) 1 in 4

   (b) 1 in 3

   (c) 1 in 2

5. When dating, 78 percent of men assume women would prefer to view "female" sports, while only ____ percent of women actually feel that way.

   (a) 7

   (b) 11

   (c) 16

6. True or False: The richer you are, the less likely you are to favor abolishing the penny.

7. Men are more likely to shave their:

   (a) backs

   (b) fronts

   (c) privates

8. _____ newly empty nesters renovate their offspring's room as soon as they spring out.

   (a) 1 in 4

   (b) 1 in 3

   (c) 1 in 2

9. Assuming they fall asleep together, a French woman will wake up _____ a Swedish man.

    (a) 46 minutes after

    (b) an hour before

    (c) several hours later than

10. On any given Sunday, in a congregation of 400, how many have their cell phones on?

    (a) Just the preacher

    (b) 8

    (c) 20, including the choir

☞ Ovulating women find other women less attractive.

☞ Americans are sad 3 days a month.

☞ Girls are 6 times more likely to fight someone they've fought with before.

☞ Only 1 in 5 Germans are binge drinkers.

WHAD'YA KNOW ABOUT PEOPLE? (ROUND 3 ANSWERS)

1. (a) 3 out of 10 kids say Mom or Dad lets the ref have it; the other 7 just don't hear it anymore. Refs and officials claim the bulk of it comes from moms.

2. (c) Midwest. An adjustment, yes; seaweed and a high colonic, only on windy days on the Lake Michigan beach. D.D. Palmer, the father of chiropractic care, first set up shop in Davenport, don't you know.

3. Pets, of course—90 minutes to 75. Still not a bad showing, all things being equal.

4. (a) 1 in 4 of the cubicled are really tired of what they're able to see from their stanchion. The rest have been there too long.

5. (c) 16 percent; sports of any sort are probably not the way to a girl's heart.

6. False, although Uncle Scrooge still has his lucky dime.

7. You're not going to want to know this, but...(c) men are four times more likely to shave their privates than their legs (16 percent to 4 percent) and no one will say why. 2 out of 3 men pay a lot of attention to ears and nose, but you wouldn't always know it.

8. (a) 1 in 4; higher after a one-semester/first-marriage grace period.

9. (a) 46 minutes, giving him just enough time to catch the SAS back to Stockholm.

10. (b) 8; although these are just the ones who confessed. Leaving it on vibrate is a sin in many denominations.

MY SIX SHOES

Ipropose that *My Three Sons* sealed modern man's fate; that is, forever to be bemused and befuddled by family contingencies in the manner of Fred MacMurray's archetypical Steven Douglas, Daddy Dumbfoundedest. True, before then we had Major Hoople, Dagwood, and W.C. Fields's Egbert Sousé, and a Spencer Tracy famously out of the loop in *Father of the Bride*, but these were caricatures and not historical place markers like Steven Douglas. Odysseus was more in touch with his kids; Ward Cleaver ruled, in part because the threat "Dad's gonna clobber you when he gets home" rang true with Methodist minister Hugh Beaumont behind it. When did Steven Douglas ever sit on Chip's, Robbie's or Mike's bed, put his arm around them, and tell them an appropriate parable that made them realize the error of buying an accordion on credit, or take Ernie aside and tell him he had joined the family purely as a ratings move? A lot of that hod was carried by Bub, but he was—Fred Mertz at heart—not the guy to inspire a young man with the wisdom of his life experience.

For Steven Douglas, those big oxfords tapping during the opening credits said it all, more so than the opening gunfight on *Gunsmoke*, or Dr. Zorba's fuzz gray head-scratching "Man, woman, birth, death, infinity" chalked on Ben Casey's blackboard like an end-around from a demented football coach. Steven Douglas was just a half-sole away from not being present at all in his household, an early '60s prelude to the absent/disinterested sitcom father and the running wild, murderous children of *River's Edge*, with no adults in sight. It's not that Steven Douglas was too much of a careerist; only occasionally do we find Steven at the office with the picture of a Titan missile behind him, so it was widely assumed he was in the Titan missile picture business—although it didn't matter any more than Mike Brady being an architect, considering the orange and brown A&W ranch house with the Astroturf backyard he was able to build his family.

Steven had to be both father and mother to the boys, and was neither—and the AWOL Mrs. Douglas—where was she? Did she flee an Oedipal uprising by Robbie? Was she living with one of the Darrens? Harriet never left Ozzie, not once since she first started singing with the band in the '40s; she hardly ever left the house with the disturbingly Germanic eagle over the fireplace and damn Don DeFore always at the back door. Ozzie was somewhat of a buffoon, but he produced the show and made Ricky a rock and roll star—if Tim Considine did all right for a while it wasn't because of Fred MacMurray. The premise he had to shoulder was never clear—was Douglas really a "widower" or was that something he just told vulnerable women who bit, hook, line and sinker, only to be caught and released. Did his wife die in the pilot? Why don't the kids ever ask about it? Did he kill Bub, too, who, we're told, suddenly "went to Ireland"? The nonstop fending off of the many hens, Stella Stevens included, who wanted nothing more than to feather his nest, what's with that? Doesn't a Midwestern guy get lonely in LA, or would a remake, today, be *My Two Fathers*? *Bachelor Father*, at least, was getting some, but then, he was the flesh and blood John Forsythe.

In the end, the failing may have been Fred MacMurray's and not Steven Douglas's, MacMurray never having been a credible screen presence—even in *Double Indemnity*, where he could have been, it's clear there's no way in hell he gets the young Barbara Stanwyck. Maybe by her *Big Valley* years, yes. Gangster moll Kim Novak having a torrid affair with cop Paul Sheridan, who turns out to be Fred MacMurray, is why you never hear about *Pushover* today. Sparks don't fly, unless it's static electricity. During the whole flubbing Disney period of the MacMurray Resurgence—flying jalopies, shaggy dogs, and all, with things constantly exploding in the basement, outcomes never foreseen but always predictable—MacMurray, father of flubber, laid the groundwork for affable but dysfunctional Steven Douglas, and the result would change the American family, forever.

One additional note of interest: Fred MacMurray is Cockney rhyming slang for curry.

SUB PRIME

All right, so I went to work in my slippers after putting my coffee in the fridge to heat it up. Who hasn't? That's, whad'ya call it, absent-mindedness. Always had it. I was the kid who washed his face with his glasses on. It's no worse as I crowd 60, the Big Oh-no-ski. On the upside, the other day I found myself genuinely puzzling over my wife's name. I knew it began with Adolf. Actually, what happened was I had just woken up and thought it was my first wife who wasn't next to me. Did you ever get that, when you've just opened your eyes and are not sure which of the many beds you've made for yourself you're currently in?

It was some time ago, true, that I struggled to carry Nora upstairs to beddy-bye gasping, "Honey, Daddy is getting old," and getting back, "Dad, you are old!" Think it was Nora. The point is, we all age; it's only a problem when it starts to show. It doesn't help that everyone feels obliged to point it out to you, the same people who wouldn't dream of patting a pregnant woman's tummy without at least asking first. The asides about being the token Jew in the Lutheran home. The loaded questions: Are you still doing whatever it is you're still doing? Still depleting vital resources? Getting the feeling that people are waiting around for your minerals, which by now, manganese alone, should be worth twenty-five, thirty dollars. Skin, another 25 cents a square foot (accumulating some wealth there), but still, you'd be better off stripping the copper wiring from the relay boxes and leaving me the hell alone.

Feeling free to reference something that happened on the Weather Channel. Finding you're attached to your wife's AARP card despite throwing away every offer sent you for your own. Resenting an

entire new generation of celebrities that you are not going to have the pleasure of outliving. Being demographically unimportant to marketers. Getting scrutinized for signs: just mishear one phrase—get "Are you dead, old dog?" for "Have you fed the dog?"—and it's a federal case. Outgrowing Youth Culture and finding no "Oldth Culture?"—it's a baby bummer, man. That Aquarius dawned and it didn't make a damn bit of difference. Reduced to being the over-the-counter culture. Well, it was bound to hit a wall once you could no longer trust anyone your own age. Instead of a Summer of Love, all we can hope for is a Summer of Levitra. I had someone who was no spring chicken herself say to me the other day, "You're getting on, now." I'll be getting on your head and stomping is what I'll be getting on, but she's right, getting on instead of getting off. Where's the love, l-u-v? Granted, the wisdom that comes with age may be knowing when to shut up, but where's the respect for the office space, if not the office? No empathy forthcoming, even from the worse off, my (way) oldest brother, Clayton, who now greets me with "The youngest—but not young anymore!" He was just pissed because I told him 72 is the new 71.

THE TEN ABSOLUTELY BEST JOBS

oney magazine, you would think, would know where the money jobs were, but, really, when was the last time one of these guys had one? The most glaring omission on the list is "consultant," a profound concept covering a host of sins, or so I assume since the consultants I've met don't seem to have a particular area of expertise. Still, if you can make decent money with a little hustle and work out of a Starbucks (despite the Paul McCartney soundtrack) you're doing all right. My job, radio host, one day a week for two hours, is not currently on the list but keep your eyes peeled, because who knows how long I can keep pulling out this plum. Without further adieu, **The Ten Absolutely Best Jobs**:

1. *Software engineer*—not too many vocations where you can start at 80.5K and get the stock! As long as there is hardware, there will be software, although increasingly we are seeing the hybrid known as limpware. If you are a truly good software engineer, you could make a lot of other people rich, and there's got to be satisfaction in that. Take the stock options, just in case.

2. *College professor*—Humbert Humbert was! Teaching assistants do all the work and you get all the glory, if there is any in Romantic Poetry. Some pressure to publish, but if you change the words around it's not plagiarism. Excellent medical, dental, optical, and psycho.

3. *Financial adviser*—122.5K on average, if you take your own advice and it turns out to be good. A relatively new field, since most bad financial advice used to come from brothers-in-law. At the very least, reduces family conflicts, until the statements come.

4. *Human resources manager*—Human resources managers never downsize themselves, making them the opposite of sea captains. Human resources used to be personnel, and before that it was Henchman. If you can look another human in the eyes and tell them you're going to have to let them go, you're already in human resources! All the benefits of working, none of the risk.

5. *Physician's assistant*—as opposed to physicians, who all pretty much hate their jobs these days and no longer crack the top ten. Unlike a college teaching assistant, pay and benefits are decent in the health care branch of the insurance industry. Plus, you can specialize and switch fields, and there's never enough of you! So you have to wear the stupid scrubs—what the hey?

6. *Market research analyst*—clean work and you don't have to be right. I don't have any idea what a market research analyst does, but they seem to be making a huge mess of it and still com-

ing out OK. The guys who handled Enron are undoubtedly analyzing a market near you. You could do market research out of your home, although maybe not with test subjects. Looks good on a card, that's for darn sure.

7. *The IT guy*—83.5K for just saying power it down and power it back up. The IT guy is the new custodian—you want something, where you gonna go? These are not the strike-it-rich nerds, but still some sense of revenge must prevail. It's hard to believe there was once a time I-T did not spell information technology.

8. *Real estate appraiser*—if you don't mind climbing a ladder. The good news is you're not slinging a roll of tarpaper on your shoulder. You can probably do real estate appraiser online school in twelve weeks on your Dell and set right out on an appraising tear. Corporate real estate is probably the way to go, what with the Abu Dubais willing to buy everything up to and including the Brooklyn Bridge.

9. *Pharmacist*—four billion illegible prescriptions per annum, but still, you get to stand on a white stage behind a podium at Wal-Mart. I don't know what they make, my school chum Jay Bubrick won't say, but he has a lot of toys. Pharmacy school can be pretty tough, unless maybe Liberty University has one, or Bob Jones. Pharmacists don't even make their own potions anymore; those are coffee beans in the mortar. Or is it the pestle?

10. *Psychologist*—one of the best ways of being self-employed without flipping blenders on eBay, depending how you feel about that. And if you help somebody, so much the better. The smart money says clinical, not research, since chronic depressives pay a lot better than fruit flies. If you're the kind of person people are always dumping on—opening up to—anyway, now you're just a two-year degree from a community college away from making it pay.

THE TEN ABSOLUTELY WORST JOBS

Hospital sharps and human parts disposal, cow inseminator, whale feces collector in the Bay of Fundy, bear assistant at the Build-A-Bear store...the usual suspects when asked the worst jobs you could have. But using Department of Labor statistics and completely selective word-of-mouth from obviously disgruntled employees, it's a no-brainer to come up with **The Ten Absolutely Worst Jobs** you could possibly have:

1. *Elephant vasectomist*—not much opportunity in the field, since the only one seems to be at Disney's Animal Kingdom.

Necessary, though, since it's almost impossible to get an elephant to wear a sheath.

2. *Bounty hunter*—once you know that nearly half of all released felons are rearrested, it's hard to resist looking into bounty hunting as a working-for-yourself option, but it's not for everyone and not in every jurisdiction. You, in fact, work for a bondsman, hoping to recoup his loss when the bad boy skips. He gets most of the money, you take all of the risk. The good news is that many states which allow bounty hunting require no training or permit—and you get to meet interesting recidivists!

3. *Repo man/woman*—that's repossession agent. Your job: protect property against people, particularly those who think they own it. America is built upon credit sales, and if we don't take that which has money put down on it seriously, the whole system falls apart, from Geo Metro to Hamptons estate. Your job: locate and recover through subterfuge, deception, and skillful use of towing—very close to legal theft. Takes a special kind of person.

4. *Chicken plant worker*—chicken plant workers of the world, unite; you have nothing to lose but your gizzards. Quite possibly the only job worse than working on the killing floor at Oscar Meyer, or as a pig sticker for Hormel. If testing positive for TB, being unable to scratch for eight hours, and being hauled off the line by Immigration routinely appeals to you, well, there you go. Tyson has some openings.

5. *Hazmat diver*—let me get this straight: you dive in sluice ponds, retention tanks, toxic rivers, and lakes with PCB beaches looking for the worst thing you can find? You're a hazardous materials diver. One man's trash is another man's treasure. Pay is good, make about as much as an accountant, albeit one who swims in nuclear reactor ponds.

6. *Turd wrangler*—job description from a gentlemen up in Door County, WI, whose job classification, sanitarian, sounds even worse: performing the very needed function of keeping the septic fields and holding tanks of a nation above water. The Honey Wagon, per se, is a registered trademark in Kansas City, where the honey boys say it's actually a clean-fingernail job due to advances in honey sucking and the cutting-edge armada of 4,000-gallon stainless steel pumpers. Regardless, your wife will make you undress in the backyard when you get home. Maybe that's not a problem for you.

7. *Biological specimen preparer*—the good news is you only have to be a junior in biology to get onto the ground floor of frog and cat embalming, which can lead to bigger things: Entry level into the exciting and open-ended bio-tech field, and without being the subject of the study yourself. Nasty work, though, quite possibly opposed to everything you hold dear, particularly if "sanctity of life" is part of your phrasebook. Not as bad as the guys down the hall testing Long Lashes on bunnies, but bad enough.

8. *Model*—It's not all glamour for models, it turns out, who average eleven bucks an hour even with such nice hair, hands, feet, and/or

teeth; fortunately, they can fall back on their $5.85 waitress jobs, which give them needed flexibility for casting calls and surplus cheese handouts. A lot of the work turns out to be dressing up on your own dime and handing out free samples, hoping against hope for entrée into the Fleet Farm catalogue.

9. *Security guards*—long been the butt of jokes and with good reason. The uniforms vary, some look almost real, but God forbid they should be allowed to carry guns. Kaplan University online (the same people preparing our kids for the SAT?) can get you into the world of security without ever leaving your home, helpful if you're still sporting the ankle bracelet. Background checks are becoming more common, but busted cops need a place to go, and why not use some of those street smarts for the good of, if not man-, mall-kind? Pay is lousy, hours are worse, but you get to carry a really big flashlight.

10. *Physician*—a surprise entry into the worst list for a profession formerly held in high esteem, at least by doctors themselves. One doctor in ten would do it again. With HMOs, most find themselves working in the insurance industry, and not liking it. The Hippocratic Oath has been replaced with insurance disclaimers; most of what physicians were trained to treat is no longer covered. Income is way down, with many doctors spending the better part of a career paying off med school loans. An increasing number of healers are cooling their heels and not practicing medicine on actual patients at all, working in the allied field of providing medical testimony on behalf of corporations, instead. When doctors are going into law, something is rotten in Denmark.

THANKS FOR THE MEMOS:
THE WHISTLER

Norm,

I think I have made myself clear lately that your whistling in the office is very disruptive to my ability to work. Even Lyle asked you to stop last week. I SERIOUSLY plead with you once again to try and stop it. I have very detailed work that needs my full attention and concentration.

Since your return from the recent hospital stay, you have been extra, extra talkative. There is nothing I can do about that if the people you are talking to do not have a problem with it. Plus, I have my headphones which I have put into high gear usage. The office has an open and friendly atmosphere that encourages interaction. But my goal at this job is to do my work efficiently between normal work hours to prevent the need for overtime.

Roger has told me that it is my responsibility to tell you that the whistling is disruptive. I partially disagree with that philosophy, since I know no one has any obligation to listen to me whatsoever. But that is the direction from the owner I must respect.

I can tune out the chatter. I have accepted that as a normal part of the office. But I must draw the line at the echoing, sometimes off-key whistling, especially since the headphones cannot drown that out. I don't know of a more annoying sound besides the stereotypical chalkboard screech. I ask that you respect this one request and try to honor others' work needs. After all, this is a workplace.

—Klaus

Klaus,

I am sorry if you find my whistling in the office disturbing. I assure you that it is a nervous habit that is completely involuntary. I will try to cease and desist. Since it is an involuntary habit, I hope you will be patient with me and politely remind me if I slip from time to time.

I had no idea it was a problem, and no one else has spoken with me about it.

Lyle's comment last week was a joke: "You are no longer allowed to whistle that song again" referring to the fact that I was a getting a bad, catchy song stuck in his head. (I believe the tune in question was "Windy" by The Association.)

I do wish you would have pulled me aside and spoke with me privately about this issue instead of going to a superior or composing a memo to me and my boss. I am more than happy to do what I can to contribute to a positive work environment for everyone in the office. We all wish to work efficiently in a friendly atmosphere to create the best work possible. If you have any other concerns about me in the office, I hope you will feel free to discuss them with me in person.

Whenever I feel afraid...

—Norm

WHAD'YA KNOW ABOUT PEOPLE? ROUND 4

1. Lipstick sales—up or down during shaky times?

2. What percentage of Americans' only exercise is running up a tab?
    (a) 23
    (b) 13
    (c) 8

3. Maybe it's errands and maybe it ain't—the percentage of working women who don't go straight home after work:
    (a) 25
    (b) 37
    (c) 50

4. How does the average woman buy her two-piece swimsuit?
    (a) Smaller on top, bigger on the bottom
    (b) Bigger on top, bigger on the bottom
    (c) Smaller on top, skirted on the bottom

5. Tattoo regret: on the rise or the fall?

6. According to *Allure* magazine, _____ men find breast implants intimidating.
    (a) 1 out of 100
    (b) 1 out of 2
    (c) a whopping 2 out of 3

7. ____ percent of men are wearing underwear that has lost its elasticity.
    (a) 30
    (b) 40
    (c) 50

RAVENMORTE'S BAD DAY

8. Percentage of wealthy women who reupholster rather than buy a new davenport:
    (a) 40
    (b) 58
    (c) 66.7

9. ____ out of 100 Americans swear they've never sworn.
    (a) 1
    (b) 3
    (c) 6

10. When asked who was more likely to go to heaven, more high school seniors said:

(a) Bill Clinton

(b) Mother Theresa

(c) the survey taker

WHAD'YA KNOW ABOUT PEOPLE? (ROUND 4 ANSWERS)

1. Lipstick sales up, hemlines down during shaky times, a look I personally like, especially if Angora is involved.

2. The Harris Poll only got (c) 8 percent of Americans to confess lethargy, although many probably counted running to the refrigerator as an aerobic activity.

3. (b) 37 percent of working women take the long way home, claiming "errands" immunity from any inquiry into where they've been. Sometimes you can find receipts, sometimes not. (*Women's Health* magazine)

4. (a) Smaller on top, bigger on the bottom. Men's main problem with swimming trunks is what level to wear them at—at a certain point, it seems pretty arbitrary.

5. Tattoo regret is actually down somewhat to 16 percent in 2008. For a lot of these dragons and mythological creatures, especially, it's going to take some time to sink in. The good news is

that girdles will pretty much cover the girls' base-of-the-spine designs.

6. (c) 2 out of 3 men involuntarily back up when they see a pair of breast implants coming at them, although we could get used to them pretty quick. It's 100 percent for penis implants…well, 90 percent maybe.

7. (a) About 1 in 3 men's jockeys should be hiked up but aren't, which accounts for the look in your officemate's eyes. 36 percent report a significant color shift and 15 percent report a pretty much formless garment which has lost the torso battle big time. (Jockey International)

8. (b) 58 percent, although you would think it would be higher, since rich women tend to reupholster themselves as well.

9. (c) 6 out of 100 Americans never swear. Dang. It is interesting that many of our swear words and phrases can be found in Shakespeare, although "s'blood!" and "zounds!" seem to have lost their currency. Chaucer knew some good ones.

10. (c) On the college entrance exam survey, 87 percent of high school seniors thought the test administrator was most likely to go to heaven, more so than Mother Theresa (79 percent) or even Bill Clinton (52 percent). They probably expected this would help them in the grading curve.

TAKING THE PLUNGE

The stock market plunges under two conditions:

(1) because things are getting better, or

(2) because things are getting worse.

This arises when the economy is either heating up or cooling down, resulting in a strong dollar, which is bad for exports, or a weak dollar, which is bad for everything else. When unemployment drops, Wall Street suffers performance anxiety, but when people are out of work and not spending, impetus is lent to the recessionary spiral and flagging occurs. This is because free-market economies dictate that when demand is high, prices increase because you can get it, and, when demand is low, prices go up due to higher per-unit costs passed along to the consumer, who is

(1) not spending enough, and

(2) not saving enough.

Flaccid leading indicators indicate a lack of virility in the private sector, impacting on a scenario where, say, foreign car prices increase and domestic car prices rise to prove they're as good as foreign cars, concurrent with spot markets selling short a barrel of oil to as little as a quart, even as pork bellies close higher. In the housing sector, Fannie Mae has been seeing Ginnie.

HUMAN RESOURCING

For most of us, work is work. Aggravation for pay. Not a calling, not necessarily what you were born to do…a job. What happens to you when school runs out. My youngest, Nora, likes school, really, is sure good at it, but resents not being paid for it. On the trail of tears to the middle school bus stop I used to say to her, "At least you're not having a rope tied around your waist to lower you into a coal mine every morning!"

"How much does that pay?" she'd always ask, adding, "I'd do it if it paid."

Worldwide, 21 percent of workers are emotionally invested in their jobs, slightly higher in the U.S. at 29 percent, which appears to suggest that 3 out of 4 American workers probably feel no pride at home or office. It is asking a lot of anyone to take pride in roller bearings or pine tree auto deodorizers, but still. Emotional investment is a tricky term, too, used as it is to describe what you're supposed to have in everything from coaching tee-ball to coupling, to emotion itself. If you're not emotionally invested in your emotions, you're in one hell of a conundrum. Emotional investment is in such demand, it's a wonder there's any left to take to work at all.

Chinese emotionally invested workers account for only 8 percent of the workforce, which means only a hundred million or so guys and gals in China look forward to going to work. Having to drink the effluent from the People's Quad Core Processor Plant has to give you pause, too, even if it does pay the water bills. And whatever happened to the "work makes you free" Germans, now at a lowly 15 percent gung-ho level that could only have been brought down by the reintegration of the East Germans, whom socialism ruined as workers. In Mexico, despite the tongue lashing they take every day from Lou Dobbs, 40 percent of the workforce are actively engaged in their jobs, even if they are in San Diego.

☞ Americans think a nurse is 9 times more honest than a car salesman.

☞ In an office of 100 people, 15 steal snacks.

☞ 3 percent of Americans suffer from "leisure nausea," an inability to enjoy time off.

☞ 6 percent of American workers would sleep with their boss, date the boss's son or daughter, pick up the boss's dry cleaning, or take credit for someone else's work for a raise.

THE CABINET OF
DR. SCHOLL

Seinfeld did it, and Portnoy, and Cindy McCain, too, as will your local teenagers if you're not on your toes—breaking and entering other people's medicine cabinets. Ointments are destiny, medications clue you into at least the most dramatic of a new acquaintance's syndromes—the treatable ones, anyway. Secrets lie within, and not just New Blue. Revelations. Have you ever noticed that Andy Rooney has no problem with us looking through his drawers but never once has given us a glimpse of his medicine chest, which has to be stuffed with jocular observations: "Beta-blockers—but can anyone tell you what your beta is?" Maybe he's a clandestine homeopath. Cracking the medicine cabinet of a friend's bathroom is the human equivalent of dog butt-sniffing protocol, a quick readout of the subject's life and times: vaginal dryness; jock itch; estro/andro-gen; horny goat weed for the big P; jimson for either cramps or seeing God; Creatine for those long waits in the on-deck circle; Cytomel for dancing pecs; Steranabol for buns of Stereel; an old bottle of Ephedra, for nostalgia; family size Metamucil; Semenax semen volume enhancer, don't know how that got in there; Glutamine; Citulline Malate; the Bs, the Es, the Ks, herbals, megas, and naturos; y los tres aminos: Alanine, Aspartate, and Asparagine. Summer's Eve, medicated. The patch, the gum, the generic cigarettes. New Freedom. Minoxydil, Botox, Dysport, Myobloc, whatever help you can get, wherever. Whiteners. Bronzers. Defoliaters. Fake 'n Bake. Good Looking Hair, aerosol. Just for Men. Teri Hatcher in a box. Large tube of KY. Viagra to Levitra to Cialis for a triple play. Zovirax? That's for herpes, no? Preparations H, W, and P, spare glass eye in solution, diaphragm the size of a frisbee, Maureen McGovern (There's Got to Be a Morning After) Pills. St. John's Wort, Prozac, Xanax, Paxil, Lexapro, Celexa, and Zoloft, in order of prescription date. Mycozil, anti-fungal ostensibly for yellow toenails. Nitrostat, just in case. Yaz—teen birth control she says she's taking for acne. Flomax, to go with the. Nembutal as a last resort.

DEAR DIARYA

Buckminster Fuller made entries every fifteen minutes between 1917 and 1983 in his (eventual) 700-volume, 140,000-page *Dymaxion Chronofile*, a personal version of the chronological ship transport records he kept as a naval aide during the First World War. Fuller regarded his "rigorous record" as being "a case history of a suburban New England everyman during the tumultuous period from the Gay '90s through the late twentieth century." Now housed at Stanford, his is a chronicle of an anything but typical life and work, which did not shy away from the mundane:

> There were times when I received a bill twenty times. Didn't have to put it in twenty times, just two or three—and then I would put in the letter from the lawyer concerning the case…

Robert Shields is the winner in the over-examined life sweepstakes, on volume alone, with a 35-million word diary leaving nothing, stools included, to the reader's imagination. Shields backed up his waking hours every five minutes, sleeping in two-hour bursts so as to record his dreams. Between 6:30 and 7:35 p.m. on April 18, 1994, for example, Shields put two Stauffer's macaroni and cheese dinners in the oven at 350 degrees, ate one while his wife, Cornelia, ate the other one, changed the bulb over the back porch, and sat down twice at the Wheelwriter to record it all before settling in for *Murder, She Wrote*. The next day was as exciting:

12:20 to 12:25: I stripped to my thermals.

12:25 to 12:30: I discharged urine.

12:30 to 12:50: I ate leftover salmon—Alaska red salmon by Bumblebee, about seven ounces—drank ten ounces of orange juice while I read the *Oxford Dictionary of Quotations*.

12:50 to 1:45: I was at the keyboard of the IBM Wheelwriter making entries for the diary. I typed diary entries since 3:00 this morning. I failed to mention that the *Tri-City Herald* weighed in this morning at one pound, eleven and one-half ounces. That was the heaviest paper we have had to my knowledge. It lacked only half an ounce of being one and three-quarters pounds. Think of it...

3:20 to 3:25 in the afternoon: I took the readings given in the margins. Humidity: fifty-one and a half. Porch temperature: fifty-six degrees. Porch floor temperature: fifty-one degrees. The study temperature: seventy-seven degrees. And the door temperature in the study, on the door jamb: seventy-four degrees.

5:45 to 6:15: I read more from the *Oxford Dictionary of Quotations*. I ate half a dozen large Archway sugar cookies while I drank two cups of milk.

8:35 to 8:40: I peeled meat labels from McCrory's to mount in the diary. Bacon is up 20 cents a pound. T-bones are terribly high.

FODDER FIGURE JS.

HELLO, FODDER

That scarecrow out in the truck patch in Dad's old clothes? Look closer—it is Dad! Fatherhood doesn't come with operating instructions, and, had it, what dad worth his salt would look at them, except to see tools needed and that you have all the fasteners. You hear about feminine intuition; well, guys have it too, but unless they come up with another name for it you'll never hear one bring it up. Fathering is locked into our RNA, and it looks like we're going to have to hacksaw the hasp to get at it. Male intuition is knowing, by your very nature, how to do the wrong thing. It compels the fledgling father not to eat the little suckers, like some species we could mention, but to keep them alive and flourishing, and otherwise keep the hell out of their and their mother's way. I'm not saying there isn't trial and error in the learning process—a while back I was attempting empathy with my youngest, Nora, vis-à-vis some disappointing friend behavior (you know, "You have to learn what you can expect from people and not be disappointed at how little that can be") and she said, "Dad, you're not a girl, and you're not NOW." She didn't want a nice fruit salad, either, and she used to love it when I made her those. Once you realize that none of your experience or scarring is relevant, it takes a lot of the pressure off fatherhood.

It's pretty much the same all over. Keller, Voelker, and Yovsi compared West African Nso and West German fathers and found quite a bit in common in how they raise their young…and in a schnitzel the Nso are quite fond of. "Father" tended to be an honorific among the Nso, and not so much anymore in the former Fatherland. West Africans tend to spread parenting over the extended family, because it takes a Hillary, so that an unrelated male can blow off a lot of things Dad was meaning to get to. African Guiessi infants are so secure in their upbringings that, when presented with anyone who looks vaguely like Dad, they will stick out their little hands for a high-five. While American kids tend to hug/kiss a parent (sometimes including the father), Ugandan Ganda children will clap, giving dear old Dad standing ovations, deserved or not. While American mothers never stop talking to and like their babies, American fathers have to talk to their offspring in asides out of earshot of their mothers; among the Gusii of Kenya, infants learn to expect their moms to do all the talking for them. Unlike Midwesterners, Efe parents do not have a problem with someone who just happens to be around nursing or comforting their children—in fact, it's rude not to. In Botswana (at least among the !Kung San) sociologists found nothing like the "Wait until your father gets home," so ineffective in the West.

Skills teaching remains a major role for African fathers, less so for western European fathers who must beg their children for help Facebooking. East German children were found to be insecure in the 1980s, but, after all, their father figure was Eric Honecker. Southern German fathers were found to be very much like southern American fathers, substituting Grand Prix for NASCAR. In addition to their increased parental responsibilities, the salaryman fathers of Japan have to juggle work and karaoke. Ho, Lin, and Fu suggest that Chinese children are raised to be interdependent rather than dependent, leaving Chinese fathers pretty much off the hook.

THANKS FOR THE MEMOS:
INCONTINENCE CAN'T BE HELPED

To: All Haulers and Transporters

From: Julio Murphy DISTRICT MANAGER

Subject: Scalehouse Behavior

Over the past few months an increasing number of drivers are removing their tarp straps, releasing turnbuckles, or untarping their loads on the inbound road prior to arriving at the scalehouse. Our policy is and has been that there will be no untarping activities or releasing of turnbuckles before weighing vehicles in. The reasons for this are that debris and liquids can be released from the vehicle, and more importantly, it exposes drivers to traffic in a potentially dangerous area of the site.

Thus, effective immediately, NO DRIVERS OR HELPERS ARE PERMITTED OUTSIDE THEIR VEHICLES PRIOR TO WEIGHING TRUCKS IN AT THE SCALEHOUSE.

Furthermore, we have had and continue to have an issue with drivers relieving themselves in the roadways at the landfill. In fact, within the week, I personally observed two different drivers engaging in this unacceptable practice. In fact, one driver from Dewdrop Trucking was observed urinating and worse in the road in front of the office and public drop-off center. Needless to say, that this is illegal, unsanitary, and it reflects poorly on Dewdrop, Taste Management, and our industries. We are not there to add to the waste. Any incontinence can't be helped.

Thank you for complying.

From everyday collection to environmental protection

WHAD'YA KNOW ABOUT PEOPLE? ROUND 5

1. Do more women like veggies than men like red meat?

2. The percentage of scrapbookers who are male:
   - (a) 2
   - (b) 1
   - (c) 0

3. Percentage of teens who make sexual choices based on the media:
   - (a) 10
   - (b) 5
   - (c) 1

4. The average American eats ____ grilled cheese sandwiches per annum.
   - (a) 8.4
   - (b) 12.7
   - (c) 19

5. While a man with a cell phone in his pocket may be happy to see you, he is risking a ____ percent reduction in sperm.

    (a) 10

    (b) 20

    (c) 30

6. Do more men or women have big TV envy?

7. What percentage of people age 35–44 regift?

    (a) 31

    (b) 43

    (c) 50.5

8. Middle-aged women underreport hot flashes by:

    (a) 20 percent

    (b) 40 percent

    (c) 60 percent

9. After age 40, ____ of all divorces are initiated by the wife.

    (a) two-thirds

    (b) three-fourths

    (c) two-fifths

10. Out of 100 women, how many are wearing the wrong size bra?

    (a) 17

    (b) 52

    (c) 80

- ☞ The average man can do a 19.5-inch vertical leap.
- ☞ If you're a teen, the odds are 2 to 1 you're bored right now.
- ☞ 2 out of 3 women prefer sleep to sex.
- ☞ 1 in 10 men wants more body hair.
- ☞ 42 percent of people sleep with their dogs.
- ☞ 2 out of 3 men have tried to make their pecs dance.

WHAD'YA KNOW ABOUT PEOPLE? (ROUND 5 ANSWERS)

1. Yes. The Grocery Manufacturers of America, who have a stake in this, find that 30 percent of women love salads and 25 percent of men lust for red meat. FYI, 8 percent of men are fruit eaters, and 8 percent of women like their meat red.

2. (c) 0; perhaps the only statistical 0 in polling.

3. (b) 5 percent of teens make sexual choices based on TV, music, and movies, but 37 percent of their parents do (!) or have, more likely. I have no idea what this means.

4. (a) 8.4. Huh. That many. Mom called them toasted cheese, and so do I.

5. (c) 30 percent, more if they're on vibrate, according to *Men's Health.*

6. Get real—men, of course, but at age 45–51 the gals, no matter what they say, know that size matters.

7. (a) 31 percent—but, to their credit, only 25 percent lie about it (*Business Week*).

8. (b) 40 percent. Middle-aged women don't feel they have to share everything with you. From my subscription to *Menopause* magazine.

9. (a) Two-thirds; they're pretty well fed up by 40 with what's probably their second mistake, anyway. This falls off considerably after age 70, when their husbands get out from natural causes.

10. (c) 80. If it's not their bras, it's their shoes, or, let's be honest, both; one bigger and one smaller than reality justifies.

WHAD'YA KNOW

ABOUT

PLACES?

PYONGYANG,
HERE I AM!

Americans wishing to visit the **Democratic Peoples** (no possessive) **Republic of Korea** must first memorize the phrase, "Raymond Shaw is the kindest, bravest, warmest, most wonderful human being I've ever known in my life." Attendance at the **Arirang Mass Performance** in Pyongyang is mandatory; with (exactly) one hundred thousand performers, be prepared for curtain calls taking up to 72 hours of your five-day "window of opportunity." (Should you be asked to hold a picture card at the stadium, act as if it is a great honor, and flip when everyone else does.) Deluxe accommodations at **Yanggakdo International Hotel** include blackout windows, closed-circuit radio in every room, and nightly **Dear Leader Hennessey Cognac** specials. The **Joy Brigades** phone in the lobby is for senior official use, only; those hankering for a taste of Pyongyang night-life need look no further than the Dear Leader Karaoke Place, just off the lobby where the pool should be. In the morning, it's on the town, under the helpful scrutiny and care of your minders, where the **Kumsusan Memorial Palace** (the final resting place of **Kim Il Sung**) is not to be missed, literally. Ditto, the life-sized at 65 feet **Grand Monument to Kim Il Sung** in **Kim Il Sung Square**, the **Grand Leader Kim Il Sung's Study House**, and **The Arch of Kim Il Sung Triumph**, not modeled after any similarly named arches. It goes without saying the birthplace of **Kim Il Sung, Mangyongdae,** is a must-see, and you will "want" to spend time in the **Victorious Fatherland Liberation War Museum**, the **Children of Glorious Kim Il Sung's Palace**, and browse for souvenirs (which may not leave the country) at the **Grand Leader Department Store**. No tour would be complete without paying respects to the **Grand Humiliation of the Hegemonists Museum** dockside at the (former) **USS Pueblo,** where an animatronic Gerald Ford does nothing. Then, on by de-luxe personnel carrier in dead of night to **Best Eastern Hyangsan Hotel** in Myohyang for a refreshing debriefing in the internment spa. Your final day in the DPRK is awash in the sights and sounds of **Panmunjom** in the heart of the zone that never sleeps, the **DMZ,** capped by a farewell re-education and buffet in Pyongyang, thence via military caravan to a point just shy of **Shenyang, South Korea,** where you're on your own.

OR OTHERWISE
DISABLING

Flying is how much humiliation you can endure and still arrive somewhere. If the TSA guys took off the gloves, it might be more fun; at least people would be lining up for a reason. I'm all for security, but I doubt that a guy who got his training at Upper Iowa Correspondence is going to provide it, his having perfected the back-of-the-hand pat aside. You can get a bazooka through security if you put it in a fly rod tube with a trout unlimited sticker on it. Airlines have the kind of contempt for their clients formerly only seen in the Microsoft/user relationship, and for the same reason—where you gonna go? Trailways? Little things, like posting "delay" as the reason for the delay. If they told you that your 747 undergoing paperwork at Sea/Tac is the reason gate B-15 at O'Hare is the default lot for the luggage haulers and fuel trucks, they'd have to kill you. None dare call it a service industry. That they stopped serving you only confirms the fact. Bearing the brunt of it, besides we, the cargo, are the flight attendants, some of whom were featured in *Come Fly with Me* in 1963 and haven't had any benefits since Eastern went under. Today's flight attendants fail to see the glamour in shuttling between Detroit and Youngstown that their predecessors, the stewardesses, did.

The worst airlines are now merging to form super-bad airlines, eliminating much lousy service replication. If you can't operate regionally, why not go global? That's like the quarrelsome engaged couple thinking marriage will smooth things over. You'd be much better off flying with your orthodontist; what the heck, you paid for the plane, if he's going anywhere near Erie. They call them carriers for a reason: you are baggage. You are free to be bandied about the country. Not that I expect to be entertained—I doubt I will ever forget the Southwest flight where the co-pilot (I hope it wasn't the pilot) came back to the cabin to pull Sacagawea dollars out of quite a few lucky ears. I'd be amazed if something similar wasn't going on on the Titanic. I don't want funny when I fly. You want funny? Feed me. I'm hilarious when I eat. Give me drink and watch it dribble down my turtleneck. For a real laugh, give me the exit row and I'll ace the Des Moines Target with the 37-pound window after giving full verbal affirmation.

TOP NON-DESTINATIONS

1. Somalia

2. North Korea

3. Aberdeen, SD

4. Yemen

5. Iran

6. Pakistan

7. Birmingham, AL, in August

8. Iraq, until corner turned

9. Nepal, until things cool off

10. Men's room near Minnesota Shines, Minneapolis/St. Paul airport

 # *OH. CANADA.*

Before Martin Short, Stephen Leacock was considered Canada's greatest wit. If you need proof, it was Leacock who said, "Canadians use English for literature, Scotch for sermons, and American for conversation." Maybe in mixed company they do, but overhear Canadians jawing among themselves and, as an American, you are out in the cold. For Homeland Security reasons alone, Americans need to familiarize themselves with our neighbors, and what they imply. Here's a start:

Click: hipster Canadian slang for kilometer; as in, "She's about a hundred clicks from Gander if the lake is still frozen."

Hoser: fake Canadianism coined by Bob and Doug McKenzie, who don't exist either.

ABM: don't be upset, it's what they go to instead of an ATM.

Double-double: two sugars, two creams. A **2–4**, however, is a case of Mooseheads.

A **garburator** is a garbage disposal.

Homo milk: whole milk.

What appears to be French fries dotted with cheese curds with gravy over it is **poutine**.

The **905ers** are right wingers in the area code which covers Peel, York, and Halton.

If a Canadian says, "**Beauty**," to you, that's good—he means "thanks."

Lotus Land is the Canadian equivalent of Los Angeles, British Columbia.

The Ontario Provincial Police are the **Piss Pots**.

Puck slut is just what the name implies, while a **rink rat** pilots the zamboni.

A Canadian **snowbird** often wings it as far south as Erie, Pennsylvania.

In southern Ontario, "take it easy" becomes **takitish**.

Tim Horton's Doughnut chain is variously referred to as **Tim's, Timmy's, Timmy Ho's, Timmy Ho-Ho's,** and **Horny Tim's.** A **jambuster** is a jelly-filled doughnut.

Off-sale is what we would call a liquor store, up where most are run by the **LC,** liquor control board.

"**Jesus Murphey**" is a Canadian way to blaspheme.

Hogtown is Toronto; **Pile o' Bones,** Regina; **Sack Vegas,** Lower Sackville.

Scare Canada = Air Canada.

Canadians order pizza "**all dressed.**"

They don't call in sick, they "**book off**" work.

ON THE ROAD TO SHAMBALA

Is this the road to Shambala? Would we want to arrive there if Three Dog Night got there first? Men have been looking for Shambala, or Shangri-la, the Taoist paradise—ever since they

realized things could be a lot better. King Mu of the Zhou dynasty found it considerably before Ronald Colman did, discovering there the Jade Palace of the Yellow Emperor, Huang-Di, the father of Chinese culture. Shambala was a pure land of enlightened beings living under the teachings of the Kalachakra tantra, a complex discipline still taught which emphasizes the correspondences between the earthly body and the cosmos. It is the Shangri-la of the Kun Lun mountains in Tibet (actually the Ojai, California, of 1933) which captivated the world in *Lost Horizon*, a land where the men resemble Sam Jaffe but the women all look like Jane Wyatt, at least at first ("Bob! Bob! Look at her face, Bob! Her face! Look at her face!") The upshot of Frank Capra's film seemed to be that if you find Shangri-la, don't leave with souvenirs.

The enlightened are more likely to find us, eventually—the 25th Kali king is supposed to reenter the not-so-ideal world in 2424 at the head of a massive army to defeat the dark forces of chaos and usher in a new golden age. So, if we hang tight, paradise may find us.

Had a gazillion Gerald R. Ford V.P. tie clips in Grand Rapids

IS THAT THE OVAL OFFICE, OR ARE YOU JUST HAPPY TO SEE ME?

For you or me, it's legacy, *shmegacy*, but not for a president. He may have only had four years to fabricate one...or less: a plexiglas time-line of the Mayaguez incident is just about the only exhibit in the Gerald R. Ford Library in Grand Rapids.

President Reagan's library is about the best, except for, inexplicably, being in the Simi Valley and not Hollywood, where they could have utilized several of those empty storefronts along Hollywood Boulevard a stone's throw from his star (right between Lassie and David Niven). The clips of *Death Valley Days*, alone, back before he became the Old Ranger, are worth the price of admission.

Twenty-Mule Team Borax, that was the ticket for Ronald Reagan before General Electric Theater catapulted him into an all-electric home and the presidency. The diorama of President Reagan greeting Nancy in which he appears to be mouthing "Mommy!" is a little creepy. The Reagan people got Air Force One—the plane, not the sneakers—parked right there in the adjacent hangar, awaiting the presidential manikin's needs, which goes a long way towards explaining why Messrs Bush and Cheney favored corporate jets. Air Force One goes back at least to Eisenhower, and the tug-of-war between competing presidential factions must have been intense. Ronnie looked better on the ramp, no doubt. The Berlin Wall, *well*, they owe him that, even though it's doubtful he ever really thought they were going to tear it down just because he told them to. Was it a headache getting it through Thousand Oaks on US 118? Yes. But worth the effort: after all, if the former Soviet Union were a soufflé, it was Ronald Reagan who slammed the door.

You have to like the Hoover Library, even if just for being in West Branch, Iowa, where Herbert Hoover was apparently from, and for the fact that you can purchase the many hats Mr. Hoover wore in the gift shop. Hoover was President Bad-Timing—just happened to be in office when the world went to hell in a hand basket. As a matter of fact, you can get the hand basket in the gift shop. Hoover was an engineer at heart and the Hoover Dam is one of the few monuments, along with the Pyramid of Cheops and Disneyland, named for the guy who earned it. The Great Depression? Nobody summed it up better than President Hoover, who said "Every time we think we can make ends meet, somebody moves the ends." History gave Hoover a better shake than Garfield, whose few months did not generate enough paperwork to line the shelves of his presidential repository, but who has a (very livable) mausoleum in Cleveland for himself and Lucretia, with the memorable sign on the stair-way "Down Stairs to Crypt and Washrooms."

FDR was originally going to be added to Mt. Rushmore, but the stone cigarette holder kept breaking off, so they put him on the dime. FDR and Eleanor each have their own libraries, and there's very little traffic between the two. The Truman Library in Independence, MO,

Down Stairs to Crypt and Washrooms

has (the) The Buck Stops Here Store, where, surprisingly, everything is not a buck. Roger Williams played Truman-style rags for the 84th birthday (of Williams? of the Library?) but Margaret, having passed away in January, did not get up to sing. Featured is the coin Truman flipped (his lucky nickel) to decide whether or not to drop Little Boy.

The Kansas History Day champion, seventh grader Cooper Self, researched his winning entry, "I Like Ike and His Compromise to Avoid Nuclear Conflict," entirely at the Eisenhower Library archives.

The Dwight D. Eisenhower Presidential Library and Museum was named one of Kansas's 8 Wonders…your line here. It is the largest native limestone structure near Abilene and was paid for, ironically, by the generous support of the Military Industrial Complex.

The Ernest Hemingway Collection is the surprising hit of the John F. Kennedy Library in Boston, surprising in that Hemingway is the one writer who did not read anything at the Kennedy inaugural. Jacqueline worked the deal, some years later. The Kennedy Library is not the fun place that the Nixon Library is, nor is it down home like the Hoover. It's a little on the Camelot side. It does, however, have a mock-up of the Kennedy–Nixon debate set with the actual infrared lights that slow-cooked the vice-president's goose, and you can go home with a JFK rocker in the store ($358 with cushion) just like the Eisenhower people did.

The LBJ library has been playing catch-up with the Nixon archivists, just having released taped phone conversations for the first four months of 1968, primetime for eavesdropping on the man from the Pedernales. LBJ's interviews while sitting on the toilet are a missed opportunity. Lady Bird's Pedernales River Chili Recipe, one of the scarier sounding chilis, is available on request. The Lady Bird Plaza is kind of falling apart, but they started restoring it to her original beauty. Worth seeing are a good number of the 4,000 LBJ editorial cartoons, including Walt Kelly's "The Lone Arranger," from Pogo. All this and just a chip shot from Willie Nelson's presidential library, the Pedernales Cutt-and-Putt Golf Club.

Best Chinese food? Nixon Museum, sticks down. It was Pat Nixon who said that China had the best Chinese food, and the Richard M. Nixon Presidential Library Commissary tries to live up to that declaration, although favoring Cantonese at the expense of Szechwan.

The Clinton Museum, despite looking like the Kubla Khan's pleasure dome on the Arkansas River, is a bit of a disappointment, what with still no presidential papers except the inaugural ball menus and several boxes of subpoenas. Ken Starr should have returned the papers by now, but, then again, you'd think Hillary's billing records would've turned up at this late day (and at those rates). The national health care card President Clinton waved at one of the more surreal State of the Union addresses (stuck it right in Newt's face, he did) is on display, even though all it was good for was slipping the lock on a motel door. Impeachment, well, you have to read between the time-line.

President George H.W. Bush seems to have gone a little mishegoss with the Born to Play Ball exhibit, which does not deal with Mr. Bush's dealings with certain parties in the Middle East, but actual, down-and-dirty major league baseball. Junior played a little in college, but I don't believe Poppy did. Didn't even play a ballplayer like his mentor/tormentor Reagan. Well, the Astros paid for it, so what the heck—supposed to be the fifty best ballplayers of all time, and Bob Uecker is not even on the bench. Have to rethink Bush I as the Baseball President.

George W.'s Libary, er, Library at Southern Methodist is still a work in progress, slowed down by the need to raze the dorms on that side of campus, and how best to make that Churchill biography he's always meaning to read not look lost on all that shelving in the reading room. The diorama of children showing none have been left behind will be the centerpiece of the exhibits space, honoring the man who wants to be remembered as the Edjication President. The gift shop will feature a faith-based bazaar and bake sale, with the proceeds going to Unplanned Parenthood. Only reference to Iraq is the Code of Hammurabi obelisk recovered from looters and on loan from the Baghdad Antiquities Museum (call for hours).

THANKS FOR THE MEMOS:
YE OLDE PARKING CENTRE

From: Kelley

Subject: Opera House Parking Centre

To: All Staff

This is a For Your Information notation. The new Opera House parking structure is to be officially referred to as the Opera House Parking Centre.

Please note spelling of Centre with an RE.

We specifically discourage any referring to the parking structure as a "Parking Garage."

Thank you,

BLM

Chief Operating Officer

WHAD'YA KNOW ABOUT
PLACES?
R O U N D

1. Divorce, annually, increases water usage in the U.S. by:

    (a) 371 billion gallons

    (b) 627 billion gallons

    (c) just a couple short of a trillion gallons

2. Least likely to weigh him/herself is a:

    (a) Singaporean

    (b) Frenchman

    (c) Wisconsinite

3. Rathakrishnan Velu of Malaysia pulled a _____-coach train with his teeth.

    (a) 7

    (b) 9

    (c) 11

4. What do the off-the-menu plates "virgin chicken," "steamed crap," and "burnt lion's head" all have in common?

5. You could go for the entry-level $50,000 in New York City or relocate to Canton, OH, and only have to make _____ to enjoy the same standard of living.
   (a) $19,000
   (b) $25,000
   (c) $14,500

6. Hugo Chavez turned back the clocks in Venezuela:
   (a) ½ hour
   (b) 3 hours
   (c) 25 years

7. The French think it's *un pamplemousse,* but we know darn well it's a _____.

8. People walk at the fastest clip in:
   (a) Charleston, SC
   (b) Singapore
   (c) Tokyo

9. Is there global warming over Kentucky?

10. Of the possible North, South, West, and East Ends, which is missing in Louisville, KY?

WHAD'YA KNOW ABOUT PLACES? (ROUND 1 ANSWERS)

1. (b) 627 billion gallons—so stay together for the sake of the watershed.

2. (a) Singaporean, the least compulsive about weight, as opposed to the Frenchman who weighs himself several times a day. The Wisconsinite only weighs himself when visiting someone with a scale in his bathroom.

3. (a) 7 coaches long, rolling weight 328 tons. They don't call Malaysia's Rathakrishnan Velu "King Tooth" for nothing. But if you think that's impressive, in Taiwan, there's a guy who can pull a 747 with his penis...King Dong?

4. Well, "steamed crap" we're hoping is a typo, but "virgin chicken" and "burnt lion's head" are dishes you had to order ahead in Beijing restaurants that were unceremoniously pulled from menus—along with dog dishes—so as not to put Olympics visitors off their feed.

5. (a) $19,000. Canton's pretty nice, really; got the NFL Hall of Fame, and Akron's just down the block.

6. (a) ½ hour; the Minister of Science and Technology, Hugo's cousin, explained that a meridian bisects Venezuela, and those west of the line would otherwise have to get up before sunrise,

which is unnatural, adversely affecting Venezuelan metabolisms and, hence, productivity.

7. Grapefruit.

8. (b) Singapore, again. The top five in pedestrian speed: Singapore, Copenhagen, Madrid, Guangzhou (China), and Dublin. NYC makes a poor showing at number eight, hot on the heels of Berlin. Singaporeans can cover a 60-foot stretch of sidewalk in 10.5 seconds.

9. No, by legislative fiat. Ironically, a researcher hired by the commonwealth determined that climate change will adversely impact the aging of Kentucky bourbon.

10. There is every End in Louisville but North, which makes sense since the Ohio River is to the north and that means Indiana can't be far behind.

HOME AWAY FROM HOME

In our quest for an earthlike planet we sometimes forget we already have an earthlike planet; maybe we should see if this one is habitable. Who knows, there could be life on Earth. The latest candidate is just like Earth if it were the size of Uranus and had plenty of affordable methane lake frontage that's not overly developed where a guy could put in a pier if he wants to. Mu Arae c is commutable in space-time, being only 50 light years away, but with the kids not even willing to drive to Door County anymore, this get-away gets away. A lot to recommend it though—the sun is much like ours, only Mu Arae light is softer and much more flattering; any life with skin can be grateful they're Mu Araen. On the downside, it's 1160 degrees today, and this is November. You could pack for the heat, but it's tough. There are three planets circling Mu Arae: one is too hot, one is too cold, and ours, Mu Arae c (we'll have to work on that—maybe Goldilocks?) is just right, almost. There is another property you might want to look at closer in, Giliese 581c, but it's not as nice—entirely ice-water, in fact, which, beyond a glass when you're thirsty, is not appealing. Meanwhile, back on Mu Arae, the

questions remain: Is there life capable of understanding we're looking for it? Is it silicone-based or did they have them removed? What
about zoning? Do the locals look more like Michael Rennie or Kang
and Kodos on *The Simpsons*? Do they want to serve mankind or *serve*
mankind? If we destroy Earth, could we stay with them for a while,
just until we find something else? Do they need corn?

WHAD'YA, AN IDIOM?

Not entirely useful phrases abroad.
What means:

1. Prenez-vous des pommes chips que je peux me marier? (French)

2. Riechen Sie meine Zehen! (German)

3. Usted desea satisfacer mi hermana? (Spanish)

4. The skeezer's spittin' nails, there. (Canadian)

5. O banheiro e abaixo que salao? (Portuguese)

6. Mne nikogda v zshizni nebelo tak harasho! (Russian)

7. Ni ting shui yao han xiang ma li qiu hun le ma? (Chinese)

8. Ana la atakellem inglieezi. (Arabic)

9. Ba'adan mibinamet gator. (Farsi)

10. Kyaa aap issey dohraa saktey hain? (Hindi)

Answers please to be found page next.

LOOSE TRANSLATIONS

1. Do you have a potato chip that wishes to wed?

2. Smell my toes!

3. Want to meet my sister?

4. Bitch is fighting mad.

5. The bathroom is down which corridor where?

6. In my life never I have felt myself so good.

7. Did you hear of the marrying of John and Mary?

8. English is not spoken of me.

9. Later, gator.

10. Say what?

MARCO! POLO!

W hile he did not invent the swimming pool game and there's some question as to whether he really brought spaghetti to Italy from China, there's no doubt that Marco Polo was one of the greatest tourists of all time—and in the thirteenth century, when connections weren't that great. His father and uncle, Niccolo and Maffeo, could have been household words as well, already having spent time in China and Asia Minor to further the interests of their Venetian trading enterprise, even becoming ambassadors at large for Kublai Khan in Europe. No slouches, these Polos. They traveled as an ensemble with the teenage Marco in 1271 through central Asia along the silk road reaching Shangdu, the Khan's summer white house, in 1275, living for the next seventeen years in Cathy, and wintering in Dadu, modern-day Beijing. It is these years Marco's *Il milione*, a grandiose take on his side trips around the provinces, covers. Kublai Kahn himself liked the cut of his jib and sent young Marco on fact-finding missions as far as Burma and the newly conquered southeastern city now known as Hangzhou. The Polos left China in 1292 to shepherd a Mongol princess to Persia (for the benefit of one of the lesser Khans) aboard a fleet of fourteen ships that sailed around the Malay peninsula, Sumatra, Ceylon, and India before docking in Hormuz, and went on from there to their arduous overland return to Venice. Marco's book, A *Description of the World*, or at least Asia as seen through the eyes of a privileged and rather unreliable narrator, was an overnight sensation in Italy. Some of the journeys—Japan, Mesopotamia, Siberia, India, and Ethiopia—were probably those of his father and uncle, and not all his facts were straight, nor his details detailed. Monks who copied the text took out some of the best parts, and there were hundreds of unauthorized and inaccurate editions circulating throughout Europe for centuries. Doubters point out that he did neglect to mention the Great Wall and the use of tea, but Marco had a lot on his mind. It was his (secondhand) description of Japan that sent Christopher Columbus off in entirely the wrong direction in 1492 to have a look for himself.

Discoveries may be, perhaps, too strong a word, but Marco Polo ran into a lot of things that were new to him, including:

ice cream

eyeglasses

spaghetti

petroleum

paper money

mail

asbestos

coal

mahjong

Ben Wa balls

opium

jackfruit

THE MICHAEL STATES
OF AMERICA

COLUMBIA, MO

Columbia, Missouri—known for its livability, columns left over from the Roman occupation, and Mizzou football (that's M-I-Z-Z-O-U-!; Tigers zealots can spell it backwards)—also does yeoman's duty keeping Kansas City and St. Louis apart. Kind of the fire door between the two gateways, east and west. Unfortunately, it sold naming rights to the arena to

Schnucks. The Columbia School of Journalism was the first to come up with the radical notion that journalists could be bred in captivity. Sheryl Crow is said to have used only one square of toilet paper her whole time at the dorm at the School of Education, not said why. Athens is known as the Columbia of Greece. City of Columbia has a very elaborate PedNet with Pedpaths and Pedobuses, all of which we hope has something to do with bike trails. So bike friendly, in fact, bikes will pedal themselves to Columbia, MO.

CLEMSON, SC

Clemson's students have been named the happiest in the nation—why not, they live on a PGA golf course and are just about guaranteed a BMW by the Department of BMW right on campus. No wonder they Tiger shag the night away—it doesn't get much better than this. Despite the significant presence of the German automaker on campus, Clemson has resisted calls (from Munich) to change its name to BMU, possibly to avoid confusion with nearby BJU, Bob Jones. Tiger mania here, where everything that isn't orange is orange and purple, from Death Valley to BI-LO. This beautiful former plantation is what Thomas Green Clemson got for marrying the Calhoun girl. The Brooks Center for the Performing Arts, donated by Robert Brooks, who proved that short-shorts and tight tees make a family restaurant, was never for a minute going to be called

Hooters Hall. They keep adding onto Tommy Bowden's church (leave the old ones right on the lawn) as the Tigers inch closer and closer to leaving the Chick-fil-A Bowl for their great reward, that BCS in the sky. While there are currently no plans for the Essie Mae Washington Institute to join the Strom Thurmond Institute on campus, Clemson is actually a confederacy of institutes which have contributed to its rise to the top in research. Clemson was recently cited as the number one academic research institution, as well as the best place to work in academia (what with the free BMW). There is a city of Clemson, as well, but nobody pays it much attention.

LITTLE ROCK, AK

In the heart of much-maligned (remember the steaming toxic dumps of the elder Bush's anti-Clinton ads?) and beautiful Arkansas, where the legislature has mandated saying SAW—still smarting from the Ar-Kansas River, I guess—the Bushwhacking never ends. Home to the Clinton Presidential Library, repository of all the artifacts Ken Starr hasn't kept as souvenirs. Very nice as far as presidential libraries go, with a beautiful view of the trailer park on the other side of the river. That would be the Clinton Presidential Trailer Park. Only 1 percent of the Clinton papers have been made available since most of the sheets have yet to be laundered. There are plaques all around Little Rock honoring Bill Clinton, mostly in lobbies of hotels, although they had to change the name of the Excelsior for marketing reasons. Huckabee and his wife Janet lived in a double wide on the Governor's Mansion lawn long after their quarters were ready. Home of the best-named infrastructure in the U.S., the Big Dam Bridge. Nearby Texarkana police run Dodge Chargers. Home of Heifer International, often confused with Clinton Foundation. Petrino keeping his bags packed.

DOOR COUNTY, WI

The only place you can get booyah—no longer just an exclamation—outside of rural Brussels in Walonia, is Door County's Brussels, imported stick by brick from the old country. Try Rouers Bar–Not the Hamburger on School Rd, and ask them to throw some tripe into the chicken stew if you dare. Door County has been called the Cape Cod of the upper Midwest, but here we think of Cape Cod as Door East, at best. Scattered around this 20-by-50 peninsula is every Scandinavian culture known to man, from the Icelanders knocking back their Angostura on Washington Island (at Nelsen's, which stayed open through prohibition, with Nelsen successfully claiming no one would drink bitters for fun); Jens Jensen's Clearing in Ellison Bay; Little Denmark, the industrious with their good looking womenfolk Swedes of Sister Bay; and the Norwegians everywhere else, if all the Johnsons are any indication. Quite a few French, too, from the original Nicolet band, one of whom may be Louis XVII, the Lost Dauphin, or, may have lost his Renault Dauphine. Within a stone's throw are Poland, Pilsen, Luxembourg, Alaska, and Dyckesville. That about covers it. If you get off the artery and vein of the Peninsula, Highways 42 and 57, the county roads will give you a hint of what Door used to look like: small farms, orchards, outbuildings just longing to be picturesque, all of which are now craft shops; potters; three-dimensional artists; birchbark canoe makers; cabbalists; weavers; basket makers; sand painters; carvers; candle, pie, and candy makers; crafters of ancient instruments and Renaissance gear, bronze age implements; natural healers; smithies; scrimshaw— anything you're looking for you can probably find off T, A, or ZZ. Be prepared for a fishboil (and be thankful the Scandinavians didn't think to add missionaries with the carrots and potatoes) and try not to notice that the kerosene seems to get into the water at flare-up. McMansions are popping up in all their taupe beauty next to Grandma's humble farmhouse near Kangaroo Lake, left standing for the quaint. You can see their cathedral beams through the clerestory from the porch. Al Johnson still has his goats on the roof, and somewhere a goat has Johnsons on the roof. Come after Labor when everybody goes back to Mundelein and see what the locals look like when they can cross the street again. Nora recommends the Confectionery in Fish Creek for all your candy needs, including candies you can't remember if you liked or not (bull's-eyes). Million-dollar getaways these days in the Door, with, as of this writing, the Saddam Hussein-inspired Chateau du Lac still up for grabs at 26 million, but that does not, it turns out, include a bowling alley, so you're way ahead at the Sister Bay Bowl for the Friday fish fry—whitefish, beer, and bowling. That's what I'm talking about. Type Xes might even want to borrow a ketch and try their skill through the Porte des Morts, but better men have tried and failed. They're still looking for the Griffin. If you have nothing to prove, Bailey's Harbor should suit you just fine.

JACKSONVILLE, FL

Jacksonville, Florida: more than Clark's Fish Camp, gators hitching on 105, and the Florida theater which sheltered Elvis from the elements for his first indoor concert. I will say, while gator tastes nothing like chicken, it ain't bad, but you can't get nothing off rattlesnake ribs. An interesting and storied place, and historied as well. Under more flags than the amusement park. Been under so many flags, someone hangs a bed sheet out, they salute. Sunken Spanish galleons nearby, ripe for the pickin', me hearties. Never known as the River City by the Gateway to the State's Interior, but could have been. City where Snow White would have had to cross seven bridges to get to the seven dwarves' Eastside bungalow. Sensible, if not imaginative, bridge naming system: Red, Blue, Yellow, Green, Orange, Ultra-Violet, and Purple. Baptists control all parking ramps for unknown reasons—look for the lighthouse ramp. Attempt by Orlando to steal Jacksonville's water known as the Big Suck. University of North Florida Osprey may not put a great team on the court, but they can dive from a thousand feet at 80 mph. Fountain of Oldth discovered in nearby St. Augustine. Seminoles (the Native Americans, not the ones in Gainesville) have taken their never-ending battle with the U.S. to the casino floor. Jacksonville is actually bigger than Miami, so all these years it should have been Jacksonville Vice, the Jacksonville Sound Machine, and Jacksonville of Ohio.

SPRINGFIELD, IL

"THEY'D HAVE TO SHOOT ME TO GET ME BACK TO SPRINGFIELD"

A. Lincoln

February 11, 1861

The ceilings in Abraham Lincoln's house in Springfield, IL, are much too law and the beds too short for a tall guy in a stovepipe hat, so he must have had to keep reminding himself to take it off before coming in. A nice but humble two-story, certainly better than the log cabin he was always going on about, although some believe the half-block walk to the outhouse is what drove Mary Todd mad. See the Lincoln house and the Old Capitol and you can be home in about four hours, depending. Springfield was originally Calhoun, for the South Carolinian of the same name, but they where already tired of him by 1832 up north and would rather be known as one of a dozen generic Springfields that dot this great and *The Simpsons'* land. Springfield is a lot like Madison: insurance men and state legislators, all that's missing is a major university and the four lakes, but it's only an hour and a half to UI and, technically, there is a lake, but it was put in by the power company and has to be full of PCBs, plus they talk about whether it's at "full-pool" or not, and that makes you think. There is the Vachel Lindsay, who nobody reads much anymore, Home, much nicer than Lincoln's, and the Dana-Thomas house, considered the biggest reason Frank Lloyd Wright got out of Prairie Style. It's sure bigger than the Italianate mansion it overran. Nice windows, especially once they were weather-stripped, but the Japanese called and want their copper roof back. Getting out, I mean around Springfield, is easy: the longitudinal streets are numbered; the latitudes start with presidents and diminish to less and less notables by the time you hit the 55 onramp. Before you do, be sure and stop at the one and only Cozy Dog, the original corn dog on a stick invented by Ed Waldmire, whose son Bob carries on the family tradition—if you're on S. 6th Street and see a place with "FOOD" on the roof, you're there.

SHEBOYGAN, WI

There is no bronze statue of Jackie Mason in Sheboygan, Wisconsin, his home town. Maybe they're waiting for his passing. They do have the world's tallest flagpole (up again after being knocked down by a light breeze off Lake Michigan): the Amity Insurance Pole of Babel, pretty darn big at 338 feet. Curiously, the flag is only four by eight. "Mention My Name in Sheboygan" was never a hit for the Everly

Brothers, but Don and or Phil may have been seeing one or more of the Chordettes (one may have been My Boy, Lollipop) who lived in town. You can get a nice schnitzel at the Elks, and the brats everybody's talking about are at Meisners, which offers a double on a hard roll, cheap. Make it all themselves, the Meisners. Home of both the toilet (Kohler) and the toilet seat (Bemis) and the continuing argument over which came first. Sheboygan, from the Indian word for "jiggle-the-handle." Beautiful setting—if Lake Michigan were the Pacific, you'd swear you were in Hong Kong. Sometimes referred to as Malibu Nort'. Sheboygan: where people who found Milwaukee not German enough came. Many think they are in Germany. The former artillery range and junky shooting gallery/dump along Lake Michigan is now Kohler's world-ranked Whistling Straits (for the anti-aircraft shells?) Golf Course, so hilly they use goats for caddies. Spaceport Sheboygan is in the works, if they can get the roof off the armory. Not clear whether launchings or landings are anticipated. Closed the shooting range at the Middle School, and now, with the dump gone PGA, there's no place to shoot a few cans. Gas said to be 2 cents cheaper in Two Rivers.

CANTON, OH

Canton, Ohio, home of the Pro Football Hall of Fame, is the cradle of football; nearby Cleveland, unfortunately, is the grave. Alright, not

fair, the Browns just had a good year—too bad it was in Baltimore. The league started in a Hupmobile dealership in Canton—try working that into your next happy hour banter. It is not uncommon to see a grown 340-pound man cry at the induction ceremonies every fall—and that's just in the audience. An amazing collection of memorabilia and a security guard dedicated entirely to watching out for OJ coming over the wall. Something about a pair of gloves. Diebold, the company famous for its Republican voting machines (the touch screens recoil from Democratic fingers) is a world away in North Canton. Because of some concerns about irregularities during the 2004 election, this time around the election commission is testing all machines to make sure the fruit lines up. Diebold also makes ATMs whose service charge goes directly to the Republican National Committee. The Hoover plant moved to China—the Hoover High Vikings are now known as the North Dongguan Vikings. The old Hoover plant is being developed by the same people who turned Akron's Canal Place into the shell of BF Goodrich. A new icon for Canton as the Colossus of Dan Dierdorff (fabricated entirely from Republic Steel Scrap) astride I-77 will soon grace the skyline.

OXFORD, MS

Estelle Faulkner had the same wallpaper (big mums on a violet background) in the parlor at Rowan Oak that my mom had in her

bedroom in Milwaukee. A big difference is that William was allowed to write on the walls of his room. A nicely restored Rowan Oak with a lot of the knickknacks from Faulkner's world travels, his Underwood portable (the curator says school kids inevitably ask where the monitor is), and even the piano reestablished in what used to be the countryside outside of Oxford, Mississippi. Faulkner was not very well liked in town, partly to his irascibility and probably more to the fact that a lot of the locals turned up as not entirely flattering caricatures in his novels. One thing you don't want is the Snopes family mad at you. Significant is the fact that doughnuts are traditionally piled around his bronze likeness at the post office to encourage the pigeons to shit on old Bill. John Grisham comes off better around town, still keeping a farm-mansion outside of Oxford, but spends most of his time on his Charlottesville plantation, where people apparently leave him alone. We'll see what happens with the Grisham statue. New Toyota plant in nearby Tupelo, which is flirting with the idea of renaming itself Tokyo. Tailgating in the Grove is still the place to be at Ole Miss, where Archie Manning's number has been raised to 25 to allow a more reasonable speed limit on campus. Trent Lott is now working full-time at the Trent Lott Leadership Center.

CHARLESTON, SC

The Feldmans go back ten generations, you know: unfortunately in Minsk and not Charleston, SC. In Minsk we go to the Ball. A Feldman actually insured Ft. Sumter. Didn't pay off, though—was considered water damage. If there's a more beautiful city than Charleston, I'd like to see Savannah...it, I'd like to see it. Secret gardens where even the bunnies need permits. There were Jews here early on: the first Reform Jews in 1841 reformed hoping to get into the St. Cecilia Society, and got this close. Joseph P. Riley is mayor for life and possibly longer in Charleston, has been since the CSS *Hunley* was still sailing. It is still only 3,954 miles to the North Pole from the Ft. Sumter Hotel, according to the sign. In Charleston, it is a misdemeanor to over-prune your crape myrtle. The beautiful and highly regarded College of Charleston is right downtown, although with nowhere to park you're either there or you're not. Many of the outstanding stately homes of Charleston are these days owned by Emirs and Russian telecommunications moguls and I bet they can't get into the Ball, either. Did make the mistake of taking Clyde Stubblefield on a tour of a nearby plantation, where he was not at all impressed that the huge mahogany dining table was rescued from the fire by slaves. "Burn, baby, burn!" were his exact words. That they stocked alligators in surrounding swamp failed to impress. Mayor-for-Life Riley's smoking ban has forced Charlestonians to inhale oyster roasts for their fix. It is not uncommon for outlying parents to list Bluestein's Mens Wear as their home address in an attempt to get their kids into Charleston schools. With Charleston pretty much taken, a clone called Ion has sprung up across the river, although to the dyed-in-the-wool Charlestonian, it more resembles Stepford.

DULUTH, MN

The heart of the Finnish Riviera, that's Duluth, Minnesota. The Coast Guard has been firing live rounds from its M-240 machine guns, part of Homeland Security re: Superior, which kind of puts the kibosh on pleasure-craft cruising. Rapid fire took out the foghorn. The Duluth Heritage Sports Center is really a hockey rink, but a darn nice one. Still a very active port where you can go down to see all the arrivals listed in the *Duluth Shipping News*, and, if you're lucky, be on the lift bridge when it goes up and the tanker goes under. The building of the aerial lift bridge, by the way, nearly resulted in war with twin city Superior on the Wisconsin side—most of the pilings had to be sunk at night when the Badgers were still in their dens. After some controversy as to which should be observed and which were voluntary, The Ten Commandments are now on display in front of the Comfort Suites, although I don't remember "Thou shall reuse towels" being in the original. Duluth offers free venison from the (world's only?) city deer hunt, although that still doesn't explain what happened to the dachshund. As they say in Dulut', it all comes out in the sausage. Strangely, a lot of Duluth residents have never been as far as Superior and seem uninterested in what may be at the other end of the Blatnik Bridge. Could be the Anchor Bar—it's worth a try. True, the people on the Wisconsin side think they're so Superior.

LOUISVILLE, KY

I love Louisville. Jews are genteel here, it's that kind of town. People love to entertain, and, hey, why pretend the seriously misnamed Ohio River is not flowing blended Kentucky bourbon? Republicans drink here, and it helps quite a bit. Just pronounce the name like you're still numb from the dentist and you'll be clasped to the bosom of Louisville. Of course home to The Most Exciting Two Minutes outside marriage, the Kentucky Derby and twin-spired Churchill Downs, where the place to be, in fact the only place to be if you can't afford to hang under the overhang with the hatted Mint Julep crowd, is the infield: just like at NASCAR, only with horses. Almost as big as the Derby is Lebowski Fest in spring featuring unlimited bowling and a Coen Brothers look-alike(s) contest. During August's Zombie

Attack, either hundreds of Louisvillians dress as zombies or in fact actual zombies walk down Bardstown Road in search of Buffalo Wild Wings or Jack Fry's, if they can get in. You can get a Jaeger and Jim Beam for three bucks at the Taproom, and, if you want to put in the time, get your beer mug up on the wall of fame. In Louisville you've got your East, West, and South End; if you're in the North End, you're in Jeffersonville, OH. I'd recommend heading over to Equus (no thoroughbred meat) on Sears Avenue for some refined American cuisine, and not merely because chef Dean Corbett always straps the feedbags on us when we're in town, but because he's a great cook, and a heck of a guy. Jewish and Catholic hospitals just merged, proving anything is possible in Louisville, KY. Yes, they do make Louisville Sluggers here, although it's hard to pull them out of the ground the way they've got them cemented into Main Street.

MEMPHIS, TN

Long distance information pointed me to the Rendezvous in Memphis, TN. I need my ribs rubbed. Boy, I like a dry rub—not everybody does, but they do in Memphis. I just want to know if they're open for breakfast. They don't call it the Cotton Carnival any more, but June would be a great time to come down for Carnival before the humidity settles in (although it's wet heat).

Any time's a good time for Graceland—we were there at Christmas, when the huge crèche on the lawn and the Elvis *Blue Christmas* tunes piped into the holding area made you swear you were queuing up for the Holy Sepulcher, which it kind of is. Not to namedrop, but we got to hang out with Wayne Jackson of the Memphis Horns (they played on everything from Otis to Elvis to the Raconteurs), who told us about hanging with the King in his self-decorated jungle room (green shag) in the big drum seat throne chair with his (short) legs sticking straight out, and sure enough, there it was in all its glory, and that was special. Stax and Sun Records were the black and white of the Memphis sound, and you can check out the Sun Quonset hut with its garage ambience that launched Elvis, Johnny Cash, Jerry Lee, Roy Orbison, and Carl Perkins, among many others. Beale Street is in renaissance, anchored by B.B. King's club at 143, and at 163 is A. Schwab's, where you can get your own bottle of love potion number 9 (or 10, for stubborn cases). The Pyramid Arena really is, as befits a city named after the capital of ancient Egypt, at least until they sell the naming rights to the pyramid-scheme people. The Lorraine Hotel, where the Reverend Martin Luther King Jr. was assassinated, is now the very moving National Civil Rights Museum. When in Memphis, stay at the Peabody Hotel, the lobby of which, as Faulkner famously said, is where the South begins. I don't mean to brag, but I was the honorary Duckmaster right after Hillary Clinton, and got to walk with the real duck man and the flock from the penthouse duck suite down to their awaiting lobby fountain, there to amaze generations of people who had never seen a duck before. We take 'em for granted around here, I guess.

WHAD'YA KNOW ABOUT
PLACES?
*R*OUND 2

1. The percentage of Italian men (including Sicilians) who live with their mothers:
   - (a) 37
   - (b) 49
   - (c) 67

2. _____ has been exempted from Google Earth imagery.
   - (a) Neverland
   - (b) Ft. Sam Houston
   - (c) Miley Cyrus's house

3. In Vietnam, you could face a fine of 30 million dong for possession of:
   - (a) a handgun
   - (b) a laptop
   - (c) a hamster

4. _____ police dogs are required to wear shoes.

   (a) Swedish

   (b) Finnish

   (c) German

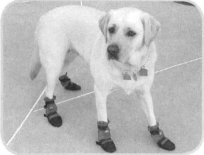

5. Who's happier, Sweden or Norway?

6. If you've gotta live some-where, where's the best place to live, according to the United Nations?

   (a) Southampton

   (b) Pierre, SD

   (c) Iceland

7. The most average—or as we like to say, representative—state in the union is:

   (a) Iowa

   (b) Ohio

   (c) Wisconsin

8. What channel are the Channel Islands on?

9. Assuming they had the shelf space, the average American would have ____ (empty) bottles of beer on the wall.

   (a) 98

   (b) 198

   (c) 228

10. In terms of cremation rates, you're as good as cinders in:

   (a) Florida

   (b) California

   (c) Hawaii

☞ The lady atop the capitol in Phoenix is Winged Victory, not the FTD flower delivery dude.

☞ Iranian Roses of the Prophets are Danish pastries.

☞ The average Indian thinks of America as a friendly bully.

☞ In Hong Kong, they sell Pantyhose Milk Tea.

WHAD'YA KNOW ABOUT PLACES? (ROUND 2 ANSWERS)

1. (a) 37 percent of Italian men still live with their mothers, or their mothers with them—sometimes it's a fine line. The Italian mother makes the Jewish mother look like a piker. For the Italian *mammoni* the food is a lot better and you can't beat the rent, although the downside for the nation is the plunging Italian birthrate.

2. (b) Fort Sam, as the command post of the Fifth Army, doesn't like to have its picture taken, although Miley sure does.

3. (c) A hamster. Vietnam had to crack down on the hamster craze, which was getting out of hand with all the hamster clubs and clandestine hamster breeding. Thirty million dong is approximately $1,900, double the annual wage.

4. (c) German police dogs will soon be sporting two pairs of very trendy Nike Woofs, designed to protect paws from the broken glass and syringes so much a part of modern police dog life.

5. Sweden is way happier than its sullen neighbor, Norway, even though the two cultures share many customs and Ole and Lena. Nobody's happier than Denmark, but Sweden cracks the top 10 at number 7. Norway is less happy than New Zealand, at 19, but happier than number 23, the USA. For the record, Burundi is unhappiest.

6. (c) Although you'd think they'd stay neutral, the UN says Iceland, which might not be so great if you weren't tall, blonde, and related. Despite its only average happiness quotient, Norway comes in second, followed by Australia, Ireland, and Sweden.

7. (c) Wisconsin, a fact we take no apparent pride in, not liking to call attention to ourselves. Across 112 different categories, including dress, headgear, verbosity, gait, and dances you can do, Badgers are pretty much the gold standard.

8. English, silly.

9. (c) 228 bottles of beer a year seems like a lot until you try to compare it to the Czechs, who drink 160 liters, which has to be a whole lot more.

10. (c) Maybe it's the volcanoes, but 70 percent of Hawaiians would just as soon leap into one when their time comes. Least likely to burn: Michiganders.

THE MICHAEL STATES
OF AMERICA, PART 2

HUNTSVILLE, AL

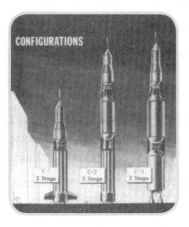

If you know any good Auburn jokes, Huntsville is the place to tell them. Bad ones work nearly as well. Founded by rocket scientist Werner Von Braun after being unable to advance in the Nazi ranks back in Germany, modern Huntsville may be the only place in America where it does too take a rocket scientist. The University of Alabama at Huntsville is the third-ranking small nation missile power, right after Iran and North Korea. History was made here. The world has never seen thrust like Saturn thrust, the equivalent of 1,000 V-2s strapped together, which in fact, it was. It was all they could do to keep it heading for London instead of the moon. Still see some Saturn boosters around used as double-wides; with the president announcing a new moon landing, the trick will be to re-convert them. Saturn technology was not rivaled again until Mercedes came in to Tuscaloosa. Through an alliance with nearby Marshall Space Flight Center, Huntsville engineering students can earn back some of their tuition without having to work in the cafeteria, and even get in on the ground floor of an exciting career in Space Science. A pretty good ice hockey team, which doesn't immediately come to mind when you think of Alabama, and the frequent host of the Frozen Four. Usually wins the concrete canoe competition, and has the longest cheer in collegiate sports, spelling out the University of Alabama in Huntsville letter by letter, then repeated, like an engineer would do it, with specs.

ERIE, PA

We were in Erie the second week of January and it didn't snow, but I wouldn't count on it. Kind of a miracle, really, here in the Lake Erie micro-clime and snow belt. You always hear about Buffalo on the other end of the lake, but the average snowfall in Erie in January is 22.8 inches to Buffalo's 23.3. Statistically insignificant. Tom Ridge must be from here, if you go by the Tom Ridge Environmental Center, Tom Ridge Field, and the Tom Ridge Chair in Intelligence Studies at Mercyhurst. Strangely, the ball club is the Sea Wolves and not the Sea Ridges. The governor went to Cathedral Prep in Erie, where he lettered in Homeroom Security. It's probably no coincidence that Erie

County is one secure homeland, not having been invaded since the Canadians tried it back when they thought they were British. They still come, but it's to save 5 percent on a pair of Timberlands. The spy school at Mercyhurst is the only one in the world where you can double major in intelligence and recreational therapy. Billy Blanks invented Tae Bo here, fighting off the skeeters on Presque Isle, the Cote d'Azur of the Great Lakes, only d'Green. Not to be missed are the Big Freddies at Tickle's Deli, which fill an entire loaf of Italian bread with ham, salami, cappicola, tomatoes, and lettuce; take two Railbenders to wash it all down. You want to eat light: perogis from Holy Trinity. The big cruise terminal at Port Erie has yet to attract much in the way of cruise ships, and, in fact, may be a homeland security decoy. Part of the Intermodal Transportation Center, which the locals know is the bus station. Come for Heritage Festival on the lakefront the first week of September, when the Erie Philharmonic does the 1812 Overture to cover the live cannon volleys towards the Canucks just to let 'em know Erie means business.

INDIANAPOLIS, IN

Besides being the capital of Indiana, Indianapolis is both the Amateur Sports and the Racing Capital of the western world. If there's a major tournament, Grand Prix, or Greatest Spectacle, it's been here. We're talking about a quarter of a million fans at the Indianapolis 500 and the Allstate 400. More monuments than anywhere outside of Washington, DC; as a matter of fact the original designer, Alexander Ralston, was an apprentice to Pierre L'Enfant, Mr. District-of-Columbia. Today there are over 2 million people living in Indianapolis, which even surprises them—they've come a long way since Judge Sullivan first joined Indiana to *polis*. Indianapolis has six cultural districts, and you're bound to find a culture that suits you. The Indiana State Fairgrounds are right in town; you won't find pig races and turkey legs on a stick in any other urban center. Local pharmaceutical powerhouse Eli Lilly has crossed Prozac with Cialis to make one happy camper. Just kidding. The Lilly-sponsored Children's Museum is one of the best anywhere, and the kids seem well-fed and cared for. The toll road to Evansville was halted when it was discovered no one wanted to go, let alone pay to do it. And, of course, gorgeous new Colts stadium, where Peyton Manning has been deified, is Lucas Oil Stadium, and not Cialis Field (where the roof might have extended for up to four days).

CLEVELAND, OH

I'm going to go out on a limb here and say Jacobs Field is the best little urban ballpark in the majors, although it lacks the older gentlemen who used to wipe the seats for you for a buck at the old ballpark. Of course, the seats needed it. Also the best cache any-where of restored movie palaces: Playhouse Square, State Theatre, and the Palace, with a lobby identical to the one in heaven. Cleveland is so much like my hometown, Milwaukee, that I feel like if I could find 58th and Center the Feldmans would just be sitting down to dinner. Similar industrial background, ethnic mix, the only difference being the (Great) Lake is straight ahead instead of on your right. Cleveland, the city Art Modell couldn't kill, although they still could kill him, now with the new Browns (in their new stadium) even showing signs of life! There is barking in the Dawg Pound! Local boy made good LeBron is settling in with the Cavaliers, and if they need additional help there's Quicken Loans right there at the Q. Don't leave town without eating at The Palazzo, where sisters Gilda and Carla Carnecelli have literally opened up their house to their dining guests, having grown up in the apartment above the legendary Palmina's, which their grandmother started in 1947. Gorgeous, with the statuary, draperies, lamps, and bric-a-brac all in the best Mediterranean taste—and the *salsicca* is to die for.

FAIRBANKS, AK

Fairbanks is so great you'll want to stay until you qualify for the permanent fund. All states should pay you to live there—Alaska's just on the cutting edge. Here you get paid just to be yourself—and—if you tough it out—the longevity bonus! Hey, it's not welfare if it comes from the oil companies. Alaska! Bounded by Canada on one side and Anchorage on the other. Denali is not to be missed—saw bears, caribou, moose, and an actual Denali (GMC). Perfect for me, up there among people who want to be among people who don't want to be among people. Makes you appreciate the people you do run into. You gotta like Alaskan women—without getting mushy, they know how to drive your team. It's paradise—they pay you to live here, throw in a pound of pot, all the lox you can eat, a Super-Cub and a snow machine, cooler wrapped in duct tape, bear bag, pair of bunny boots, a bike with a chain greased to 60 below, a good dip net, and your choice of firearms. All you have to provide is the Phantom Pro-Series WK-340 Digital Moose Caller capable of doing a bull in rut and a cow in estrus simultaneously in stereo. Survival skills—using flares to start a fire, lining the crapper seat with Styrofoam, using your trunk for a freezer—you can pick up. Ice-caving is optional, you don't have to. Look, here's an '02 Honda Rubicon, with wench, for $4,200. Why, the wench alone is worth that. You don't get the wench with a Raptor. And, if it's security you're worried about, Ft. Greeley has enough missile power to launch a pre-emptive strike against North Korea within minutes. Sure, there was the bridge(s) to nowhere controversy, but that will all be forgotten once the Colossus of Ted Stevens spans Ketchikan to Gravina Island.

IOWA CITY, IA

They say in the rainforest of Brazil they've recreated an Iowa cornfield, as part of Vision Brazil, but I might have gotten that backwards. The remarkable and unexpected Iowa Rainforest has been renamed—now it's the Kum & Go & Rain. There's also the Mt. Swisher Pretty Active Volcano that's unexpected and worth seeing. Eventually they're hoping to complete the entire complex: The Rainforest Casino, Supermax, IMAX, and Aquarium of Iowa. Herky the Hawkeye was actually bred in captivity down here, but they won't say how. There was the little matter of painting the visitor's dressing rooms pink, like they do at the prison in Phoenix, but a sensitized Badger team can still kick your ass. Oops, editorial comment. I like Iowa City; it's like Madison must have been a hundred years ago, before the lakes formed and all the New York commies moved in. Writer's Workshop is still the place to kick-start your Great American Novel. Big research center for biofuels, although one day the truth will come out: ethanol is people! They're working on the Corn Fusion Project at the High Energy Kernel Collider. Another thing I like about Iowa is they put your county on the license plate—like putting your mother's maiden name on there. If her maiden name was Pocahontas. Or Calhoun. Johnson, more likely. Web appearance of nude Iowa baseball players begs the question: can they lay down a bunt?

HARRISBURG, PA

They have really fixed up Harrisburg; if you don't say something about it they get really peeved, although to their credit they get over it quickly. The only problem we had on our bus tour was getting into Harrisburg, which looms like the Celestial City behind a 12-foot 6-inch train overpass, as seen from our 13-foot 4-inch tall scenic cruiser. It was a little like Kafka: we could see the castle—the state capitol—in the distance but whichever approach we took we couldn't get any closer. Finally, you guessed it, we pumped some air into Harrisburg's tires and rolled right under. And it was well worth it—boy, they really fixed the place up. Gentrified, a lot of great restaurants, continental *sur la terrace* dining downtown. Last time we were there it was only the Harrisburg East Mall or the Spot, and only street people ate on the street. It's a Renaissance, Mayor Reed is a Doge, and Harrisburg is the new Venice. No easy solution to the unmistakable Three Mile Island being on your left when you land at the airport.

BOISE, ID

The hot button in Boise right now is dog poop in the foothills; since Boise is surrounded by foothills, this is no small button. Four hundred pounds per annum, they say, stays behind. Other than dog doo from free-ranging pets in the foothills, not much that's disturbing

the tranquility of Idaho's Treasure Valley and Democratic preserve. And those foothills are darn pretty in the distance, Boise keeping its mountains located conveniently next door in Owyhee county, inexplicably named after the Hawaiian Islands by missionaries with a really bad sense of direction. Around 200,000 people, mostly from Ohio, not counting state legislators, who are part-time and so only ruin three months of the year. You can tube around Boise on the Boise along the Greenbelt, and, if you're damn lucky, catch the rooster tail excess water blast at the Lucky Dam. Picturesque Shosone Falls, once Niagara's Rival and now Cedar Falls, is nearby, and it's not that far to the real deal, the Snake River and its wet and wild world of wilderness and whitewater. Only place in Idaho Larry Craig jokes still get a chuckle. Quakers in nearby Greenleaf are armed by law, so be careful, or not. Downtown, there's the continuing saga of what to do with the Big Hole left behind from a failed office tower which may receive national landmark status if it goes on much longer. Boise has a large Basque population, and every five years hosts the huge Jaialdi festival, the next being in 2010. If you'd like to try a little Bacalao al Pil-Pil or yearn for a side of Pimientos de Guernica, Leku Ona is a good place to find it, along with local pols of both colors co-existing over cod and red beans. When in Boise, stay at the Modern, an updated version of a Basque rooming house trance-channeled by the former Travel Lodge. Home of the Boise State Broncos, whose game-winner in the 2007 Fiesta Bowl is the only known successful use of the Statue of Liberty play. Only field in any league to boast blue Smurf turf which has reportedly lured ducks to their deaths. If it's cowboys you're hankerin' for, head for the mechanical bull at Grizzly Rose, where the name says it all.

PRESCOTT, AZ

Prescott is special to me: it's the only place that ever made me feel like a cowboy. Well, they gave me the hat and boots, I bought the shirt at Prairie Rose Boutique and brought the Lee's boot-cuts with me. Didn't actually ride any horses out there, but neither do most cowboys nowadays. Prescott was named a top ten True Western Town by *True West* magazine, who should know. And Yavapai is an authentic Indian casino, Yavapai Downs an authentic Indian race-track. Arcosanti, the futuristic—because it will be done sometime in the future—urban environment that Paolo Soleri first imagineered in 1970 is worth seeing, and if you don't walk away with wind bells you just don't get it. After doing Whiskey Row downtown, you may also be tempted to walk away with wind bells, just don't do it. Boy, there are a lot of antique stores in Prescott—nobody must have any junk at home anymore. I expect Phoenix Krispy Kremes may be bartered for Prescott chamber pots. A lot of squabbling between Cowboy and Indian art galleries, but, so far, no victors. There's no better place to watch overweight guys line dance than the Texas Roadhouse, featuring legendary service and legendary side items, although the Rattlesnake Bites are really battered jalapenos. Embry-Riddle Aeronautical University is nearby, where they figure if you can land at Prescott's Love Field, you can land anywhere. Prescott is a very friendly town, amidst some beautiful and rugged terrain well worth clambering over—and at least twenty degrees cooler than Phoenix any time of year. Stay at the Hotel Vendome just like Tom Mix did when he was makin' them cowboy pictures.

MANKATO, MN

Mankato is the kind of place where they have a Yard of the Week—recently won by Don and Pat Schmidt on West 9th the day we were there and very nice: borders, trellises, reflecting balls, birdbaths, the whole nine yards. The Schmidts are now eligible for the Quality of Life drawing in September, and could win trellises, reflecting balls, birdbaths, and more. A generous $200,000 from the Fallenstein estate paid for the animal petting zoo in Sibley Park, so that young urban Mankatons can experience the joy of farm animals formerly available only to the youth of N. Mankato or New Ulm. And what about that old town stone in the middle of Riverside Drive? The reminder of Mankato's heritage is well worth the occasional axle and more often, realignment. *Site Selection* magazine named Mankato tops for micropolitan areas…well, fifteenth, and some Livability guide pegged it as 14th most livable class C city anywhere. The city theme, "Make It in Mankato," considered well-intentioned but somewhat ambiguous, has been replaced with the mildly disturbing "Show Your True Colors." The Minnesota Vikings train here in the summer since the microclimate most closely resembles that found in the Metrodome. The R.D. Hubbard House on Broad St. is the one surviving example of Mankato Victorian, and the Judge Lorin P. Cray and his wife LuLu mansion on 2nd St.—the only Queen Anne—is the YWCA. Local Maud Hart wrote her *Betsy-Tacy* books in Makato, fictionalized as "Deep Valley"; her childhood home and that of her best friend on Center Street are open to the public, call for hours.

NASHVILLE, TN

Go into any bank in Nashville and you'll see not just the usual money market offers and socket wrench inducements, but gold records by the score covering the walls, from every country star who's had to put up collateral in the past fifty years, which was pretty much all of 'em. The Country Music Loan Capitol of the world is Nashville, because a nice Delgado Hutzel guitar or a spangled Manuel ensemble don't come cheap. Hatch Show Print on Broadway attracts nearly as many visitors as the Opry with its fabulous poster archives of country star bills from Hank Williams to Keith Urban, and the presses are still rolling for hopefuls who keep a-comin' in the hope of working for HCA hospital or Bridgestone, or maybe, just maybe, becoming a Gaylord Entertainment Star—Smiles, Teamwork, Attitude, Reliability, and Service—in catering, housekeeping, or security. A lot of country songs come from worse. You never know who you'll see at Tootsie's Orchid Lounge—one time Brooks came in without Dunn and nobody recognized him. Don't stand on the crate at the bar, though—that's Little Jimmy Dickens's and you will have to deal with one or more of the Kung Pao Buckaroos. Mostly waitpersons are discovered at the Bluebird these days, and Opryland has literally made a circus of the heart of country music which used to beat at the Ryman between doses of Little Liver Pills and all the good things you'll find at the Cracker Barrel (which more than one wag has accused the Opry of being). Nashville has gotten a lot more diverse these days, what with Tim McGraw getting down with Nelly and Faith Hill covering "My Milkshake." Nashville has its own football team now—disappointingly not called the Nashville Cold Hoppers—the Tennessee Titans, and, frankly, you'd never know they were the Houston Oilers. Al Gore, author of *Unrealized Expectations*, lives not too far away (look for the columns with solar panels on top), and Vanderbilt is the Yale of the mid-South.

CHICAGO, IL

I'm not sure what a toddlin' town is, but Chicago is my kind of town, too, although I've always liked it more than it cared for me. But you can't measure a city by one monumental career setback at WGN radio in the mid-'80s. When I was a kid riding the North Shore Line down from Milwaukee to the Loop, I thought the Magikist lips puckered just for me. The City of Big Shoulders—has to be, since people drive on 'em—of Studs Terkel, Larry Lujack, and Harry Caray, of the Magnificent Mile and Grant Park with its magnificent view of the cityscape, the riveting bridges, the Marshall Field's clock still at State and Randolph, even if Marshall Fields isn't. Dreams of a playboy apartment swaying high atop the Hancock. Mummies, like family, waiting at the Field. Just walking down human-scale Clark Street along every nationality of food, shmatte, antique doorknobs, taverns with the original bars and patrons intact, and manna from the Vienna beef carts. The expanse of public beaches ringing the lake, and the cops ringing the beaches who know good duty when they see it. Lincoln, with the giant balls, in Lincoln Park. The El, where you can get where you're going and look in people's windows along the way. Uptown, where Hispanic transsexuals walk hand in hand with hillbillies; Wrigleyville, where nuns take a vow to park cars; Wacker, for the name, and for the dynamic river bend financial heart; the Tribune tower in case you're looking for a missing rock; the Wrigley building, which stayed lit during blackouts, and Wrigley Field, which stayed blacked out during peacetime. The little sandcastle that could, the Water Tower, which stood up to Mrs. O'Leary's cow. Rush Street, where you can get roaring drunk and blend right in. Chinatown, where it's possible and even likely to order duck's feet from the hieroglyphic menu on the wall; Andersonville, for Swedish pancakes; Vernon Park, where three generations of Tufanos erupt from the kitchen with Chicken Vesuvio. The Northwest territories for things perogi; Bridgeport for beer and colcannon; blues at Lee's, the former Queen Bee's, on S. Chicago; and the Pump Room at the Ambassador East, for cabaret. Theater which makes Broadway Off-Steppenwolf—Chicago is!

MILWAUKEE, WI

Who says you can't go home again? You can, but you'll discover they've put green siding on it. I'm not kidding; our old house looks like a record-breaking avocado. When I think of all the times I risked a heart attack watching Dad go up on that three-story ladder to paint it tan. The cement block retaining wall he built—The Great Wall of Dave Feldman—looks like Joshua's been there. That was a great wall, too—you could crouch behind it and rain snowballs (plague-like) on Uptown Motors across the alley with nearly complete impunity, in an attempt to see if you could startle the salesmen into dropping their feet from their desks and running out into the lot long enough to slip in and grab the keys to a sharp-looking Hudson fastback. We never got that far, but a guy could dream. The alley's even in disrepair, if an alley can be in disrepair...I don't know, I've never seen a new one. That alley was the world to me—playground, escape route, toboggan slide. With proper icing, you could sled all the way from 58th Street to Ruth's Sweet Shop on 51st, knocking Rabbi Twerski off his feet on 53rd if you cut it too close to sunset. If you got past Twerski, it was a round of wax lips for everybody.

I didn't knock on the door. I was afraid we still lived there and I'd be back in the damn bedroom with my brother Arthur, my Moriarty, trying to sleep in the beds Dad built in during the built-in craze, all without benefit of box springs. I used to pool up at night like a blob of mercury. Arthur in those days was a night creature that only came up from the basement to bed in the wee hours, flipping on the light and whistling while he filed between his toes with his sweat sock. The upside was that my bad dreams, by comparison, didn't seem so bad. There were actually worse accommodations in the house: Howard slept in the sunroom, which was on Highway 41. We felt like the only Jews on the Santa Fe trail, since an amazing number of cattle moved past our house.

Mother was the only one who liked the house. It was head and shoulders above living over the drycleaners on 27th Street, and with all those strings of lights over the used car lots, she didn't have to put on the kitchen light at night. It was convenient; in winter, Barger's bakery was only a black-and-blue fall and swollen knee down the alley for Kaiser rolls and hot ham, our concession to prevailing custom. Plus, it was on all the major bus routes, particularly the number 27, which enabled you to make it downtown as far as Boston Store and back with one transfer. They were supposed to tear the house down for the East-West freeway, during the freeway craze which stopped dead once they weren't tearing down slums.

Milwaukee has changed a lot over the years, almost enough to allow me to move back, but not quite. Country Stadium, the pride of the county during my youth, was torn down for the retractable beast fashioned from crane parts from Harnischfeger. Love the new Calaveras art museum, a giant seagull which flaps its wings to the lake every day at noon. The east side could be someplace else entirely, and the Third Ward is all gussified, and some breweries have even moved back in, although they will never make Milwaukee famous. Red Star Yeast has moved from the edge of the industrial valley and now it will be impossible to know when to exit for downtown by smell. Milwaukee Casket ceased to add a sense of foreboding to the Plankinton exit. Maybe the biggest change is that people in New Berlin think they live in Milwaukee, and Muskego is a local call. It's a brave new world, that Milwaukee.

MADISON, WI

Madison is the high ground in the swamp, most years. Lady Forward atop the state capitol is as high as you can get in Madison, although many have tried. From the penthouses of all the new high-rise student condos you can look up her skirt, which is shocking. Home of the University of Wisconsin, former home of Bucky Bolshevik, currently a hotbed of student rest. It's not so much that Madison thinks of itself as a liberal town, it's that the rest of Wisconsin thinks of it that way, radical even, despite the fact that the last riot of any size was entirely beer-induced. The only reds you see around here now are the ones carrying their matching cushions to Camp Randall for a Badger game—there are legions of them, advancing on the ramparts of the alumni ghetto behind the goalposts. Even the former radical mayor is now a financial counselor, and in this economy. It's a long way between the Shining Path and what you see walking out of the state office buildings, where there are cubicles, not cells, although I see how you could make the mistake. Former radicals are retiring from state agencies left and right; one or two probably will go Grey Panther.

These days we have more animal activists than human ones. Makes you wish you were an animal. The old hippies have to worry about their hippie replacements, although it seems like a few of them haven't had three squares a day since the Green Lantern eating co-op shut down. Well, go to the Haight-Ashbury and you'll be disappointed, too, particularly if you're looking to buy. Madison always has been surprisingly town-and-gown, more Columbus or Bloomington than we care to admit; there's a substantial population that works for a living, although it's not clear where, outside of American Family Insurance and the State Legislature (hey—not always synonymous). You see guys coming home in work clothes, but maybe they've been sitting in the tavern all day waiting for an imaginary shift change.

Used to be townies tended towards the army and gownies towards army surplus. Now that I resent college kids, myself (how dare they wear my clothes wrong?) I can see how it was possible for them to have resented us; by now most of their kids have gone through a UW long since purged of outside agitators (many of whom came from as far away as Boscobel)—these days, what's not to like, tuition aside? Madison also has an east side, west side thing going on, but since I moved to the (near and not so bad) west side years ago, I can't say much about it. I don't think we're better. Better off, maybe, but there's some pretty nice places in Sun Prairie and Fitchburg. I used to think of the east side as where the proles defied the sex police by trysting in camera-free flats above antique stores, but I was reading way too much Orwell for my own good. War is Peace, indeed. It's not like the ruling class lives past Hilldale Shopping Center—I don't see how you can live on what used to be the experimental farm a few years prior and think you're hot stuff. Who knows what they left in the soil?

I'm not admitting that Madison has been my Shangri-la, but each time I make the turn onto I-90 I immediately turn very old and withered and have to make an illegal U-ie back home to Mad Town.

THANKS FOR THE MEMOS:
THE MEMORIZED ONES

TO ALL: We asked an Italian Software Engineer to translate part of the instructions for the new machine that we had purchased from his company. Abbondanza!

"THE MANAGEMENT DEALS HIM WITH TO CREATE THE CHART OF THE MEMORIZED ONES TO ADJOURN, AFTER THE RECOGNITIONS, TO CREATE A CHART (AND BIT) OF PRESENCE ALARMS NEW ANCHOR TO BE RECOGNIZED, AND TO REMOVE FROM THE CHART OF THE MEMORIZED ONES THE TO HAUL DISAPPEARS ME AND ALREADY PREVIOUSLY RECOGNIZED. An actual alarm (instant) it immediately enters the chart of the memorized ones, therefore it lifts the bit of new alarm, and it enters the chart of the new ones, subsequently you/he/she is recognized with PB ACK and it passes in the chart of the recognized ones and you/he/she is removed by the new ones—if the actual one and "already" disappeared you/he/she will be removed by the memorized ones, otherwise it automatically stays however us thin to real disappearance and to that point you/he/she is removed by the memorized ones LOAD 5 IN THE REGISTER FOR to do OPERATIONS with INDEX."

WHAD'YA KNOW ABOUT PLACES?
ROUND 3

1. At Ohio State, in Columbus, ____ percent of incoming freshmen come to orientation with a parent.
   - (a) 49
   - (b) 53
   - (c) 85

2. In France, can you name a pig after Napoleon?

3. You could buy 1 gallon of gas in Eritrea, or ____ gallons in Venezuela.
   - (a) 10
   - (b) 40
   - (c) 80

4. Speaking of France, there are 4 rats for every Parisian—how many chickens are there for every West Virginian?
   - (a) 10
   - (b) 25
   - (c) 50

5. In Idaho, if a wolf is really bugging you, can you kill it?

6. Peachtree Rd. in Atlanta—is it misnamed?

7. A comely lassie offers you a digestive in Scotland—what is she suggesting?

8. In the Singapore phonebook, which name are you most likely to find?
    (a) Wing Ho
    (b) Zhang Min
    (c) Chen Jie

9. Percentage of male New Zealanders who feel comfortable in a pink shirt:
    (a) 20
    (b) 25
    (c) 75

10. Is sangria legal in the Commonwealth of Virginia?

☞ 60 percent of Brits use a scissors to pick their teeth.

WHAD'YA KNOW ABOUT PLACES? (ROUND 3 ANSWERS)

1. (c) 85 percent, says the National Survey of Student Engagement. Fierce as the Buckeyes are on Woody Hayes Dr., that's how close

they are to their parents, leading the Big Ten in dragging Mom and/or Dad to registration and sometimes to class with them.

2. *Mais, non.* Since 1993, French parents have been free to name their children anything they want (providing it does not subject the child to ridicule), but pigs—and Napoleon—are another matter entirely. You can, however, name your bloodhound Napoleon, so ce qui vous savant?

3. (c) 80. It's up to 12 cents a gallon in Venezuela and about $10 in Eritrea. If you wanted to fill up in Caracas, it would cost you about $400 going down and $12 coming back—although Hugo would insist on driving.

4. (c) 50. If you are a chicken-less West Virginian, it means your neighbor has 100.

5. Yes. Wolves have been reclassified in Idaho from "endangered" to "big bad." If you see one worrying you or your livestock, you can shoot it, as long as you report it within two days.

6. No. The *Atlanta Journal–Constitution* reported the last one, on Peachtree Ridge at Fairview Circle, bit the pit in May of 2008, victim of disease, pollution, and wear-and-tear. Popular history has Atlanta's peach trees planted to commemorate those fallen to Sherman's troops in defense of Atlanta in July 1864.

7. It's just a cookie. No biggie.

8. (c) There are 4,000 Chen Jies, making it the most popular name in the Shanghai white pages.

9. (c) 75 percent of Kiwi men turn out to be comfortable in their skins and the pastels that grace them—also, half hand-wash their own pink things.

10. Yes—for the first time since 1934, when the legislature deemed that, while booze may again have been legal, nobody in Virginia was about to mix spirits and wine, which pretty much rules out sangria. Now you can have a pitcher with your tapas, but still no Kir Royales or Beer Cocktails.

THE NAZCA LINES

The Nazca Lines have suffered the same fate as the Easter Island heads, Stonehenge, and Chichen Itza: namely, being linked to ancient astronauts, trod upon by hordes of crystal worshipers, and featured in dubious meaning-seeking specials on the Discovery Channel, all of which tends to obscure the fact that no one knows how or why the Nazca people some 2,000 years ago carved their beautiful giant totemic images of whales, hummingbirds, spiders, condors, and some creatures which either don't exist anymore or never did on the arid Pampa Colorada in southern Peru, or why they had to be so darn big they can only be seen from the air. Maybe so the gods could see them without their bifocals. This was way before environmental art, so the thinking is the carvings are religious in nature. Some seventy images in all, including animals, plants, and geometric shapes preserved by the dry climate (it rains for half an hour every two years) and re-etched by the constant winds. Not much is known of the Nazca themselves, classified as belonging to the seemingly contradictory Early Intermediate Period (*c.* 200 BC–600 AD), except that their pottery had four or more colors with typically red or white backgrounds of naturalistic design not unlike the glyphs, and they favored open bowls or double-spouted jars. The patron saint of the Nazca lines was German mathematician Maria Reiche, who lived on the plain for fifty years until her death at age 95 in 1998, mapping and studying them and attempting to protect them from the encroachment of Range Rovers. The figures radiating through the desert from the cultivated Ingenio valley overlap and are incised through the red oxide surface with precision and a sophisticated knowledge of surveying—astronomical observations made big enough for proofreading by the heavens.

ONE MICRONATION, UNDER TINY GOD

A s we say in Sealand, One If By. God bless this sceptered pontoon, this derelict gun platform, this Sealand. Technically a principality, Sealand was founded in 1967 by Major Paddy Roy Bates, a pirate radio broadcaster pirating the former HM Fort Roughs six miles off Suffolk from other radio pirates. The War of Sealand Independence, September 2, 1968, was three shots over the bow of a British Merchant Marine skiff attempting to relight a nearby navigational buoy. An English court the following year ruled the floating fort beyond its three-mile jurisdiction, and so a micronation was born, one with a constitution, flag, postal stamps, passports, and ambassadorships available at popular prices, and a benevolent dictator, Prince Roy. It is not Roy in drag, but Buccaneer and Third Earl of Cumberland George Clifford pictured on the stamps and folding currency. His Royal Highness Prince Michael serves as head of state while father and Princess Joan live in exile in Essex. The biggest challenge to Sealand's sovereignty was an insurrection led by the former Prime Minister Professor Alexander G. Achenbach, a German with dual titles and citizenship, imprisoned for treason by Bates loyalists for several weeks before a release was negotiated by the Germans in return for inferred (wink-wink) recognition. In 1990, the Royal Maritime Auxiliary vessel *Golden Eye* took fire from Sealand's national guardsman enforcing its 12-nautical-mile sea claim, which would extend its jurisdiction to Stowmarket in Norwich. In June of 2006, the topmost platform of Sealand caught fire due to Bates's (unlicensed) electrical work, and was put out by a local fireboat from Harwich, which unsuccessfully billed the principality for services rendered. Sealand has been on the micronation market since 2007, and was very nearly reconstituted as a Bit Torrent Republic by Pirate Bay, whose offer of stock and first-run Hollywood films was deemed inadequate. The little bit of heaven-on-sea goes for 750 million euros.

PANACHE, HEY

A Midwest peace agreement would have to be brokered between the flatlanders to the south and the cheeseheads, whose territory they routinely invade to purchase and drive up cabin prices. Along our free highways, I might add. Yet, as Condi Rice might discover on her shuttle diplomacy 'twixt Brodhead, Crystal Lake, and Fergus Falls, we are all Midwesterners, every Monterey Jack of us. Prick us, do we not leech butter fat? Are we not large boned? Is this not a Leinie's I see before me—come let me clutch thee! Is the speed limit not 55? Do not my taxes pay for the left lane, knucklehead? And so forth. Unpretentious and, Minnesotans aside, not ones to call attention to ourselves, we pretty much have replicated the values and foodstuffs of Northern Europe on the prairies and forests of the glacial till of the Wisconsin (mind you) Age. Your Germans, your Poles, your two kinds of Scandinavians—Swede or Norwegian—a few Finns and Icelanders, your Chippewa, Oneida, Potawatomi, sprinkled with Jews and Hmong…not so much a melting pot as a fish boil of hard working, liquor-fearing (make that God-fearing), hearty folk saying, "Come by the house, later," spelled "b-y," by the way, you guys from Mundelein with the bank rolls.

Midwesterners are thought to be rather self-contained, but the truth is, shake us, you'll hear something rattle. We just don't let someone shake us until we've known them for a while. Extremely friendly if you know what to look for, outgoing, even, although "demonstrative" may be a stretch. A lot of it is subtle, a facial-tics-and-inflections kind of thing. Seed caps open or clipped in the back. Tendency to hunker down past highway 29. Go off the well-maintained free highway into the cow culvert in your Volvo, speeding to your four-season cabin in Rhinelander, one of us will be there on a John Deere in a half-hour or less with a chain to pull you out, and your thanks is thanks enough. We just want you out of the goddamn culvert, worrying the cows.

Major exports of the Midwest: corn, soybeans, dairy products, machine parts, and talk-show hosts. People assume this last one is because we have no accents to speak of, but really it's because we have all these things we've been holding back that come spewing out once we hit New York or Los Angeles. Still a lot of families living on the land, although increasingly on Lands' End. If you're on the phone trying to get help with your network problem and you're not talking to someone in Mombassa, you're probably talking to a Midwesterner; same with On-star. We are the least likely to say anything when you've locked yourself out of your running Buick on the freeway. Hey, it's happened to us. We're from around here.

THE STICKY WICKET
OF NATIONAL CHARACTER

Germans believe in national character, and think theirs is to their credit, but that's just typical of the German *über alles*, all upside and no down, as far as they can recall. Parisians are born believers in their own largesse, finding the rest of France provincial, duh, by definition. To feel good about themselves, the Polish pretend they're French, while the Swiss, when not being neutral, get to choose between being French or German, based on food preferences and number of kilometers above sea level. Many of the English are most convinced they are really French, of all things, if they could only bring themselves to admit it, although more than one Saxon has had a brush with that stiff upper lip. Very few native Angles left, having played them all—the few remaining are mostly in men's haberdashery. The contiguous Irish, Welsh, and Scots, however they got that way (the wayfaring Picts, Celts, Vandals, and Vikings), have by now pretty much made it their own.

British women care least about wasting water during long showers, while only 35 percent of their significant others give a fig about contaminants in the water, perhaps because it's always cold by the time they get to it. Two-thirds of Spanish women conserve water and care deeply about what's in it, whereas the Germans have purity laws governing only water in beer. One in seven British men goes to work without a shower, due to the abovementioned British women. Thirteen percent do, however, moisturize, another 6 percent just a little base and a hint of shadow. A little more than half comb their hair. 72 percent say their mums have not influenced their grooming choices. The average British male spends 46 euros a year on personal care products to the average Frenchman's 68 euros, the Germans and the Dutch falling between them and feeling pretty uncomfortable about it.

Germans are not above injecting themselves with pharmaceuticals; the Brits are oral, while the French and Belgians both find suppositories strangely rewarding. In the European theater, no toilet habits have been studied more extensively than those of the Germans, 52 percent of whom find toilet time inspirational. Thirty-four percent of German men spend up to ten minutes on the toilet at a crack, whereas the hausfraus are in and out in under five. Twenty-six percent of German youth text on the toilet. Ten percent of Germans from Saxony-Anhalt sing show tunes on the crapper, while half of those from Mecklenburg-West Pomerania daydream.

French cooking and its relationship with the French has been looked into nearly as much as German WCs—in 1978, the average French meal lasted an hour and twenty-two minutes; today it lasts 38 minutes, fast food being such a timesaver, the downside being the French have gone from "How come nobody's fat?" to the current 12 percent obese and 40 percent overweight, and, increasingly, are being mistaken for Germans. Heartening is the fact that only 9 percent of French men have a problem with women of weight, while 22 percent of increasingly beefy British males do. Spanish men—43 percent, if you must know—are the least tolerant of body odor among the European states; British men, at 27 percent, have learned to live with it. What they can't stand are hairy armpits, which the French find *de rigueur*.

GENDARME, OU
EST MA FEMME?

Any broadening you may see is not from travel. My only overseas trip was the ill-fated 1990 conjugal visit to France and Spain, ill-fated in the sense my wife survived. I know that sounds cruel, but you travel with a woman who packs only open-toed sandals for the dog-*merde* streets of Paris, who speaks French just well enough to have a Parisian laundromat owner hurl a fistful of 20-franc pieces at us for complaining the dry cleaning machine stole her money by looking like a washer (*"comme une machine à laver!"*), who gets so mad at you for getting a direction wrong (*vers la droit? la derrière?*) that she hovers alone through the Rodin Gallery, *Thinker* to *Balzac*, purposefully appearing insubstantial, causing many to swear she was the ghost of Camille Claudel, haunting the place.

It was like entering Paris with Hitler, except he was all excited to be there. All right, the hotel, Champs Elysées, was not on the Champs Elysées, not anywhere near it, but it was not my fault she brushed her teeth in the bidet and used the wrong closet to make ze wee-wee. We couldn't seem to see anything together—I went to Notre and she went to Dame. Up the Eiffel Tower we were bisected by a throng of Indiana basketball fans who thought they were in Terre Haute (French, too, you know), completely ruining the illusion that I was Franchot Tone and she Burgess Meredith. Certainly no reason, once we made Nice (after the farmers celebrated a bumper crop by burning it on the tracks of the TGV, so we had to go back to Paris backwards at 320 km/h), to attempt to book a flight back to Madison in the USA to retrieve her Timberlands and amoxicillin.

We were not speaking in any tongue by the time we took the train from Nice that changes gauges at the Spanish border because Franco liked HO scale, and the Spanish border guards came on board thinking one of us was Peter Ustinov in disguise. I have had my belly poked playfully, and that was not it. I will say her Spanish inflections very nearly passed for Catalan, and should not have propelled the Barcelona cab down the Ramblas and into the Mediterranean, just missing the Ibiza Ferry. She thought the Sagrada Familia gaudy, and I couldn't convince her otherwise (Catholicism in a termite mound, ¡es maravilloso!), and was a very bad sport when the live eels in their own juices she mistakenly ordered arrived tableside. We can never eat at Las Anguilas again, that's for sure. *¡Que lastima!* Barcelona would be a great town with the right person, or not with the wrong one; even under her circumstances I liked it a lot better than Paris, since jugglers don't follow you around and mock you like mimes. Being condescended to by your wife is nothing compared to being mocked by a Parisian mime, whose little bailiwick on the cobbles of Marais ("Centrally the diverse communities of Jewish, artist, and gay give the area a cosmopolitan soul," the guide book says) you were forced to tramp through while pursing her in a huff, giving him all the license he needed to imitate an ugly American who walked on the balls of his feet, and came close to getting my foot in his.

After agreeing next year no Marienbad, we parted in Madrid; I, to sign up with the Republicans, she to the Prado to see if her portrait was still up (you can see her in Guernica, next to the horse holding a torch: that's Sandy). She wouldn't come to the bullfights, and the bull felt the same way. In my opinion, the Madrinos are more approachable than the Parisians, perhaps because everything is closed during daylight hours and they never have to serve tourists. You couldn't find a sangria or tapas until 10 p.m., when I was already tapas-ed out, and although nobody invites you to their siesta, nobody harasses you cooling your heels on the Puerta del Sol, under the clock of the famous 12 Sour Grapes waiting out the next Iberia to O'Hare.

THANKS FOR THE MEMOS: NEXT YEAR IN MINOT

To: All Staff

Subject: National Meeting

Re: Spouses at Tahoe

Date: 11/29

It has been brought to our attention that even though the company **will NOT** be able to pay for your spouses to go to Lake Tahoe, some of you are trying and planning to have them attend at your own expense. Due to the arrangements that have been made (airport transportation/tickets, group activities, meetings, etc., etc.), we do not see how or where you would have any time to spend with them. Every day from the day you arrive until the day you leave (excluding Thursday), we have activities planned as a group, from 9:00 a.m. until at least 10:00 p.m. We believe that any spouses attending would only be distracting to our National Sales Meeting.

Please be aware that **ALL** air travel, hotel accommodations, and group activities **ARE** etched in stone as a group, with absolutely **NO CHANGES** possible. We are sorry that we cannot accommodate any of your spouses in Lake Tahoe. Bottom line is: if you continue your quest and it interferes with our National Sales Meeting plans in any way (**OUR** sole discretion), disciplinary action will follow.

Don't worry, be happy, next year we're planning to go to Minot, North Dakota, so we won't have any of these problems.

WHAD'YA KNOW ABOUT
PLACES?
ROUND 4

1. Although officials couldn't be reached for comment, workers in which state are the biggest slackers?

    (a) Minnesota

    (b) New Mexico

    (c) Missouri

2. The town of Yelm, Washington, has barred citizens from saying what at council meetings?

    (a) Slander

    (b) Lord's name in vain

    (c) Wal-Mart

3. Qatar in the United Arab Emirates plans to use _____ as camel jockeys.

    (a) neutered boys

    (b) robots

    (c) monkeys

4. Do the French or the Brits have more liaisons?

5. Road rage rages the most in:

    (a) South Africa

    (b) India

    (c) Greece

6. Who has more boats per capita, Aucklanders or Minnesotans?

7. Cleveland can save you _____ over living in Ginza, Tokyo.

    (a) $1,559

    (b) $2,214

    (c) $8,016

8. Even though it seems like a lot more, even the town with the most Starbucks per 10,000 residents, Falls Church, VA, only has:

    (a) 8

    (b) 13

    (c) 3

9. Cincinnati chili goes up to:

    (a) 4-way

    (b) 5-way

    (c) 6-way

10. Percentage of Italians who would sunbathe nude if their neighbors did:

    (a) 70

    (b) 80

    (c) 90

WHAD'YA KNOW ABOUT PLACES? (ROUND 4 ANSWERS)

1. (c) Missouri. Salon.com claims they spend 3 hours, 12 minutes of the average 6-hour workday on the Internet: forwarding funny articles, watching tournaments, Facebooking, etc.

2. (c) Wal-Mart. Gotten pretty contentious regarding the new Super Store. Can say "Big Box," though, in a normal tone of voice. No yelling.

3. (b) Robots. Responding to international concern as to the well-being of imported Arab pre-adolescent camel jockeys in races, Qatar has decided to go with robots, who don't seem to have a constituency.

4. If *liaisons* means what I think it does, surprisingly, it's the Brits (60 percent) over the French (30 percent), who invented the darn things. This flies in the face of the stiff upper lip, but there it is. Only 17 percent of Chinese have liaisons.

5. (a) South Africa. 2 out of 3 South African drivers are blowing their horns, screaming, and riding the bumper of the car that cut them off at this moment. Too closely followed by the UK and Greece.

6. C'mon—Minnesotans, hands down, 1 out of 6 as compared to 1 out of 11 in New Zealand.

7. (a) $1,559 a month—not including Cleveland Heights—over the Ginza.

8. (a) 8—for a town of about 10,000, it doesn't seem adequate.

9. (c) You can go as high as 6-way on your chili in Cincinnati: spaghetti, chili, cheese, onions, kidney beans, and garlic/jalapeños.

10. (a) 70 percent; it's all set and setting for the Italians, 5 percent of whom (male) don't like seeing nude women on the beach. From the Naturalist Federation, and I guess we know where they fall on this.

 GWYNAETH

Nothing may be rotten in Denmark, often ranked, suicides aside, as the happiest place in the world, but no place has more *gwynaeth* than the 25 Welshmen per square kilometer of Powys (rhymes with "cow-piss," according to local wags), named the happiest place to live in Britain by the University of Sheffield. Buffered on the north by Gwynedd, Denbighshire, and Wrexham; on the west by Ceredigion and Carmarthenshire; to the east by Hereford; and resting gently on a cushion of Rhondda Cynon Taff, Merthyr Tydfil, Caerphilly, Blaenau Gwent, Monmouthshire, and Neath Port Talbot; who wouldn't be happy?

The former Kingdom of Powys, having gotten all the battles out of the way between this Æthelfrith and that Æthelfrith, has been resting on its scenic laurels since the thirteenth century, and lovely laurels they are. Green, forested, astride the rolling Cambrian mountains dotted with unimproved villages, unblemished by cities and motorways, thought by some to have inspired Shangri-la in *Lost Horizon*...why be anywhere else, unless it's Cardiff, for the night life. Julie Christie lives there, and lady in waiting to Princess Anne, Shan Legge-Bourke of Glan Usk. No crime rate, only the occasional spot of bother from a Birmingham vagabond, so close to Swansea (number 269 on the list) and yet so far away. In Powys no one comes or goes, one of the markers of happiness being not changing addresses in five years—what about in eight centuries?

In Brecknock, Montgomery, and Radnor, gwynaethiest of the gwynaeth, everyone stays put, creating what sociologists call social cohesion, a shared sense of well-being, here underscored by a revival of all things Welsh not seen since Peter Sellers and Mai Zetterling in *Only Two Can Play*. Insularity with scenery is the Powys prescription for gwynaeth, in the largest county with the smallest population in Wales, ethnically 99.3 percent purebred Welsh, the 0.7 percent being Christie. Bronllys Hospital makes electricity from pure sunshine, wind farms like the one at Camddwr dot the pristine Cambrian slopes, and mountain bike trails in the forests of Brechfa, Afan, and Cwmcarn are the envy of the UK. Meirionydd Oakwoods Habitat Restoration is well along and a model for all of Europe, while the bovine husbandry of greater Powys more than justifies the council boast, "Powys is Cowys!" The tilting harvester at Nant yr Arian is considered one of the wonders of the modern world.

There are, of course, detractors. Ogwr, perhaps the only unhappy place in Wales these days after coming in a disappointing number 22 on the happy list, behind Cumbernauld and Kilsyth, was vexed enough to have released this statement: "Llefydd prin iawn ar y daith, felly'r cyntaf i'r felin gaiff falu!"

BIG TOP CIRCUS ACT

CAN YOU BEAT THE MONKEY?

pop. 19

MONKEY'S ELBOW
KENTUCKY

CAN YOU BEAT
THE MONKEY?

You probably knew that Truth or Consequences, NM, was named to attract the popular quiz show, but what about Paris Hilton, TX? How come nobody thought of that? Could draw her the way Braselton, GA, did Kim Basinger. Town names are funny things. Take Modesto, CA, which should, by all rights, be Ralston, after developer William Ralston, who declined the honor to shouts of *"muy modesto!"* It may have been something other than modesty, however, since the town was already called the Filth Capital of America for its abundant gambling, opium dens, and brothels. Eclectic, AL, was the name proposed by a resident of Coosada who had taken an eclectic course of study at school and was proud of it. Conversely, no one in Muck City, AL, had, or was. Chicken, AK, was named for the abundant ptarmigans, but they couldn't agree on the spelling. Technically, it should be Snow Chicken. On the other hand, no body remembers how Eek, AK, on the edge of the Yukon delta, got its name, but one could conjecture. Toad Suck was, of course, named for the river men who got plied while plying the Arkansas, drinking so *durn* much whiskey they swelled up something amphibious. Whereas Romance, AR, was a blatant attempt by the business community—namely, the post office—to drum up Valentine's Day covers. No Name, CO, is named for No Name Creek of the same no name. There's a No Name Tunnel as well, but don't try to ask for it by name. Yeehaw Junction, FL, was originally Jackass Junction. 'Nuff said. Normal, IL, is what happens when you tire of being called North Bloomington; while Buddha, IN, that's *boo*-dee, got that way from a traveling salesman's wisecrack regarding a stout fellow asleep on the rooming house porch. Could just as easily have been Farmer's Daughter, IN. Monkey's Elbow, KY, has a population of 19, none of whom was ever told about the name, but they will sell you a "Can You Beat the Monkey?" tee for twenty bucks. They haven't suffered for being named Hell in the Michigan town of the same name—people from there are forever yelling Hell! Story is, since George Reeves and his seven daughters lived there first, in their grist mill, when time came to incorporate they naturally asked George, who said, "Call it Hell, for all I care," and, damnation, they did. There is both running Coldwater and

Hot Water in Mississippi, the former having cold water thrown on it by the building of the Akabutla Dam, and the latter more the result of cattle relieving themselves in the pond. Embarrass, MN, which had a *near*-record low of –54° in 2007, was named after the Embarrass which runs through it, a difficult patch of water known for embarrassing canoeists, or bare-assed canoeists—something like that. Disco, TN, is inexplicable, but Dismal is not—it was just trying to distinguish itself from Tatter Knob.

Sea cucumber, on the hoof

VARY IT UP!

Surprising, still, it is, when someone comes to Wisconsin and is astounded by deep-fried cheese curds, or calls a brat a *braat*. Sometimes you get so used to it, you don't know you're sitting on a cuisine. You think only the French have a cuisine, because it's their word, but *au contraire*. There is Icelandic cuisine, somewhere amidst the blood puddings, fermented whale, and broiled puffin. There is the deep-fried horsemeat fondue associated with Swiss good eating, the *dun hoi sum*, Szechwan sea cucumber stew—best when the ovaries they shed when annoyed are re-added. The simple Turkish breaded and fried brain, *beyan tavasi*, compared and contrasted with Lamb's

Brains Neapolitan, a casserole with capers, garlic, and olives. If cod's head and shoulders are any indication, there is even an English cuisine head and shoulders above the haggis of their neighbors to the north. To be fair, people who like haggis really, really like it, even if it hasn't been flung across the Firth of Forth before serving, like the directions say. Would it be too eclectic to wash it down with some Uzbek *kumyss*, the 100 proof fermented ass's milk (talk about a kick) you cannot find in a liquor store around here…maybe they can't keep it on the shelf. The only thing that comes close, people say, is Moroccan *smen*, which is not, as is often assumed, fermented spit, but actually butter cooked up with spices and buried in jugs until somebody gets married. In Morocco a household is regarded by the amount of *smen* they have in the ground. Perhaps it's unfair, but you can judge a culture by what they do with pigeons, from shooing them away with cannon blasts to calling them squab.

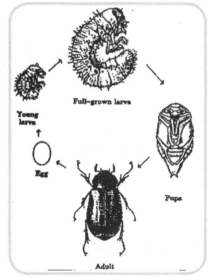

The Germans, Japanese, and Chinese all tend to call pigeons squab, and cook them accordingly: *Gerbratene junge Tauben,* breaded and fried for the Germans; *Waka dori no yaki tori,* named like a disclaimer, marinated and broiled pigeon for the Japanese; and five-spice infused and wokked *Su tsa*

nen kuh for the northern Chinese, plus a nice little *pigeon a l'orange.* In Belgium, it's pigeons and chestnuts roasting on a open fire and Father Christmas nipping at your *nez.*

There are some ecumenical dishes that never get the credit they deserve, like the Locust Soup of both the Arabic and Jewish (God gives you locusts, you make soup) North Africans. Supposedly can't be told from beef stock, properly strained. To extend the metaphor, a very similar stock was made by Brigham Young's party when the Lord gave them Mormon crickets. When locusts are unavailable, grasshoppers may be substituted. To the Vietnamese, palm worms are manna from heaven, dipped in the versatile *nuoc-mam* sauce, fried twice, once in lard and again after wrapping in a spring roll; a different approach from that in the French West Indies, where the grubs are skewered and roasted, then rolled in seasoned bread crumbs and roasted again. Not to editorialize, but I might roast them a third time as well. The closest you can get in France, proper, are several ways of looking at Cockchafers, the ingeniously-named scarabaeid beetles, which, if not eaten, would threaten the entire Eure et Loir Forest. You may fry the grubs live in butter, wrap them in parchment and bake in a wood fire, or remove the heads and wings of the adults, pestle-ize the pests, and, that's right, make soup.

BORN IN THE UAE

Remember when you thought a Qatar was a fretted string instrument with either a hollow or solid body? That the Emirates were a Phillies farm club playing in Montgomery, AL? Today they own the Chrysler Building, which, with enough booster rockets strategically placed on Lexington Avenue, could make the suborbital flight to splashdown in the Persian Gulf in less than 27 minutes. The first I heard of the Emirates was when we were doing a show in Lexington, KY, and someone mentioned that Sheikh Mohammed bin Rashid Al Maktoum, Himself, had just been in town buying racehorses and watermelons (apparently they hadn't yet cracked growing melons in the desert, but they will), reiterating the local concern that both were consumables, and, moreover, you couldn't find a watermelon for love nor money in Bourbon County. Turns out the Dubais, while not abandoning camel racing, their bread and butter, are heavily invested in Arabians, which seems only fair. Al Maktoum is not called the Crown Prince of Arab Horsemen for nothing: his stable regularly sweeps European tracks, and one day the Derby, even if he has to buy it and move it. A far cry from the sheiks of old who made a living pirating passing vessels instead of watermelons and signature skyscrapers, when the gulf was known as the Pirate Coast, until becoming a British protectorate in 1853 in exchange for letting their opium through. Independence didn't come until 1972, but it came with a vengeance, and much making up for lost time, as the United Arab Emirates—Abu Dhabi, Ajman, Dubai, Fujairah, Ras al Khaimah, Sharjah, and Umm al Quwain—smart, as in all things, to go with the acronym, UAE. They've come a long way from camel herding, pearl diving, and living in mud huts, if the 2,684-foot Burj Dubai, conveniently located in downtown Dubai, is any indicator, all ready for businesses and residents in fall 2009. Office space goes for $4,000 per square foot, and residences go for a slightly more residential $3,500. Even so, it will soon be surpassed by Bahrain's Murjan Tower, still on the drawing boards—where it keeps getting redrawn bigger—but currently at 3,353 feet and 200 floors, with square footage priced at if-you-have-to-ask-you-can't-afford-it. Then there's a little friendly competition from the $3 billion Abu Dhabi development of Khaldoon Khalifa al Mubarak—three skyscrapers, two five-star hotels, and an upscale souk to die for. Mubarek says he is importing the Sorbonne, Guggenheim, Louvre, and Cleveland Clinic as well, although it's not clear whether in whole or in part.

But, friends, in the Emirates the fun doesn't stop at water's edge— entire new cities are accreting like sandbars, which some of them are, but none on the scale of Dubai's Waterfront City, a real estate developer's wet dream, home and work to 1.5 million, assuming everybody currently living in the Emirate moves in. Centered by an island resembling Manhattan on steroids, Waterfront City features a 44-story sphere and an 82-story ziggurat, and still has plenty of room for the Chrysler Building among the forest of Trump Towers, and more ocean-view condos than anyplace on Earth. If Waterfront City is all about conspicuous consumption, Abu Dhabi's Masdar City, about a third of the size for a population of 30,000, will be a zero-carbon, zero-waste city filled with wind farms, solar arrays, plantations, fields of biofuel, composting plants, and treatment plants that will recycle nearly all of the desalinated water. You will have to park your Range Rover in the outer city, though—the core of Masdar is one huge pedestrian mall. If successful, and that's pretty much a certainty, the Burj, Murjan, Waterfront City and Masdar will not go unanswered in the Emirates—it's just that kind of place.

THANKS FOR THE MEMOS: FURTHERING INTERNATIONAL MISUNDERSTANDING

To: All Villages

Re: Transport Torino Olympic Games

I understand there are still questions regarding using the TOROC transportation system to access the mountain venues. In today's report we will try to simplify the system for you. First of all, don't get on the ATV if you want to go to a venue, you need to get on an ATM. The ATM is for athletes, which you catch at the Transport Mall, not the MTA or the OVAC, unless of course you arrive on the ATV2 from OVT which rotates arrivals between the MTA and the VBS. Don't take the SUS or the WKF, as they are for the locals, unless you want to go to Borgata. If you want to take the OFMS, you need a T 4 credential or you need to take the DOM6, no credential required, which goes to most mountain venues except of course the SSF. If you are departing from OVB, you can take the ATM3 to A BDY2 and the A CSS1 to Cesana San Sicario. Now, if you want to go to Fratieve and get on the ATM4 by mistake, you will be SOL as it goes to the APT Caselle. So ultimately, to sum up, the TOROC system is very usable as long as you give yourself time to be familiarized.

WHAD'YA KNOW ABOUT PLACES? ROUND 5

1. Who's, you know, *quickest*, among men?
   (a) Turkish
   (b) Dutch
   (c) British

2. Turns out the eruption of Mt. Vesuvius may have been a blessing, since researchers discovered the sauces favored by Pompeians were made from:
   (a) bat droppings
   (b) goat skulls
   (c) fish entrails

3. The brandy capital of America is:
   (a) Wisconsin
   (b) Utah
   (c) Washington, DC

4. The president of Turkmenistan (that's central Asia) has banned:

    (a) humming

    (b) air guitar

    (c) lip synching

5. They may not be swallows and this might not be Capistrano, but what returns to Hinckley, OH, on the Ides of March?

    (a) building inspectors

    (b) turkey vultures

    (c) Norway rats

6. Percentage of Clevelanders who have posed nude:

    (a) 0

    (b) 9

    (c) 14

7. Number of flies allowed in a Beijing toilet:

    (a) 1

    (b) 2

    (c) 3

8. Of the seven deadly sins, which is first for Italians?

    (a) lasciviousness

    (b) sloth

    (c) gluttony

9. Onalaska, WI—is it the "crappie capital of the world"?

10. Number one globally in per capita ketchup consumption:

(a) Pittsburgh

(b) Venezuela

(c) Sweden

WHAD'YA KNOW ABOUT PLACES? (ROUND 5 ANSWERS)

1. (a) According to the *Journal of Sexual Medicine*, which won't reveal its sources, a Turkish male is in and out in 3.7 minutes. The Dutch stretch it out to 5.1, and the Brits a leisurely 7.6 minutes. American males break the tape at 7.0 flat.

2. (c) Garum, fermented fish entrails, predated tomato sauces. The Romans stole this delicacy from the Greeks along with everything else. It is featured in just about every recipe in *Apicius, The Joy of Ancient Roman Cooking*.

3. (c) Between the streets and the Capitol Lounge, DC's number one.

4. (c) Lip synching. Never one to shy from eccentric decrees, President Saparmurat Niyazov cited the "negative effect on the development of singing and musical art."

5. (b) Hinckley's turkey vulture spotter, Robert Hinkle, announces the arrival of the first of hundreds who find springtime in Medina County to their liking. Not true that they are attracted by the annual collapse of the nearby Cleveland Indians.

6. (b) Speaking of Cleveland, 1 in 11 residents admits posing nude—the figure is probably higher. Go figure.

7. (b) As part of the preparation for the Olympics, only 2 flies were allowed to go to the toilet in Beijing at the same time, during the Great Flush Forward.

8. (c) Gluttony seems to bother Italians the most, at least among others.

9. No; the city fathers of the western Wisconsin town decided against it and went with sunfish.

10. (c) You could have knocked me over with a bottle of Heinz, but the average Swede consumes 3 liters of ketchup a year to our measly 16 ounces—I guess we're playing ketchup.

THANKS FOR THE MEMOS:
AND THE BAR THING, TOO!

From: "Mr. PAO"

Subject: The superelevation price ratio hand coffee grinder and the bar thing help your commodity to be sold immediately

Dear Sir or Madam: Breezing from China

I am come from the Chinese Zhexiang production coffee grinder and the bar thing independent production factory, today suddenly contacts with you, will disturb your life and the work, regarding this inconvenient which will bring to you, will ask you to forgive.

My factory is located the famous consumable manufacturing industry base China Zhexiang, here has the massive skills level first class but the salary level to be lower than the very the developed country many is outstanding technical worker! Therefore our hand coffee grinder and the bar thing quality and the world well known trademark product is same, but my factory hand coffee grinder ax factory price generally about 3～4 US dollars, but the bar thing also absolutely is the high quality low end, so Pao Xingjia compared to the product recommends to you, you have the interest to understand the more exhaustive product information? I will be anticipating your deigning to inquire!

Respect gentleman or madame, 1 am the independent production factory, if we directly cooperate, will be able to save the very big middle link expense for you, you will say?

Looking forward from you soon

Best wishes,

Mr. PAO

JINJUA WONGDANG ARTS AND CRAPS PACKING FACTORY

THINGS *YOU* SHOULD HAVE *LEARNED* IN

SCHOOL

THINGS YOU SHOULD HAVE
LEARNED IN SCHOOL
ROUND 1

1. Who said "When I use a word, it means just what I choose it to mean, neither more nor less?
    (a) Shakespeare
    (b) Wordsworth
    (c) Humpty Dumpty

2. Force a dyne one centimeter and, voila, you've got a(n):
    (a) erg
    (b) dynamometer
    (c) British Thermal Unit

3. Why did Prometheus get his liver gnawed?
    (a) It was too near his onions.
    (b) For stealing fire.
    (c) For paying a little too much attention to Athena.

4. If you wanted to illustrate peristalsis, you might use:

    (a) lead shot and the Tower of Pisa

    (b) a milk bottle, a candle, and a hardboiled egg

    (c) a mongoose and a gerbil

5. A Petri dish is:

    (a) a dish prepared by Laura for Rob

    (b) a medium for growing bacterial colonies from cheek swabs

    (c) hand-painted and very expensive

6. A flying buttress is:

    (a) a masonry arch supporting a Gothic cathedral vault

    (b) the same as (a), but in rebar

    (c) an undergarment for Rita Hayworth designed by Howard
    Hughes

7. When Lauren Bacall said, "Put your lips together and blow,"
   she was illustrating:

    (a) mimicry of the Bluestreak cleaner wrasse

    (b) the pretty obvious

    (c) Bernoulli's principle—a fluid stream creates a partial
    vacuum in Humphrey Bogart

8. What is wrong with the following:

   All penguins are black and white.

   Jim is black and white.

   Therefore, Jim is a penguin.

       (a) It has an undistributed middle, as does Jim.

       (b) Absolutely nothing; Jim is a penguin.

       (c) Jim is Jim.

9. "Look on my works, ye mighty, and _____."

       (a) plotz

       (b) relax

       (c) despair

10. Let's say you commit a crime so original they have to invent a law for it. Continuing the tribute, they decide to prosecute you. Can they?

       (a) You bet; they can do what they want.

       (b) No, because it's ex post facto and unconstitutional.

       (c) Yes, but only in Mississippi.

☞ Jesus was probably born in 5 BC.

☞ When you think Leibniz, you think binary arithmetic.

☞ If you're bathetic, you're insincerely pathetic.

☞ "Obfuscate" does what it says.

THINGS YOU SHOULD HAVE LEARNED IN SCHOOL (ROUND 1 ANSWERS)

1. (c) Humpty Dumpty, whose ego was easily bruised. This quote comes not from the nursery rhyme (a mockery of the egg-shaped Richard III) but from Lewis Carroll's *Through the Looking-Glass*, where Humpty tries to teach Alice semantics.

2. (a) Erg; from the Greek, meaning *work*—or, in the Maynard G. Krebs, "work!" To make for easier work, you can convert your erg to 10^{-7} joules.

3. (b) For stealing fire. Similar to how they got Capone, you know, taxes, when they could have nailed the P man on any number of things. Zeus had it in for him for eons. Prometheus was the first humanist, since who do you think he gave the fire to?

4. (c) A mongoose and a gerbil; although personally, I'd use a boa constrictor and my neighbor's cat. Without rhythmic contractions this would be hard to swallow.

5. (a) and (b), even though you'd have to be old enough to remember *The Dick Van Dyke Show* and appreciate what a dish Laura was. Julius Petri invented the Petri dish in 1887 when he neglected to wash his Jell-O bowl.

6. (a) Without flying buttresses we'd speak of the great Gothic huts of Europe. How else would you transmit the thrust of your

vault across space? On second thought, don't tell me.

7. (c) Bernoulli had his principles, but Betty Joan Perske (Lauren Bacall) had Bogart from the moment she demonstrated the art of whistling.

8. (a) Illustrates the undistributed middle, as does Jim. A logical fallacy.

9. Well, I always heard it "plotz," but the irony Ozymandius left behind carved on his headless statue was (c). Shelley wrote the little ditty for a sonnet-writing competition which he lost, but not to history.

10. (b) No, because it's ex post facto, i.e., "from something done afterward." Article 1, Section 9 of the Constitution…look it up. And you're entitled to a free phone call.

THANKS FOR THE MEMOS:
TERRORIST BAKE SALES

Attention Faculty and Staff,

At the conclusion of the current Bake Sale here at Don Wilson Elementary, I am directing that NO further Bake Sales take place this year. My reasoning is threefold:

First, we are currently at war with terrorist groups that are looking for heinous acts to inflict harm and pain on Americans. Is there a more heinous way to make a point than to inflict pain and suffering on children via poisoning food and treats that children love to eat?

Secondly, even before this crazy time of war, we have had people poison Halloween candy, over the counter medicines, and other food items for who knows what reason. Most all bakery goods purchased at modern food chains can easily be tampered/poisoned/altered without detection. Next time you are shopping, take a close look at the plastic bags and containers that bakery goods are marketed in.

Lastly, after living on this planet for over fifty years, my experience is that many people don't utilize modern sanitary cooking and cleaning methodologies that can lead to gastrointestinal problems associated with microorganisms, organic biocides, and entomological fecal matter.

If you have concerns/questions with my policy, please take a minute to visit with me.

Mr. Holmes

REUBEN, REUBEN

study at Brandeis should have grade school boys and girls singing "Reuben, Reuben" across the country. It concludes that
boys should not be allowed in the same classroom as girls because
they hamper the girls' growth, and suggests they be admitted to
school only after reaching the threshold of "emotional and physical
stability." Well, maybe you can lead a forty-year old man to P.S. 47,
but you can't make him sit; after all, a guy gets pretty long in the leg
by the time he's emotionally stable.

Of course, it's no secret that boys hamper girls' growth. We've
been at it for years. I assume it's part of the gender system of checks

and balances intended to prevent the female from climbing the next rung of the evolutionary ladder alone. I hadn't realized, however, just what a drag we had become until reading that Professor Mortrude of St. Cloud has implied that girls could be probing the very origins of consciousness were it not for the boys behind them sticking their shoes through the seats.

Girls are, on average, two years ahead of boys, or just entering fiscal 2011. Developmentally speaking, girls, with their propensities for the arts, languages, and insightful thinking, are Renaissance and better, whereas boys are late Neolithic. Girls tend to use more of the right side of the brain, the side where everything that's right comes from. Boys are limited largely to the reflex actions of the cerebellum, allowing them to make surprisingly realistic belches. Girls have sophisticated motor control, permitting them to master folk dances at the drop of a hat, while boys dance only when threatened with a rolled wet towel. During the formative years, boys like to be physical in dramatic ways, a tendency modern schools have taken into account with windows which don't open. Creative powers differ as well: given macaroni, glue, and construction paper, boys inevitably glue the noodles to girls. There's even a memory gap—girls have complete recall, as boys soon discover.

Girls continue to outpace boys until about the sixth grade, when, ironically, they begin to pay attention to boys. Some girls regress at this point, and turn in language arts themes written entirely in eyebrow pencil. Seizing the moment, boys pick up the slack, learn to feel their way around a dance floor, and begin the search for females to hamper throughout their adult years.

ALEXANDER
THE GREATEST

For a time, the world belonged to Alexander the Great, son of Philip the Pretty Good—in fairness, it was Philip II of Macedon who conceived the civil and military innovations his son would loose on the world. Alexander picked up where his father left off after his assassination, with a weak Greek coalition incapable of taking on King Darius and the legions of his number one and rising higher Persian Empire. At the Thrilla' in Gaugamela, in present day Iraq, Alexander routed Darius's troops, although the Persian once again eluded capture (Alexander never did get him; Darius died, to his great surprise, of natural causes). Darius's much-feared weapons of mass destruction, fifteen long-range elephants, seem to have had little effect on the outcome other than crushing Alexander's dog, Peritas the Greyhound.

It's hard to conquer the world, even if it's only the known world, and not get grandiose. Alexander had his handsome (at least that was the official rendition) beardless visage painted, stamped, or chiseled on the appropriate medium wherever he went and even became a god after conquering Egypt—where it took little convincing to persuade him that he was not Philip's son, after all, but Ammon Ra's. He never did much of anything with the world after winning it, unless it was the symbolic marriage of Europe and Asia when a thousand of his closest field commanders took Asian women in troth, Alexander characteristically adding insult to injury by choosing one of Darius's daughters (the thin one). After enjoying the fruits of his labors on the banks of the Euphrates in 323 BC, Alexander fell asleep drunk and woke up dead, the cue for all his extended family members to murder one another, for the coins to go out of circulation, and for all the known world to relax for a while before the next great white, yellow, or black hope (or his son) came along.

HYGIEIA WAS HERE

The first bath was taken in about 2500 BC at Mohenjodaro in the Indus Valley, the cradle of bathing. While the Hindus bathed religiously, the ancient Egyptians bathed only when the Nile rose, or when held under by the Romans. The Greeks not only sported with the gods, they bathed with them afterwards; while only the patrician upper classes bathed, the lower classes were allowed to pass water. Hygieia was the Greek goddess of cleanliness, which, for them, was the same as godliness.

Modern science was buoyed by a discovery in a bathtub, when Archimedes realized he would have to fill the tub less full or risk losing the cleaning lady. While the Greeks may have been clean, the Romans had bath *complexes* which they installed in all places overrun in their effort to make the world safe for a nice soak. Soon, most of the empire boasted hot and cold running aqueducts. You may have been a slave to the Romans, but you had plumbing. According to Plutarch, the changing room at the Baths of Caracalla with its one hundred thousand lockers was the eighth wonder of the world. Surprisingly, in the centuries that followed, bathing did not wash with many Europeans, due to the prevailing attitudes of the Church, which held that bathing was an immodest activity in that it was done naked. As a result, the truly devoted had to make their baptisms last.

THE CHINESE
HELL FROM HELL

Traditional Chinese mythologies conceive of hell as a cross between Dante's *Inferno* and Chicago's city council. The netherworld consists of ten courts, each ruled by a king and subdivided into sixteen wards. The king with the most clout is Yen Lo of the Fifth, who, as plenipotentiary of the lower regions, dispatches officers of the court to bring in and book the dead. The book used is the *Book of Destiny*, an unauthorized biography dredging up all the individual's doings from his or her most recent lifetime.

THINGS YOU SHOULD HAVE LEARNED IN SCHOOL
ROUND 2

1. Which Greek God was too good a doctor?

    (a) Moe

    (b) Asclepius

    (c) Mercury

2. What's wrong with this sentence:

    Every cowboy has their own heifer to wrestle.

LACTOSE TOLERANT

3. Kangaroo babies are called:

    (a) Bennys

    (b) Freddys

    (c) Joeys

4. "In the room women come and go / Talking of _____"

    (a) Michelangelo

    (b) Barack Obamo

    (c) Bloom, Orlando

5. What do calories—say, the 500 in a quarter pounder with cheese— actually measure?

   (a) the effort required to eat it

   (b) how much heat you'd produce if you burst into flame

   (c) nothing if they're empty calories.

6. Which president, not known for his intellectual prowess, said, "I know somewhere there is a book that will give me the truth, but hell, I couldn't read the book!"

   (a) Gerald Ford

   (b) Martin Van Buren

   (c) Warren Harding

7. *Howdah*: a seat on the back of an elephant or a form of greeting in Muscle Shoals, Alabama?

8. What do Iran and Nebraska both have in common?

   (a) the Cornhuskers

   (b) a unicameral legislature

   (c) a nuclear arsenal

9. The one thing that prevented the Yaps of Micronesia from having vending machines was:

   (a) their stone coins are twelve feet across

   (b) they're off the electrical grid

   (c) the difficulty in finding individual serving sizes of monkey brain

10. If a peduncle isn't married to your aunt, what is it?

    (a) the sound a parking meter makes as it's thrown into the Rock River

    (b) the bulbous fistula in the X-ray of your colon

    (c) a flower stem

THINGS YOU SHOULD HAVE LEARNED IN SCHOOL (ROUND 2 ANSWERS)

1. (b) Apollo's kid, Asclepius, came up with the serpent rod, which to this day seems a fitting symbol for the medical arts. Asclepius was so good he could bring patients back from the dead, for which a jealous Zeus exiled him to duty as the constellation Ophiuchus, the serpent guy—not even a very good one.

2. First of all, not all cowboys care to wrestle heifers; secondly, it should be "his" own, to make it agreeable. It's an English thing.

3. (c) Joeys. Everybody knows this one. It's a gimme.

4. Barack Obamo (sic) as of this writing, but (a) "Michelangelo" the way J. Alfred Prufrock overheard it, as told to T.S. Eliot.

5. (b) You can blame the joules, I don't mind, since that's what a calorie really is: a unit of heat, specifically the amount needed to heat up 14.5°C water one degree, a little more than four joules.

Calories are used because otherwise the quarter pounder would weigh in at 2,000-plus joules.

6. (c) Warren Harding, who should be given credit for his candor, if nothing else. At least until some recent candidates, he was regarded as the man most unfit for the presidency of all time. And that's quite a distinction.

7. Both.

8. (b) A unicameral legislature; since Johnny Carson's boyhood home is not in Tehran. There's absolutely no reason you need two houses to make a legislature—look at the House of Lords, or the Senate. Nebraskans had the good sense to realize that, and I guess Iranians, too, to be fair.

9. (a) Their stone coins are twelve feet across; another gimme— who hasn't hoped for a Yap money wheel to be rolled up to his hut? The Yap call themselves the Wa'ab (you know?) or "locals." There are five denominations of Rai, stone money: Mmbul, Gaw, Fe', Yar, and Reng. The Reng is the smallest unit, but making change is almost impossible.

10. (c) Your peduncle supports your inflorescence, and it's about time somebody told you. Calling it a stem cheapens the whole process.

War of Griffin's Pig Reenactor

THE WAR OF
GRIFFIN'S PIG

The longest conflict in American history was The War of Griffin's Pig, the curlicue tale of a British hog in an American potato patch on San Juan Island, near Vancouver. On June 15, 1859, an unnamed black boar of British national Charles Griffin was discovered rooting next door in the patch of American Lamar Cutler. Acting upon what he believed to be his rights and under "the impulse of the moment," Cutler shot the hog. Griffin cried murder, since if he cried pig no one, certainly not the hog belly, would come running. But it wasn't over by a long shot—Griffin appealed to British authorities who, never guilty of under-reacting, dispatched the warship *Satellite* to arrest Cutler. Cutler sought the protection of Brigadier General W.S. Haney, the American Army commander, who was kind enough to land nine infantry companies with artillery on San Juan. The British anchored five dreadnaughts offshore and landed over 2,000 Royal Marines. While pondering his next move, Haney was relieved of his command by President Buchanan, who thought things were getting a little out of ham.

The dispute was not actually settled until 1872, when an unlikely arbitrator, peace-loving Kaiser Wilhelm I of Germany, awarded San Juan Island to the United States and a black boar to Charles Griffin.

A PIG IN A POLKA BAND

PIGS GONE WILD!

Wild pigs are actually more intelligent than their domestic offspring, from the *Sus salvanius* (pygmy hog) to the *Sus scrofa*, the wild boar of *Lord of the Flies* fame. English zoologist Harry Miller reports they are also very responsive to human affection and make excellent pets "if you get them young enough." Pot-bellied pigs are the delightful result of mating with their farm brethren. Related to the hippopotamus, they are gregarious family-centered creatures devoted to their young and mating for life—their sounders, extended families, include the sows, piglets, and young adults, and consist of several generations. Altruistic, courageous, intelligent, and resourceful mammals might be more accurate than "nasty, mean animals with tusks." They had been thought to have been hunted to extinction in the UK until one showed up on Paul McCartney's estate about the time of Wings, and a herd of free-range swine are now annoying an island nation of gardeners very nearly as much as "Silly Love Songs." I'm rooting for them!

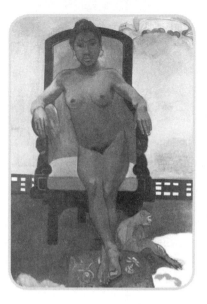

OH, GAUGUIN!

Gauguin was the one who didn't cut his ear off—that was his roommate-from-hell Van Gogh, after first going for Gauguin's. It may well have been this incident which propelled Paul Gauguin from Arles to Tahiti, although the prospect of abandoning a wife, five children, and a bank job had to have been appealing. Once in paradise, Gauguin was disgusted to receive a letter from Van Gogh, not so much because of its contents (the usual kvetching) but for the realization that primitive Polynesia had a postal system, government officials, and an Archdiocese that had already succeeded in humiliating local girls into wearing sarongs which he had to cajole them out of...you know, for art.

Gauguin was a stock broker by trade, a tremendous advantage for a painter which he was never really able to capitalize on; returning, briefly, to France, he was reduced to selling pots at art fairs. True, his naked Polynesians were a bigger hit than twenty ways of looking at a haystack, and for a while Gauguin had his own school going, the Synthetists, considered the visual equivalent of the emos Rimbaud and Verlaine. His style was a rejection of the Impressionists, because you could not float a naked lady on a lily pad. Flat, two-dimensional forms suffused in unnatural color does not really convey what I get from *Annha, the Javanerin*, nor does synthetism help to unravel *Where do we come from? What are we? Where are we going?* of 1897, which, economically, put the entire spiritual progress of mankind on one canvas. In 1901, Gauguin retreated to the Marquesas, where, like Kubla Khan, he built his House of Pleasure, a carved and be-decked Maori-influenced work of art to live for, which he did for two years, dying of the natural causes of syphilis (Gauguin did not clean his brush) in 1903.

SIZE MATTERS

T he biggest pothole known to man is the Archbald Pothole, of the Pennsylvania state park of the same name, left over

from some rough riding glaciers some 15,000 years ago. The Archbald is 42 by 24 by 38 feet deep, elliptical, and could eat up the axle on Paul Bunyan's oxcart. City workers would need 18,600 cubic feet of loose asphalt to fill it, and then come spring…

A snowy winter, you say? How about the 1,140 inches of snowfall the Mt. Baker Ski Area in northwestern Washington reported for the winter of 1998–99? That was a snowy winter, or so thought the National Climate Extremes

Committee, which goes all out to record extremes in weather events. And this one was unanimous, beating out the once thought unbreakable record at nearby Mt. Ranier, a paltry 1,122 feet set in 1971–72, and exaggerated over the years by those who lived through it. We had a record 100 inches this past winter in Wisconsin, a small figure except for the fact that it had to be removed from the sidewalks by noon of the following day.

Deserts are generally assumed to be pretty arid places, which allows people in Arizona to claim theirs is dry heat. But to find the driest heat of all you would need to retire to *El Valle de la Luna*—The Valley of the Moon—in the Atacama desert of Chile. If you find lunar landscapes attractive, this could be your own private Mare Tranquillitatis, and a lot closer than the moon. Here lies a gorgeous wind-carved dry lake that hasn't received a drop of rain since Santiago declared its independence from Spain. The prototype of the Mars Rover was tested here, for obvious reasons. It's the driest, man.

Rocks are like people. All kinds, all backgrounds, all ages. This one, however, a gneiss zircon discovered in the Australian interior twenty

years ago, is the granddaddy of all rocks—4.4 billion years old, answering the age-old question: which came first, the diamond or the zircon? Zircons need standing water for a long, long time to form their requisite isotopes— so first there was Australia, then there was no Australia, then there was. Down underwater, mate, or as they say in the outback, what in the Jack Hills is that? Gneiss work, if you can find it.

THE BEST OF THE -EST!

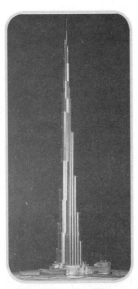

TALLEST manmade structure on Earth—the brand spanking new, 1,680-foot Burj Dubai Tower in Dubai, UAE. Built in only 1,276 days—that's nearly a foot and a half a day. One of Sheik Mohammed bin Rashid al Maktoum's many pet projects, which include re-creating the Earth as an archipelago of artificial sand islands in the Persian Gulf and six brand-new theme cities in Dubai. The least of it, really, is the

LONGEST yacht plying the high seas—*Golden Star*. At 525 feet, it's longer than some cruisers, but you need room for a helipad and submarine hold. The *Star* was the brainchild of the former richest man in

the world, the Sultan of Brunei, who ran into some financial difficulties early in the millennium when the yacht extras ratcheted up costs to over $300 million. The Sultan's setbacks, in fact, served to crown a new

A GATES·LIKE MAN
ATTRACTING GIRLS WITH......

$

....HIS SECONDARY SEXUAL CHARACTERISTICS !

RICHEST human on the planet—the self-effacing Warren Buffet, able to catapult himself over Bill Gates even with $62 billion on his back. Pretty athletic. One share of Berkshire Hathaway spiked as high as $150,000 in 2007, making it a 15-million penny stock. The Oracle of Omaha lives rather humbly in Nebraska, shunning the

LARGEST house somebody actually lives in—Ira Rennert's 110,000 square foot Southampton estate, Fair Field, which, to be Fair, is only 65,000 square feet or so without the outbuildings. Technically, the Biltmore Estate in Ashfield, North Carolina (that's *Vander-*

Biltmore, son), is larger at 175,000 square feet, but it's not a single-family residence any (Bilt)more. Ira and his wife Ingeborg raised three children, but are currently 110,000-square-foot empty-nesters. While the Rennerts do collect some art, they don't own the

COSTLIEST, if not the ugliest, piece of art ever on the market—the 4 by 8 fiberboard drop cloth of Jackson Pollock's *No. 5, 1948*, bought from David Geffen for $140 million in 2006 by corporate debt artist David Martinez, who also holds the record for paying the most ever for a Manhattan *pied-à-terre*: $54.7 million, parking not included. For the record, Martinez denies owning the painting; if a rumored anonymous German financier owns it, it's still a lot of dough, even in euros.

THANKS FOR THE MEMOS:
CLEAVAGE AMONG STAFF

Topic: CLEAVAGE!!!

Subject: It's a ladies-only email!

Okay, ladies, I've been asked by three different people to address this, so I am doing this in the least threatening or embarrassing manner that I can. I hope that I have all the ladies identified within our schools, as it is intended to be sent to everyone. I believe, with fall and winter approaching, this issue may quickly resolve itself, as more sweaters will be worn. In the meantime, however, we need to be more aware of cleavage showing with T shirt tops or low cut or wide cut shirts. This is especially an issue when you may feel discreetly covered standing or sitting upright, but end up bending over to assist a student or bend down from a chair to a reading circle. I am aware that the popular trend is to have one or more T shirt or tank tops with multiple layers; these, however, may not be appropriate or your best choice for school.

Please consider the following guidelines:

1. No cleavage at all, not even a little. That will be at a different height for different women, but if you can see any kind of line or space or delineation, your top is too low.

2. Check yourself in front of a mirror. Bend over into the mirror. You may be surprised that more is visible than you had considered. If this is the case, obviously, please reconsider what you are wearing.

3. Check yourself if you are wearing a shirt but the buttons are undone too far down. Sideways glances still reveal the color and frills of Victoria's Secret, even if you have a shirt and sweater or jacket on.

4. If I show up in your room and hand you a sweatshirt, even if it is 90 degrees out, you'll know what the issue is and nothing more will need to be said, except, perhaps, my asking you to put the sweatshirt on.

Thanks for thinking about how you can best meet today's fashion trends and still be the prudish female staff member!

THINGS YOU SHOULD HAVE
LEARNED IN SCHOOL
ROUND 3

1. It's the 25th anniversary of which emoticon?

   (a) :-)

   (b) ☹

   (c) (;>/}

2. "What pleasure does it give to be rid of one thorn of many?" complained:

   (a) Pliny the Elder

   (b) Henny the Youngman

   (c) Horace

3. Use *pwn* in a sentence to show you know its meaning.

4. If you are having Saddle Seat Pleasure, what are you having?

5. Who in all likelihood didn't say on his deathbed, "Either those curtains go or I do"?

   (a) Oscar Wilde

   (b) Truman Capote

   (c) Rodney Dangerfield

6. Did Marco Polo invent polo?

7. Ponce de Leon should have been looking for the Fountain of:

    (a) Heighth

    (b) Oldth

    (c) Smarth

8. Leonard Skinner, the real one, was a high school:

    (a) counselor

    (b) shop teacher

    (c) gym teacher

9. Where would you hope to see your fovea?

10. Leap year was the leap of faith of:

    (a) Ben Franklin

    (b) Julius Caesar

    (c) Pope Gregory

☞ Warren Harding won the presidency with the slogan, "Let's be done with the Wiggle and Wobble."

☞ By law, the possessive form of Arkansas is Arkansas's.

☞ A decision by a court in Scranton, PA, extends First Amendment protection to cursing at an overflowing toilet.

☞ "Revenge is a dish best served cold" is attributed to *Star Trek II: The Wrath of Khan.*

THINGS YOU SHOULD HAVE LEARNED IN SCHOOL (ROUND 3 ANSWERS)

1. (a) :-); discovered a quarter of a century ago at Carnegie-Mellon by Scott E. Fahlman, the first man to have an emoticon.

2. (c) Horace—who, besides being a philosopher, was a drama critic and thus pincushioned with thorns. BTW, he was born in 65 and died in 8, and you can't say that about everybody.

3. "I pwn these guys on Halo," or something like that—"to own" in *leetspeak*, as in to commandeer someone's Commodore.

4. Arabians horses are usually trotted out saddle-seat style, and, apparently, it's a pleasure.

5. (a) Oscar Wilde should have said it, but neglected to at the last minute. Wilde did say, "Alas, I am dying beyond my means."

6. No, although he probably encountered it on the Persian leg of his journeys, as polo was first known as chaugan; a match is play-by-played in *Omar Khayyam*. The Mongol hordes, whatever else you can say about them, were excellent polo players, even if the ball had hair and ears.

7. (a) Heighth; Ponce de Leon was only 4 foot 11 inches, and required all his crew to be shorter, or face alteration.

8. (c) The now immortalized gym teacher back in Jacksonville, FL, who told Bob Burns and Gary Rossington they "would never amount to nothin'."

9. In your eye(s), hopefully, being the focal point on the retina.

10. (b) Julius Caesar liked to micromanage the empire, right down to the time. In the Julian Calendar, the first leap day was in 45 BC. In 44 BC, on the Ides of March, the calendar ended, for Caesar.

WHEN DOCTORS
WERE GODS

The only Greek deity to be god-napped intact by the Romans (who stole everything Greek, right down to whatever you wear under the tunic) was Asclepius, the god of medicine before the health care industry. Asclepius was the child of Apollo and the always-entertaining sea nymph Coronis. If you must know the sordid details, Coronis swam in and out of a number of god's lives—never letting being hitched to the god of truth slow her down; when Apollo learned the truth from Raven, he broiled her, but spared Asclepius, sensing doctor material in him. Apollo was already the god of healing, but he was hoping to turn the day-to-day over to his son and concentrate more on his poetry. One of the Centaurs, Chiron (a sea nymph, like Asclepius's mother) took Asclepius in as a resident (part of a notable medical class which included Achilles, Heracles, and Jason). Then comes the inevitable Greco-Roman turning point: Jupiter, always protecting the franchise and fearing that Asclepius might be such a good diagnostician he could make men immortal, reared back and thunderbolted him, making it look like an act of nature. Asclepius was famous for having cured Philoctetes of his snakebite, despite (or because of) where he was bitten.

COME ON BABY,
LOAD MY GUN

Iknew Emily Dickinson and I could have been tight the minute I read:

> My Life had stood—a Loaded Gun—
> In Corners—till a Day
> The Owner passed—identified—
> And carried Me away—

A type, normally, too mystical for me, Emily Dickinson, "a little plain woman" who dressed in white and spoke in a "soft frightened breathless childlike voice," belied all that by inventing her own poetics and filling it with a lyrical, original, and assured voice. She was from the Amherst Dickinson's, never close to her parents; strongly resisted demonstrating a more conventional religious attitude even at the convent, Mt. Holyoke Female Seminary; was tutored in poetics and who knows what else by Ben Newton, supposed to be working for her father; and possibly had a Hester Prynne with the Reverend Charles Wadsworth, lifelong "dearest earthly friend" and Calvinist lifeline.

Emily Dickinson began writing verse of a conventional Brontë-light type at age twenty, but within a few years was taking chances with form (she likes to vary her meter) and rhyme (favoring those that don't) and liking to throw in the occasional *non sequitur* to see if you're listening. During the Civil War she produced over 800 poems, and she left 1,775 overall in her body of work. That being said, she might have been more ambitious professionally, only publishing seven poems in her lifetime, five of those turning up in the *Springfield Republican*. But then she wouldn't have been my Emily.

TFOF: TEXTING
FOR OLD FARTS

BY NORA FELDMAN

For those of us completely unexposed to texting, it is a form of communicating by sending written messages from one cell phone to another. Texting is a major part of almost every modern teenager's life. I mean, what would they do without texting—actually call people? I, being a very text-involved teenager, would know. These days the common "call me" has been replaced with a "text me" and the cell phone has become the only source for phone numbers. Some people may be afraid to enter the complex and confusing world of texting, which is probably a good thing if you're over 25. But if you must text, there are a some things you need to know.

My dad occasionally texts me, which I find very amusing. I was shocked that he was so confident with the texting lingo. (Rule number one: never say *lingo* in a text—not cool.) Right off the bat he was throwing *btw*'s (by the way's) and *lu*'s (love you's) my way. Where he learned these, I haven't a clue. Luckily for you, you have the guide to texting right here. So, slap on those reading glasses and let's go!

TEXTING ACRONYM AND ABBREVIATION DICTIONARY

lol—laughing out loud (this one's a biggie!)

hbu?—how about you?

idk—I don't know

ik—I know

ic—I see

idc—I don't care

idt—I don't think (usually followed by a "so," depending on the person)

bs—bullshit

s/o—sleepover

bf/gf—boyfriend/girlfriend

bff—best friend forever

lylas/lylab—love you like a sister/love you like a brother

ttyl—talk to you later

bbl—be back later

brb—be right back

gtg/g2g—got to go

jk/jp—just kidding/just playing

k—OK (it makes sense!)

nm u?—not much, you? (whad'ya know, Dad?)

np—no problem

omg—oh my God

pda—public display of affection

phat—pretty hot and tempting

rotfl—rolling on the floor laughing ("t" is optional)

wtf—what the fuck?

ppl—people

skool—school (that one saves a lot of time!)

sup?—what is up?

what is up?—what is new?

b4—before

cya—see you later

ne1—anyone

thx—thanks

w/—with

w/out—without

w/e—whatever

w8—wait

lmao—laughing my ass off

The text is a mysterious thing, but with a lot of practice and patience it can become a helpful tool you won't want to live without!

WHAT'S IN A NAME?

While given names may reflect your mother's predilection for romance novels or mellifluous sounding household products (our youngest daughter was very nearly named Cremora), surnames often stem from accolades or abuse heaped upon our ancestors generations ago. A lot of English names are flotsam and jetsam from the Norman invasion, actual Lord-love-a-duck French places and persons upon whom the Brits take their revenge cold with misspellings and mispronunciations. The town of Montfort Sur Risle in Normandy, alone, begat the Montforts, Montfords, Mountfords, Mundfords, and Mumfords, all of whom believe they're as English as kippers.

Occupations provided a legions of surnames: Taylors, Glovers, Saddlers, Cooks, Butlers, Barbers, Bakers, and so on, but here, as well, a Rosencrantz is not always a Rosencrantz. Marshall, sounding to God and man like there's status and possibly a stipend involved, actually refers to the servant who marshaled guests into the drawing room, while Steward comes from sty ward, or keeper of the pigs. Nicknames were popular in the Middle Ages, and, happily for suc-

Nigel Steward

ceeding generations, not all of them stuck: Crookshank, Handless, Onehand, Neck, Blind, Daft, Mutter, and Stutter being a few of the kinder noms de plume given physically challenged forebears. The ones that did stick—King, Pope, Abbot, and Duke—were often ironic, if not as funny as calling a fat guy Slim. The good news is, it might not be such a challenge to uphold the family name after all.

The Declaration of Dependence

Sometimes, in the common run of things, one must accommodate circumstance; times change and, so, people. Yet nothing in
the Laws of Nature or of Men says one need go off half-cocked.
The British are coming, indeed. That would be us. We come from
England, making us, de facto, English. The Canadians, living on
the edge of a polar ice shelf, don't seem to have a problem with it.
The prisoners of Australia, between aborigine and the deep blue
sea, have fewer complaints and more gratitude. Some truths are
self-evident, that all Englishmen are created equal, and endowed
by His Majesty with certain Rights, and so on, with as much Liberty
as a man can abide, jolly well enough to Pursue Happiness, if not to
grab it by the Tail. One is born with these rights and within them.
No Jefferson-headed, goat-hoofed satyr need hand them out. One
cannot abolish one's birthright because one cannot abolish one's
birth. Even the recent Philadelphia boilerplate acknowledges that
Prudence (note the capital P) dictates that Governments long
established not be changed for light and transient causes—and
the tea tax is as light and transient as they come. Rather, let us
dress like savages and dump a shopkeeper's livelihood into Boston

harbor! Boys, let us purchase a team of Hessians and invade New Jersey! And so on. The Crown has been more than patient with these delinquent Colonies, as the French in Africa and the Spanish in South America, where the taste of steel is representation, have not. Our British family worries about their profligate American fathers and sons, who fled the mother country to escape debt and paternity, and now would flee again, and take America with them. When ne'er-do-wells speak of Liberty and Freedom, it is liberty from debt and freedom from providing for the abandoned. In other words, a Democracy. From this Congress of Scoundrels, the inmates run amuck through the UNTIED States of America. Abracadabra, a colony is an independent state, and, poof, all debts, personal and public, disappear. Oh, the Glory! Divine Providence is not too strong a phrase; perhaps with a snifter or two and some captured lightning, Franklin can distil something stronger, or be content to stick a feather in his cap and call it macaroni. The United States of Macaroni.

THANKS FOR THE MEMOS:
THE CALL OF DUTY

Dear class teachers,

We have noticed that some students are not hygienic in disposing their used sanitary napkins. We would like to seek your help to teach our students the importance of personal hygiene and of showing respect to their fellow students and the maintenance staff.

Please demonstrate the proper way of handling used sanitary napkins during the home room period within this week. You can obtain a piece of clean sanitary napkin at the teachers' counter when you come in for your register tomorrow morning. For male class teachers, Mrs. Harriet will arrange a female teacher to demonstrate to your students.

Thank you for your assistance and cooperation.

Regards,

ADMIN

THINGS YOU SHOULD HAVE LEARNED IN SCHOOL

ROUND 4

1. Out of a dozen teenagers, how many think Columbus set sail in 1792?
   - (a) 1
   - (b) 2
   - (c) 3

2. All right, the block and tackle, the screw, the heat ray—but did Archimedes invent the odometer?

3. Famous in his time for never missing a spittoon, "Old Rough and Ready" may have been poisoned. Who was he?
   - (a) Teddy Roosevelt
   - (b) George Rogers Clark
   - (c) Zachary Taylor

4. To a cowpoke, a stew of calf brains and internal organs is a specialty known as:

(a) son of a gun

(b) calf fries

(c) Mexican strawberries

5. Why can't you begin a sentence with "Hopefully..."?

    (a) because you are not in the least hopeful

    (b) because it's an adverb, that's why

    (c) because *Kirkham's Grammar* says

6. What does ϖ actually represent?

    (a) Avogadro's other number

    (b) how many quarters go into a dime

    (c) the ratio of a circle's circumference to its diameter

7. Everybody knows there are a _____ nanoseconds in a second.

    (a) million

    (b) billion

    (c) trillion

8. How much more do you get in a heaped bushel than a stacked bushel?

    (a) a heap

    (b) a peck

    (c) a heap and a peck

9. 20 percent of US college graduates are unable to do fundamental computation; that's equal to:

    (a) 1 in 4

    (b) 1 in 7

    (c) 1 in 5

10. In reproduction by budding, is a buddy involved?

THINGS YOU SHOULD HAVE LEARNED IN SCHOOL (ROUND 4 ANSWERS)

1. (c) 3, or 50 percent...I mean, 25 percent. They're probably confusing the event with Marco Polo's discovery of polo.

2. Yes, by special request of the Republican chariot pool, who felt that vehicles were being used for personal use. Archimedes' device clicked off a counter with the turn of the wheel; as a result, many Athenians would hitch their chariots backwards before selling them.

3. (c) Zachary Taylor. Mexican war hero Taylor was the first president elected who had held no previous electoral post. Taylor was known for the Territorial Bypass, allowing California and New Mexico to shoot the moon for statehood, while a gastric bypass might have saved him from the suspicious gastroenteritis in 1850, his second year in office. Vice President Millard Fillmore had the most to gain.

4. (a) Son of a gun; an apt description for the mouth-feel of the delicacy. Recipe's pretty simple: "throw ever'thing in the pot but the hair, horns, and holler." "Overland trout" was bacon, a spoiled egg a "souvenir," "calf-slobber pie" sounds appealing, and "son-of-a-bitch-in-a-sack" (steamed fruit, really) was a real treat.

5. Technically, you're supposed to use an adverb on a verb. Some people get unusually upset if you don't. It is to be hoped they get over it. Probably they won't.

6. (c) The ratio of a circle's circumference to its diameter, roughly 3.14159. Archimedes (again), who was pretty much obsessed with calculating it, inscribed circles in 96-sided polygons until he was able to do it…a great day for math until he was murdered by an invading soldier who was standing on his figures in the dirt. The world record for the most decimal places to which pi has been calculated is 1,073,740,000 by Yasumasa Kanada of the University of Tokyo in 1989, using an early Hitachi.

7. (b) Billion. It goes second, millisecond, microsecond, nanosecond, picosecond, femtosecond, attosecond, zeptosecond, and yoctosecond—one-quadrillionth of a second.

8. (b) They figure a peck for heaping. To further complicate things, it depends on a bushel of what—oats are 32 pounds; barley, 48; malted barley, 34; corn, 56; and 60 pounds each for soybeans and wheat. Plus, of course, your peck.

9. (c) 1 in 5; a trick question. Not.

10. No buddy method in budding—it's when you reproduce without anybody's help. Also called burgeoning, which is putting it nicely. Happens a lot in plants, but in animals it's mostly seen in sponges and hydra, and whatever a yeast is. All I'm saying is, it's an option.

PANGAEA

If the world seems like a puzzle to you, rest assured that the pieces all fit nicely together into the proto-continent Pangaea, at least as conceived by the early twentieth-century German paleo-meteorologist (old weatherman?) Alfred Lothar Wegener, who died trying to wrap Greenland around North Africa to put the final piece in place in 1930. Wegener was not the first to notice that the outline of the Americas was the inline of Africa: the German naturalist von Humboldt was pooh-poohed for saying much the same thing in 1800, and the Frenchman Snider-Pelligrini was told to keep his heresy about fossil plant similarity between New World and Old to himself or eat alone at the Academe. But it was Wegener who gave the unifying theory a name and a history, postulating that for most of geologic time Pangaea was the only game in town; until late in the Triassic, maybe 210 million years ago, when things began to go south as the Americas headed west (young man), India went equatorial to put the sub in subcontinent, and Australia parted ways with Asia once and for all. The primal supercontinent looks kind of like an ax head with the blade in the northern hemisphere. A body of water, the Tethys Sea, was enclosed within, and European animals could freely associate with African and Australian, before they drifted apart about 180 million years ago, first into Gondwana (to the south) and Laurasia (to the north) and eventually into whatever shape we find the world today. Those were heady days, with entire continents moving willy-nilly across the vast Panthalassic Ocean. In our neck of the woods, the micro-continent Avalonia divested itself into England, New England, and the Upper Midwest after colliding with Laurasia somewhere around West Virginia. Southern Europe fragmented from Gondwana smacking dab into Euramerica, and the rest is manifest destiny. North and south China were actually on different continents, accounting for the gap between Szechwan and Cantonese cooking. It all broke up due to a big rift, which has so often been the case in the history of the planet.

IT'S ABOUT
GREENWICH TIME

Not so long ago the world was one big Indiana—every village, municipality, and fiefdom kept its own time without regard for what neighboring clocks might say. It wasn't until the coming of railroads in the 1850s that it became clear timetables would be pretty hard to keep if the time at each station were different. Clearly, a convention was needed, and in 1884 one was held in Washington, DC, called the Prime Meridian Conference, during which 41 delegates from 25 nations were successfully lobbied by the prestigious Greenwich Royal Observatory—founded by Charles II in 1675 to attain "the so-much desired longitude of place" on the still sunlit empire—for the honor to go to the London borough of Greenwich, which at the time only had the gasworks going for it. Longitude demarking is pretty much inseparable from timekeeping, and it seemed obvious to the British that the Prime Meridian to base it all could only run through Royal Astronomer Sir George Biddell Airy's Transit Circle Telescope, whose crosshairs have their sights set precisely on the vertical equator, the Prime Meridian at longitude 0 degrees 0 minutes 0 seconds, which bisects East and West Greenwich between hemispheres. Greenwich, by the by, was prime in another sense as well, being where many of your biggest Tudors were cranked out, including Henry VIII and Elizabeth I, at the curiously named Palace of Placentia. During the English Civil War, Placentia was a biscuit factory/prison, and it was eventually torn down when Charles II thought it needed too much work. But the Royal Observatory was his baby; Charles laid the foundation stone on August 10, 1675, and established the Astronomer Royal as time-keeper to the world.

THE DOGS OF WAR

On March 5, 1770, the first canines—believed to have been mixed breeds—gave their lives in the American struggle for independence, when two dogs, along with seven colonists, were killed by the British in the Boston Massacre. The scene immortalized in an etching by eyewitness Paul Revere, shows a dog in the forefront of the American ranks as they face British rifles. The senseless slaying of the friendly mongrel did as much to raise colonial hackles as the Intolerable Acts.

The Deity's position in the War of Independence was arguable, but both armies could claim dog was on their side: Francis Marion,

the Swamp Fox, smelled out Lord Cornwallis with dogs, and a colonial rival of Washington's, Charles Lee, was said to trust no one
but his dogs. Washington himself was a dog lover, although Martha
cared not a whit for hounds Chloe, Forester, Lady Rover, Searcher,
Taster, or Sweetlips. The Battle of Harlem Heights in Manhattan
was delayed when British General Howe's foxhound, Duchess, was
kibbled and returned to Howe after wandering into Washington's
command tent. In gratitude, Howe sent Washington a bottle of
claret and the battle continued.

MY LIFE IN FICTION

My character is fictional. A critic might attribute this to the chronic lack of event, drama, or turning point (other than south) in my real life, but to that I give a hearty Walter Mitty, "Ta pocketa pocketa pocketa." I'm a vulnerable reader and have to be very careful what I pick up; I say this as one who would have watched helplessly as Joyce Carol Oates murdered his family had not his eyes already been spooned out by Jerzy Kosinski. I'm a serially monogamous page-turner, and have to really like an author before I'll crack his spine, let alone go all the way. Whenever I've tried juggling several authors, one of us always gets hurt. Once

I like a guy, I'll pretty much do his oeuvre until I beg for mercy (begging off only on Updike's heartbreaking psoriasis diary and the Nabokov with the butterflies, White Russians, and blank verse) so it's a big help if the author's either dead or Salinger so I can get on with my life. Oh, I've made my mistakes (McInerney, Kotzwinkle, post-Yossarian Heller), but very rarely will I read someone I don't deeply care for or think I could, and you've got to admire that.

I've often thought (well, once) that if John Stuart Mill had been my dad I could have been a utilitarian today, or, at least more useful, more of a reader, and in Greek (εὑρηκα/ηὑρηκα!). Under Dave Feldman we had access to all the Geographic's graphics (to this day, I expect to find a girl with plates in her lips who loves me), the complete paperbacks of Mickey Spillane (I can still mentally retrieve the cover of *I, The Jury*, and do), and the poorly concealed copy of Paolo Mantegazza's erotic groundbreaker, *The Sexual Habits of Mankind*, which made the nuptial huts of Malawi as real as Chicken Delight on the corner. We did have a bound set of Twain, but that was for pressing pansies.

From those humble beginnings, and as an aid to literary psychologists of the future, here is my literary history: *Danny Dunn and the Anti-Gravity Paint* made me an early believer in overselling technology, while *Dr. Doolittle* startled me with the revelation not so much that it was possible to talk to animals but that, unlike humans, they might listen. For me, S.J. Perelman bridged the gap between intellect and whoopee cushion, and taught me that big words were funny. It might be that I got to it at the wrong stage of adolescence, but *The Catcher in the Rye* only made me want to assassinate Paul Anka. During junior high school, I awoke more than one morning to find I had not been transformed into a giant dung beetle but could not say the same for my brother Arthur across the room. Thurber fleshed out my father's bare bones muttering on the opposite sex ("Women!") and for a time convinced me both that I was going blind and could draw. Twain made it clear that you've really got to be good to write dialect, and Faulkner that you've really got to be good to live somewhere where they speak in it.

Thinking back on it, it may have been Henry Miller and not Mike Feldman making impromptu and violent love on a radiator in the hallway of a Parisian apartment house in 1923; I'll have to check Anaïs's diary. Kafka was kind enough to render high school meaningless, Beckett made meaninglessness meaningless, and I'm forever indebted to William Carlos Williams for proving a piece of paper about the size and shape of a man was not a man by driving over it. I've had days like Raskolnikov, but without the resolution, and unlike Gogol's character, if I saw my nose on another person, I would not pursue it but gladly let it go.

My great love for the Protestant people, specifically their women, comes to me by way of the Ivy League swappers in Cheever and Updike, who led me to believe that a Jew might get in on some of this action, even though Zelda Fitzgerald caused me to marry in the faith. I have yet to see the best minds of my generation, let alone in the condition Ginsberg found his, so I guess it's a trade-off. Early on, Roth and I pulled in tandem, although he got a lot farther with his stroke. Martin Amis reassured me that a dismal view of human nature and an impenetrably bleak worldview need not keep you from being a laugh a minute, and Cormac McCarthy that life, while a succession of massacres, impaling, and disemboweling, has its charms.

THE MICHAELCOSM

Democritus again, this time armed with the golden ratio to justify the golden means to the golden end we find ourselves at today, came up with the **microcosm/macrocosm**—or the other way around, if you prefer—dichotomy (gee, it's been a long time since grad school). This is not your *cosm* from Milwaukee, but **all that is** and most of what **isn't** in one easy-to-swallow capsule. Large world, small world. Simple as that. No medium, family, or economy worlds. To the Greeks, (Greek) man **was** the microcosm.

Plato said that Socrates said that the four elements—Earth, wind, fire, and water—are present both in the great big world, and in little old us. The mechanism of the thing, the windy-uppy spring, is the soul in man, and in the big picture, the *anima mundi*, "**Soul of the World**"; both souls having the wisdom (*sophia*) and intelligence (*nous*) to ruin everything inside and out. The cosmic reflects the individual, and not the other way around, a workable enough delusion to enable the Athenians to flourish until the Romans, with their arches, showed up. Their estranged cousins, the Stoics, were horses of a different color, seeing the cosmos as a *mega zoon* or really big animal they alternately appeased and tried to ride. A Jewish fellow, Philo, then took "man made in God's image" to mean that God looks uncannily like Philo, and that can't be bad. As Philo's mind rules his body, so God rules the universe, and both work in strange ways. Philo goes so far as to say **man** is the microcosm and God is just a **big man**. Seneca the Younger (the "What fools these mortals be!" one) played around with the idea of an Earth with the same organs and complaints as man, both passing stones and water. Here's where the Plotinus thickens: Plotinus, the Greek thinker who trademarked "The Soul of the World," said that this Übermensch, God, didn't Sistine the whole ceiling, but simply *emanated* existence, jack-o-lantern-like. The Plotinus trio featured **unity**, **intelligence**, and **soul**, and if that sounded a lot like Plotinus, at least to Plotinus, so be it. Self-knowledge, Plotinus-knowledge, is, ergo, knowledge of the cosmos, and is free to assume whatever he wants with impunity, at least for a while. Plotinus came up with but neglected to trademark "**Being**," as well as the supreme, transcendent **One** lording over it, the details of which we are still wrestling with today.

Sam Jaffe as neo-Platonist Dr. Zorba

WHAT REALLY HAPPENED
TO THE DINOSAURS?

D inosaurs, the most successful reptiles the world has known,
flourished for two hundred million years, ruling the Earth
one hundred times longer than my wife. There are several possible
explanations why the orders *Saurischia* and *Ornithischia* disappeared
some seventy million years ago. One scenario has Earth bombarded
by the intense fatal radiation from an exploding supernova. Another
suggests a reversal in the Earth's magnetic field allowed ultraviolet
radiation in lethal doses to penetrate a depleted ozone layer. Most
recently, a persuasive theory based on satellite views of a huge impact
crater in the West Indies depicts a meteor strike of such magnitude

that huge clouds of dust were borne skyward, causing a "nuclear winter" which sealed the dinosaurs' fate.

A poetic possibility is the suggestion that the evolution of flowering plants from more primitive gymnosperms deprived the dinosaurs of certain essential oils found only in naked seed plants, causing the dinosaurs to perish due to a monumental case of constipation. This would account not only for the extinction of the order, but for the surprisingly small size of fossilized dinosaur dung.

WHO FIRST MADE MONEY?

While jade, salt, amber, skins, and gold were bartered as early as 3000 BC, the first universal medium of exchange was probably cattle, the breeding of which produced a good deal of interest. The nomadic Aryans traded oxen and consequently drove a hard bargain. Indeed, the Latin word for money, *pecunia*, comes from the word *pecks*, or cattle. While cattle were more portable than the heavy iron ingots exchanged by Macedonians, their disadvantage was that it was nearly impossible to make change without a butcher.

Although the Hebrews had money, nobody else ever saw it, so the first coin of the realm became the silver shekel of the Babylonians, so much the rage of the ancient world nations lined up to conquer Babylon for more. In about 2000 BC, the Servants of the Temple of the Moon God of Ur, the original traveling salesmen, took a giant step for mankind by never leaving home without letters of credit incised on clay tablets advising creditors to see the Moon God for payment. The Carthaginians, first modern global traders, developed "leather money," a promise on parchment to pay the bearer on demand the stipulated amount of gold. Unfortunately, the bearers all showed up at once and Carthage was sacked.

The Yaps coinage was macro for Micronesia, some of the larger denominations being eight feet across. Eventually the Yaps tired of the inconvenience of a one ton cartwheel, and now use plastic for everything. Small change was the innovation of the Athenians, who minted exceedingly small silver coins, some barely the size of a pinhead, which (due to pocket-less togas) were carried in the mouth. Often as not, when money circulated in Athens, it really circulated.

☞ The term "money" was fist uttered in Hera's temple in Rome.

☞ Aristotle said that Midas's wife, Demodike, came up with the idea for coinage, what with everything having turned to gold.

☞ China invented paper money right after inventing paper. Before then, coins were strung together on a lanyard to reach the higher denominations.

☞ The first European banknotes were paper coins cut from hymnals during the Spanish siege of the Netherlands in 1574.

ANIMAL QUESTIONS AND QUESTIONABLE ANIMALS

ARE DOGS PLEASURING THEMSELVES WHEN THEY... YOU KNOW?

Most dog psychologists agree that it is not self-pleasuring but just a sitz bath, doggie-style, although there are exceptions, particularly with some schnauzers. Dogs are just naturally fastidious, in their own way. Butt-sniffing is strictly a matter of protocol.

YEA, THE SCENT IS FRESH, BUT I WISH IT WERE 'APRIL FRESH!'

ARE TABBIES RELATED TO JUNGLE CATS?

Yes, cousins, although many times removed. House cats all go back 10,000 years to just five African wildcats, *Felis silvestris lybica*. Tabby is and always will be an obligate carnivore, a flesh-eating hunter, and don't forget it.

WHY IS "BIRD-BRAIN" AN INSULT?

Should be a compliment, since birds have larger brains per body size than all but the biggest brained, smallest humans. Cormorants can count, crows can covet, cuckoos remove a host's eggs before laying their own, pigeons can spot a patsy, Egyptian vultures use stone tools, striated herons fish with bait, and Alex the Parrot, may he rest in peace, spoke several languages with the proper accent.

WHY DO SNAKES CRAWL? SHOULDN'T THEY HAVE KEPT THEIR LEGS?

Snakes descended from lizards, who discovered that legs just got snagged on the underbrush, while rectilinear motion (lateral undulation, if you prefer), flexing through use of opposing muscles, cuts right through it. It's speedy,  it's quiet, and it's surprisingly efficient in terms of power consumption. If there's nothing to push against: sidewinding.

WHAT'S THIS I HEAR ABOUT A FISH THAT CAN CHANGE SEX?

The clownfish is always clowning around. Clownfish, *Amphiprion ocellaris*, live in a matriarchy, and when the clown queen goes to her great reward, odds are even that one of her ambitious male attendants will be willing to go to any lengths to ascend to the throne. If you'd like to look further into this, it's known as sequential hermaphroditism, and occurs in any species in which the individuals are all of one sex or the other—in the case of clowns, male. Very common aquarium types who can now be looked at in a new light.

TERMITES CAN TEAR DOWN, BUT CAN THEY BUILD ANYTHING?

Can they! Witness the great cathedral mounds of the African Savannah, often thirty feet tall, engineered with flying buttresses, columns, a high-rise of chambers and fungi farms connected by highways.

RAIN OF TERRIERS

J.S....

A DATE WITH HISTORY

Sunday, October 23, 4004 BC – The first day of Creation, according to Archbishop Ussher of Armagh, which is the sound most often made when people are told. He worked it out in *The Anals*—check that, *Annals of the World*. To give you some idea of the pace of life at that time, Adam and Eve were told to leave Eden on November 10 (a Monday, wouldn't you know it) *of the same year!* Paradise never lasts—but seventeen days?

Fall of 454 BC – Herodotus publishes the first history, plural in fact: *The Histories*, a travel history and views on the Greco-Persian wars. Herodotus establishes the Black Sea in the offseason and the principal of "I only know what I've been told." Still, it's a whole new discipline with a lot of possibility for manipulation. It was Herodotus who dismissed reports that Phoenicians, while sailing westward around Africa, saw the sun on the right side.

October 1, 331 BC – Alexander the Great finishes conquering the world by defeating his nemesis, Persian King Darius III, at Arbela near Nineveh (turn right at the two large mounds), despite the Persians' cutting-edge technology, the height of which was scythes on the chariot wheels and optional captain's chairs. Alexander did go on to conquer Turkistan afterward, but that was pretty much icing on the cake.

March 14, 42 AD – After which Caesar was known as The Divine Julius, which had its plusses and minuses, as he discovered two years and a day later. Brutus and the boys were actually guilty of deicide, a much more serious charge. Ironically, Octavius, taking over where Julius left off, first became Augustus and next The Divine Gaius.

February 12, 877 – Louis the Pious, of the Franks, deposed in favor of Charles the Fat, with the inevitable resulting humor. To try to get people to like him, Charles the Fat was a hearty laugher (although his catchphrase, "I'm no Charles-le-Magne," became quite tiresome) and established the right of hereditary succession—which, hey, becomes pretty important, although it didn't work for Charles the Fat's Kid. Other than that, he was Charles the Fat then, he's Charles the Fat now.

1337–1453 – The Hundred and 16 Years' War. In case anyone asks, it was primarily a French internecine deal between the Plantagenets and the House of Valois over who was entitled to be beheaded once the Revolution came. If you subtract several periods of inexplicable peace, it should have been known as the "81 Years' War, 35 Years' Peace." Joan of Arc instilled *esprit de corps* in this one by being burned at the stake.

First Quarter, 1690 – Clarinet invented in Nuremberg, Germany; John Flamsteed is the first to see Uranus; and John Locke invents the "self." Locke is the first to suggest that personality disorders arise due to having a personality, and the radical notion that individuals are individuals. Locke said we are born with a blank slate and die with a cracked one, and that all ideas are derived from some experience.

September 5, 1793–July 28, 1794 – The relatively brief but efficient Reign of Terror, the marked downside of *Liberté*, *Fraternité*, and *Egalité* of the French Revolution, but as the French say, if you are wanting the omelet, you must to crack the eggs. The cutting-edge guillotine made it possible to separate as many as fifty thousand royals and hangers-on from their blue blood. In the end, the Terroristes, including Robespierre, were themselves 'tined and the dreaded Reign of the Civil Service began.

June 16, 1895 – D.D. Palmer performs the first chiropractic adjustment on janitor Harvey Lillard, in Davenport, Iowa, who was deaf and had to stoop quite a bit in his work. After the adjustment, Lillard found some relief after returning to his stoop work with his hearing loss. Palmer's friend, the Reverend Weed, coined the phrase, from the Greek, *chiro*, or hand, and, *proctos*, or anus, which, for many years, impeded its growth. His son, B.J. Palmer, was, understandably, very popular.

January 3, 1929 – Patent for the Zerk fitting, the grease nipple which made the industrial revolution possible, granted to Kenoshan Oscar Zerk. Before Zerk you had to take the damn wheel off and repack the bearings every time. Zerk got the idea from a baby bottle, which became the world's first grease gun. A talented machinist, Zerk solved the tricky mechanics which had eluded many others, including Henry Ford, in the race towards the grease nipple.

December 21, 2012 – The Apocalypse, as predicted by the Mayan calendar, marking the completion of the thirteenth B'ak'tun cycle in the Long Count. Also set to be the Yule Solstice, and bound to put a damper on festivities. For the Mayans this marks the end of the current Creation World and the beginning of the next, in which basketball will once again be played with human heads.

THANKS FOR THE MEMOS:
AND THAT WAS JUST THE FACULTY...

Subject: HALLWAY SUPERVISION

Teachers, please step out of your rooms and supervise the hallways during transition times. We have kids spitting, throwing items from the top floor, throwing Gatorade in the halls, wandering around aimlessly, hitting each other, running, yelling, touching each other inappropriately, disturbing finals, etc. This information comes from your colleagues who are concerned that we all need to work together on this one. It is only going to get worse if we don't put a stop to the *ensuing chaos* right now. One other suggestion: please give your students a break from a double period after transition times and please monitor the students for a short stretch break. Keep smiling!

James Morel
Dwight Johnson Middle School

THINGS YOU SHOULD HAVE LEARNED IN SCHOOL

ROUND 5

1. Former conquistador Juan Cabrillo discovered _____, California.
    - (a) La Jolla
    - (b) San Diego
    - (c) Otay

2. The Earth wobbles because:
    - (a) of its bulge
    - (b) of the impact of solar winds
    - (c) it's heavier on the Eurasian side

3. If an English girl is a good ten stone, she's a good ____ pounds
    - (a) 120
    - (b) 140
    - (c) 160

4. Which one's the flotsam and which one's the jetsam?

5. What's the difference between *blatant* and *flagrant*?

6. A gas is noble if:

    (a) a nobleman discovered it

    (b) it wins a Nobel

    (c) it's inert

7. What did Charles Townes invent while sitting on a park bench in Greenville, SC?

    (a) the stadium cushion

    (b) the theory of inertia

    (c) the laser

8. Who's bigger, the manatee or the womanatee?

9. What do you call a female duck?

10. The Tepidarium, Calidarium, and Frigidarium are elements of what Roman innovation?

☞ The top selling college coffin for the diehard fan is the U of Oklahoma Eternal Sooner.

☞ William Henry Harrison and his grandson Benjamin were both president.

☞ Do not thrash violently in quicksand—just relax.

THINGS YOU SHOULD HAVE
LEARNED IN SCHOOL
(ROUND 5 ANSWERS)

1. (b) A late-bloomer as an explorer, Juan Rodriguez Cabrillo departed Navidad, Mexico, in 1542 and discovered San Diego Bay while looking for the seven cities of gold. Unfortunately, he died after wiping out at Imperial Beach.

2. (a) The Earth doesn't like to talk about it, but it is an olblate spheroid, bulging at the equator about 26 and a half miles, due to its rotation and some settling during middle age. For that reason, the top of Mt. Chimborazo in Ecuador, and not the Everest summit, is as high as you can get on the planet.

3. (b) 140 pounds, perfect for her height. The British peoples are actually composed of stones, each weighing 14 pounds.

4. Flotsam—float-some—is the nautical refuse floating around; jetsam—jettison-some—are items thrown overboard by the crew...which probably float as well. If they don't, they become "lagan": sinkers.

5. Blatant is what you do with disregard: without caring what anyone thinks. Or it could be a trombone. Flagrant is when you do something really bad, like Watergate or Monica Lewinsky—low behavior at the highest levels.

6. (c) It's inert. Your helium, neon, argon, krypton, xenon, and radon, although they're making new ones all the time. What happens when our outer shell of electrons is full: no combining for you.

7. (c) The laser; in downtown Greenville, SC, a bronze Charles Townes sits on the very bench he had his Eureka on: not, surprisingly, a way to sterilize pigeons, but a way to make wavelengths shorter. The schematics of such a device fit nicely on the back of his Greenville Power & Light bill.

8. The womanatee has as much as 400 pounds and 3 feet in length on the male manatee, who also must suffer the embarrassment of being a sea cow. This would put her at 1,300 pounds and 10 feet; as a result, when things fit here, they don't fit there. Early reports of mermaids turned out to be manatees, which shows you how disappointing life can be.

9. A duck. And if she walks like one and quacks like one, so much the better. Actually, it's very insulting to call a male a duck—he is a drake.

10. Quiz show set…kidding, the essential three elements of a decent bath: Tepidarium, the warm water, Calidarium, the hot water, and the chilly Frigidarium. The Romans were very picky on the schematics and often quite lavish in the décor—much of the bric-a-brac now graces Vatican bathrooms.

...and this is just the tepidarium

286

WHAD'YA KNOW

ABOUT

J. Siegel

SCIENCE?

THE SECOND
TIME AROUND

January 19, 2004—in a dramatic challenge to what he calls America's inge-*moon*-ity, President Bush pledges an American will walk on the moon by the end of the decade, although it is not clear as to which. Next one, most likely. Neil Armstrong is unavailable for comment, but Gene Cernan, still suited up, is anxious to go, thanks to funding from GmbH Pharmaceuticals for testing Flomax in lunar gravity. The biggest challenge to Mission Exxxon (for Excellent Extra-terrestrial Exploration On) will be re-outfitting *Saturn* boosters currently serving as double-wides in Alabama, as well as finding a former Nazi still living who knows how to fire the damn things up; NASA teams have been scouring the Parañena plateau of Paraguay for personnel. Exxxon resources will be significantly augmented by equipment left behind from *Apollo*, including several Commodore 64s with dot matrix printers, Garden Weasel "Golds," Radio Telemetry Shack transmitters, and, of course the lunar rovers, excluding Cernan's, known to be pretty banged up from doing donuts on the *Mare Tranquilitas*. With the driving range and practice tee undisturbed, it will simply be a matter of bringing up another set of clubs, a bucket of balls, and an MTV flag, MTV a proud sponsor of Mission Exxxon. As back-up transport, economy-minded exxxonauts (their lander, dubbed the *Super Saver*, is sponsored by the store in Council Bluffs, Nebraska: Super Saver, Where You Save So Much We Should Add Duper) will take along BMX bikes and two Segways the Bushes don't use any more.

The president sees the moon as a broad yellow disc from his porch in Waco, where the barn is being cleared out (luckily there were no animals, just bales of switch grass the president has stashed as a hedge against inflation) to serve as Mission Control for Project Exxxon. Seen as the major and perhaps only legacy of his time in office, Mr. Bush spoke eloquently (for him) of the moon being "one big ol' step for mankind to galaxies far, far away, in all directions, really, handing us inter-galactic start-ups and undreamt of mineral resources to break America's dependence on terrestrial oil and yellow cake from Africa on a celestial platter. The Exxxon Mission—from Exxon Mobil: Taking on the Universe's Toughest Energy Challenges—is the start of a hop, skip, and a jump across the back forty known as our cosmos, and the biggest thing to hit the moon in four billion years." Mr. Bush was visibly misty-eyed as he signed the nonbinding initiative, leaving the details of this, along with everything else, to his successor.

NASA is well into the requisitioning necessary to put four men on the moon by 2018, although still a bit short on the funds to return them, the estimated arrival being well ahead of the Chinese plan to reconstruct Bird's Nest Stadium on the Sea of Fecundity in 2020 in hopes of drawing the first Lunar Olympics, and of the Mexican moon landing, Project Tecciztecatl, scheduled for mañana. Working within reduced funding parameters, NASA will cannibalize outgoing shuttles, old *Titans and Minutemen*, ICBMs available from North Dakota silo-downsizing, Eastern Airline's mothballed 737s, and eBay'd Soyuz surplus to cobble together a new generation of launch vehicles capable of putting a man on the moon for pennies ($15 billion in 2018 dollars) a day, but only if we act now. Once on the moon for their seven-day, six-night stay, our exxxonauts will acquire mineral rights and conduct test borings, all the while living off the land, putting in low maintenance crops like Jerusalem artichokes and shitake mushrooms for the new Whole Moon brand of organics, using bauxite-rich moon dust to make aluminum mission medallions, and melting the south pole for catfish ponds—sponsored by the Mississippi and Nam Viet Catfish Consortium: "One World, Many Catfish"—which will serve as a staple for future Exxxon missions, with the excess sold to restaurants across the Southern Earth turning a nice little profit as well. At Mission Exxxon, The Sky's Not the Limit!

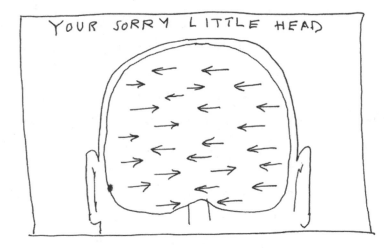

SHADES OF GREY MATTER

Researchers find the human brain to be seven times larger than expected. Who woulda thunk it? By popular mammalian convention, out brains should be about the size of cocktail onions. The equivalent of three or four ferrets or a badger and a wolverine. For our oversize noggins to pay for themselves, the average man would be approaching 42 feet, and the average woman—were there one—38 foot, 6 inches. A good-size toddler would run 14 feet, slightly higher in Canada. Thought of another way, each of our brains should be able to power another six adults comfortably and with plenty of legroom.

We don't need that much brain, or that much SUV, but if the cranium wasn't exaggerated, the wiggle room would have to be made up with packing peanuts. The brain may be vestigial—like our little bobbed tails—or be considered the Univac of early dendrite hubs. Today those 1700 ccs (on a good day) could be replaced with a nanochip you could inhale and be Vista capable until you sneezed. As it turns out, our heads are largely ornamental—some more so than others—figureheads, the heavy lifting done on the Q.T. by the so-called primitive forebrain (in the sense that Grandma Moses or George W. Bush is a primitive), the *medulla oblongata*. The *medulla* takes its *oblongata* seriously, running the entire business without notice, since giving credit is a function of a prefrontal lobe stubbornly refusing to recognize the brain stem. I don't know what stalk they think they're hanging off of. Our forebrain is identical to the one in cows, and is what allows us to chew cud and all face in the same direction.

SCIENCE YOU CAN EAT!

Thanks to the growing field of Molecular Gastronomy, it is now possible to live, breathe, and eat science. Molecular gastronomy, the edible science, was the rumbling first heard by Hungarian (!) Nicholas Kurti (but the crackling is superb). Kurti was fond of quoting Brillat-Savarin, whose *Physiology of Taste* appeared in 1825:

> The discovery of a new dish does more for the happiness of mankind than the discovery of a star.

Kurti was famous for complaining we know more about the atmosphere of Venus than what goes on inside our soufflés to a lunch crowd at the Royal Society in 1969, who were probably expecting to hear something about his atomic bomb research during the war. Kurti then made meringue with a Hoover, electrocuted bangers on an auto battery, and radar-ranged a "Frozen Florida," a reversed Baked Alaska (hot inside, cold out) to a mixed reception. Kurti championed low-temperature cooking, that last leg of lamb reaching perfection only posthumously. If molecular gastronomy is where chemistry and cookery meet, Kurti was somewhat unique in being an epicurean as well as a chemist. The torch is carried today by Hervé This who, looking for colloidal solutions, formulated his famous chocolate chantilly using whipped cream physics...O/W + G → (G + O)/W... where G is gas, O is oil, and W is water: voila, an eggless chocolate mousse (you can use *foie gras* if you don't have chocolate!):

CHOCOLATE CHANTILLY

Serves 2 (you); 1 (me)

Using complex disperse systems formalism, place 250 g (8 oz) of a nice, coarsely chopped bittersweet chocolate into a saucepan with 200 ml (¾ cup + ⅛) water; heat while stirring till melted. Fill a large bowl with chopped ice. Remove the chocolate-water colloid from the heat and pour into a second smaller bowl. Immediately set the smaller bowl on top of the ice and whisk like it's going out of style to aerate the emulsion. Stop at chocolate mousse.

WAS IT MR. WIZARD?

Without a paternity test, it is all but impossible to pin down the father of science, let alone the mother. There are no shortage of suspects—Abu Rayhan al-Biruni, for starters, was named as the father of geodetics (Earth-measuring) and anthropology (people-measuring) and at least the uncle of chemistry, psychology, geography, encyclopediology, and pharmacy. Al-Biruni vies for the title sheik of the scientific method with Ibn al-Haytham, who lived in Basra at about the same time, and invented a regimen for finding the truth, what science used to be about before the cosmetics industry. Experience, conjecture, deduction for the purpose of prediction, and testing, hopefully not on rabbits, was the Haytham approach, not so different from the Greek uncle of science Aristotle's method of *observation* followed by *pontification*. When he was wrong—the Earth being the center of the universe, for example—he was very wrong, but his heart, like Archimedes' lever, was in the right place. Aristotle believed that men have more teeth than women, that heavier objects fall faster than lighter ones, and that math was not worth taking. Galileo, the father of astronomy and physics, made a nice living (before the little fallout with the Church) simply adding the "… not!" to Aristotle's conclusions, and taking whatever else he needed from astronomy's birth father, Nicolaus Copernicus, cutting-edge heliocentrist (that's sun, son) and widely rumored to be commander in chief of the scientific revolution.

☞ T-Ruth, recently of Montana, is the first ovulating female dinosaur fossil ever discovered.

☞ The ancient Syrians sacrificed acrobats.

☞ The earliest traces of life have been found in zircons.

☞ The centers for love and lust are widely separated in the brain.

☞ Four glasses of milk will reduce PMS by half.

☞ There are three sunsets on planet HD 188753.

☞ Rodents' beady eyes are 61 percent the size they should be.

POPULAR SCIENCE
FICTION?

May 1955—*Popular Science Monthly*—Mechanics—Autos—
Homebuilding—promises technological advances that will
rock our world, and soon. Bible of the forward-looking man of the
'50s who wanted the body of Charles Atlas, yes, and who might
just make concrete planters in his basement or learn TV repair in
his spare time, but who wanted more, who stood in the driveway
looking at the stars, *Popular Science* promised a better future through
SCIENCE. Could they have been lying for their 35 cents?

Let's take a look.

Promise 1: *Space Elevator*. One end of a cable to be hooked to the Earth's surface, and the other to an artificial moon in stationary orbit around the Earth. A guy would have to attach a pretty good sized counterweight (a '55 La Salle?) to keep the cable taught, but that was doable. The elevator could then ride the cable into space without any rocket engines needed. Express elevator to space!

Where is it? Stymied by needed advances in cable technology, the space elevator was never actually built, but does keep cropping up, most recently using carbon nanotubes with the needed tensile strength. The space elevator has been re-imagineered as Skyhook, since "elevator" was never very sexy (JFK never dreamed of pledging we would have an elevator going into space by the end of the sixties). The LiftPort Group, or so it says on their prospectus, believes they can, with proper financing, have an elevator to the stars operational by 2014.

Promise 2: *Gyrocopter* personal commuter craft. The nicely rendered gentleman in the business suit lifting off from the roof of his suburban ranch wrapped in a cocoon-like flying machine, to begin his dash over the clogged pre-Interstate class B highways to his high-paying job downtown. A win-win for what was not yet known as lifestyle and for post-war productivity.

The reality: Autogiros, as they are now popular-sciencely known, exist, but have yet to catch on with commuters, perhaps intimidated by FAA regulation of air space and the F-16 interceptors standing alert at nearby Air National Guard bases. Unlike the powered rotor of a helicopter, the autogiro blade is actually free-spinning, alarming to some popular scientists not onboard with autorotation, which gives lift without separation from the frame. A powered prop aft pulls the craft through the air, while a joystick controls the angle of the autorotor to make it go up, down, or bank all the way to the bank. Unfortunately, the autogiro needs a runway for takeoff beyond the pitch of the average homeowner's mansard. The verdict: came to pass, but not in a home version.

Promise 3: *The Home Atomic Pile.* The exciting possibility of the clean and economical personal nuclear reactor hit home for many popular scientists. Many were disappointed when Ronald Reagan's all-GE electric home in Pacific Palisades did not include one, due to zoning restrictions. The Brits were the first to jump on this bandwagon, heating offices at their experimental plant in Harwell with heat exchangers over the core, making enough hot water to heat the place for five thousand years! The North Sea oil could stay where it was. A tough sell to the British public, amid fears of nuclear proliferation in Epping Forest.

Outcome: Unavailable at Harrods or Menard's, pending a possible McCain administration (2012?).

Promise 4: *Fallout Shelter/Rec Room.* It was 1955, and Americans were understandably worried about the Russians and body-snatching watermelons from space. The elegant *Popular Science* solution: a *Make Room for Daddy*, reinforced concrete, lead-sheathed, filtered, ventilated recreation room, stuffed with canned goods and canteens, an empty spackling pail comfort station, homemade Geiger counter (see page 218) and optional gun rack to discourage "neighbors" dropping over without calling first. Looks exactly like Rusty Hamer's room on *The Danny Thomas Show*, adding to the reassurance factor. The promise of dual-duty, in war/peace, made it quite an attractive home addition for the do-it-yourselfer, coming in at under five hundred 1955 dollars, plus supplies and furnishings.

Did it come to pass? Quite a few dual-purpose rumpus rooms were built in the wasted space where the coal chute used to be, more still in the back yard using vintage submarine hatches wedded to storm cellar plans. Most backyard models were decommissioned due to groundwater and rat problems; in-home varieties made excellent reconversions into wet bars, as seen in the June 1960 PS.

Promise 5: *Studebaker Bass Boat*. Early Volkswagen Beetles, the commercials claimed, could float, but, despite German ingenuity, they couldn't paddle once they hit the frink. Being able to drive right into Pewaukee Lake to fish had long been a dream of *Popular Science* subscribers, spurred on by 1955's challenge, "Fish From Your Car!" The marine-like Studebaker seemed particularly suited for aquatic duty—tarring it up, running a propeller off the differential, and dropping a rudder through the back seat didn't seem like too much of a big deal, albeit impacting resale value. Some guys undoubtedly tried it; I seem to remember one from *My Weekly Reader* who appeared to be towing a skier from a Studebaker Lark.

What then? The Germans triumphed with the people's Amphicar in 1961, powered by a 43 horsepower Triumph engine that could do 7 knots and 70 mph, two-door cabriolet with fins, naturally, and lifted skirts. The Amphicar steered with its front wheels on land or water, making navigation problematic—two crossed the English channel in 1968 and haven't been seen since.

Results: Three of five *Popular Science* promises from May 1955 have been kept, while two others—home atomic piles and space elevators—may still have their day. Thank you, *Popular Science!* You are so much better than *Popular Mechanics*, despite Mimi!

Photographed by Peter Gowland

Dear Reader,
    Here you catch me playing a round with my new steady—the Babco Electric Caddy, which goes so straight you just point it down the fairway and follow it. You can pre-set it so the motor cuts off in 0 to 40 seconds. It climbs sturdily, is almost tip-proof. It has three speeds and a handbrake for downhill. From Babcock Mfg. Co., 5632 Shafter Ave., Oakland, Calif. It's $199.50. With battery and charger, $264.40.

Mimi

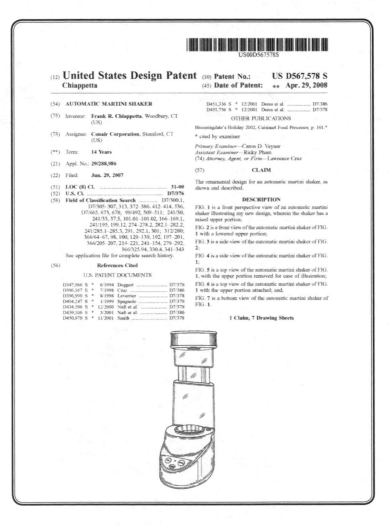

IIIIIIIIIIIIIIIIIIIIIIIIIIIIIIIIIIIIIIIIIIIIIIII
US00D567578S

(12) **United States Design Patent** (10) Patent No.: **US D567,578 S**
Chiappetta   (45) **Date of Patent:** ** **Apr. 29, 2008**

(54) **AUTOMATIC MARTINI SHAKER**

(75) Inventor: **Frank R. Chiappetta**, Woodbury, CT (US)

(73) Assignee: **Conair Corporation**, Stamford, CT (US)

(**) Term: **14 Years**

(21) Appl. No.: **29/288,986**

(22) Filed: **Jun. 29, 2007**

(51) LOC (8) Cl. **31–00**
(52) U.S. Cl. **D7/376**
(58) **Field of Classification Search** D7/300.1,
D7/305–307, 313, 372–386, 412–414, 536,
D7/665, 673, 678; 99/492, 509–511; 241/30,
241/33, 37.5, 101.01–101.02, 166–169.1,
241/195, 199.12, 274–278.2, 282.1–282.2,
241/285.1–285.3, 291, 292.1, 301; 312/280;
366/64–67, 98, 100, 129–139, 192, 197–201,
366/205–207, 219–221, 241–154, 279–292,
366/325.94, 330.4, 341–343
See application file for complete search history.

(56) **References Cited**

U.S. PATENT DOCUMENTS

D347,966	S	*	6/1994	Doggett D7/378
D396,167	S	*	7/1998	Cruz D7/386
D396,990	S	*	8/1998	Leverrier D7/378
D404,247	S	*	1/1999	Spagnolo D7/378
D434,596	S	*	12/2000	Nafl et al. D7/378
D439,106	S	*	3/2001	Nafl et al. D7/386
D450,978	S	*	11/2001	Smith D7/378

D451,336	S	*	12/2001	Deros et al. D7/386
D451,756	S	*	12/2001	Deros et al. D7/378

OTHER PUBLICATIONS

Bloomingdale's Holiday 2002, Cuisinart Food Processor, p. 101.*

* cited by examiner

Primary Examiner—Caron D. Veynar
Assistant Examiner—Ricky Pham
(74) *Attorney, Agent, or Firm*—Lawrence Cruz

(57) **CLAIM**

The ornamental design for an automatic martini shaker, as shown and described.

DESCRIPTION

FIG. 1 is a front perspective view of an automatic martini shaker illustrating my new design, wherein the shaker has a raised upper portion;

FIG. 2 is a front view of the automatic martini shaker of FIG. 1 with a lowered upper portion;

FIG. 3 is a side view of the automatic martini shaker of FIG. 2;

FIG. 4 is a side view of the automatic martini shaker of FIG. 1;

FIG. 5 is a top view of the automatic martini shaker of FIG. 1, with the upper portion removed for ease of illustration;

FIG. 6 is a top view of the automatic martini shaker of FIG. 1 with the upper portion attached; and,

FIG. 7 is a bottom view of the automatic martini shaker of FIG. 1.

1 Claim, 7 Drawing Sheets

THINGS WE DIDN'T KNOW WE NEEDED
MARTINI SHAKER

WHAD'YA KNOW ABOUT
SCIENCE?
ROUND 1

1. What excited NASA scientists about Saturn's moon Enceladus?
   (a) it's Saturno-synchronous
   (b) the geysers shoot out of its south end
   (c) it's shinier than Uranus

2. Viagra, I'm told, also works for:
   (a) hot flashes
   (b) jet lag
   (c) an after-dinner mint

3. Do sparrows ever do medleys—just to mix it up?

4. Bacteria who've been into space come back:
   (a) nicer
   (b) much the same, maybe a little wiser
   (c) nastier

5. So, you're telling me the Juan de Fuca plate is lubricated by Old Faithful?

6. What did the rostral anterior cingulate cortex say to the rostral posterior cingulate cortex on a slow day in the brain?

    (a) It's gonna be all right.

    (b) Make like a tree and leave.

    (c) I'm hungry. You hungry?

7. Thanks to forgiving research, you are now allowed ____ extra pounds without a health penalty.

    (a) 5

    (b) 10

    (c) 25

8. It looks pretty much the same, at first glance—but the universe has, in fact:

    (a) lost a few pounds

    (b) filled out

    (c) maintained its girlish figure

9. All right, they never cut class, but are chimps smarter than college students?

10. Dinosaurs last roamed the Earth:

   (a) 100 million years ago

   (b) 6,000 years ago in Kentucky

   (c) 60 years ago, if you consider the Packard

WHAD'YA KNOW ABOUT SCIENCE? (ROUND 1 ANSWERS)

1. (b) It's Old Faithful all the time at the south end of Enceladus. Cassini could hardly believe her eyes on the pass by—a national park waiting to happen. Steam absolutely spews from the south pole of the 300-mile wide moon of Saturn, where unknown heat sources melt subsurface water to a frenzied boil and all hell breaks loose.

2. (b) So if your jet's lagging it, too, there you go, getting that old circadian rhythm going.

3. Sparrows are forever doing medleys of their greatest hits in both copulative and territorial situations, if those aren't one and the same. They mix it up for mates and adversaries, if those aren't one and the same.

4. (c) Nastier; this is a little alarming in a science-fiction scenario sort of way. Salmonella which got the chance to go into space were, upon touchdown, three times as likely to kill mice. Travel does not broaden salmonella, or, really, any of the enterobacteriales.

5. So says Richard Allen at Berkeley. Got a problem with that?

6. (a) It's gonna be all right. Hopefully the cingulate will not think it's Gerry and the Pacemakers, and sing the song over and over. NYU has found that the rostral anterior cingulate is the optimist in the brain, even putting a good face on the rostral posterior cingulated, which has nothing good to say about anybody.

7. (c) Possibly the only thing the government has done for us lately is give us a 25-pound hedge against obesity. The Centers for Disease Control and Prevention collated body-mass indices with what people died of and found that putting on a few makes you no more likely to die from cancer or heart disease, and a lot less likely to die from pneumonia, emphysema, infection, and injuries.

8. (a) The universe has actually dropped a few, or at least our appreciation of it has, since there appears to be a higher percentage of dark matter than was thought. Comes to a 10–20 percent weight loss, since dark matter weighs but a farthing.

9. Yes, at least on the AC-as-in-chimp-T conducted at Kyoto University, which look at memory reaction time patterns suggesting that chimps think about something other than sex 24/7.

10. (b) 6,000 years ago in Kentucky, according to the diorama at the Creation Museum in Hebron, which means that *Caveman* with Ringo Starr was historically accurate.

BETTER LIVING
THROUGH SCIENCE!

Remember *Science Fiction Theatre*, with your host Truman Bradley? Remember Mr. Wizard always showing kids cool stuff in his garage? Remember *GE Theater* hosted by Ronald Reagan, proud owner of an all-electric house? You're pretty old, aren't you? But you look good, probably due to science making your life better just like it promised it would. True, we don't have the atomic-pile home heating plants that don't have to be refueled for 50,000 years, or personal gyrocopters for commuting like *Popular Science* strongly suggested we would by now, but we can talk on the phone while driving, or drive while we talk on the phone. Robots can replace us on the assembly line and at the office, and routinely do. Stepford wives are within earshot. Our kids can text one another in an unbreakable code, while the recording industry of America can sue us for the intellectual rights of an iPod, a crime that didn't even exist when we were young and stupid. Our health records can now be googled, which sounds like the rant of a delusional just a few short years ago, here, and purloined along with our identities—well, he who steals my health can have it. It's Science and its cohort Technology we have to thank for a lot we take for granted:

Post-its—Eureka'd by 3M researcher Arthur Fry while singing in the choir at St. Paul's North Presbyterian Church, whose little store-receipt bookmarks kept falling out of the hymnal. Borrowing a colleague's Magic Tape adhesive, he went crazy with little squares of paper, and the rest is history. "It's a paper world, out there," he's often said.

Teflon—Chances are Teflon wouldn't have become so omnipresent or so nearly the descriptor of Ronald Reagan if it were marketed under its original moniker, polytetrafluoroethylene. On April 6, 1938, DuPont researcher Roy Plunkett accidentally polymerized some freon he was playing around with, and found he had a pretty darn slippery plastic on his hands. The real hero of the story, however, is the wife of a Parisian fisherman, Adele Gregoire, who used the stuff her husband had been applying to his fishing tackle on her saucier pan. Voilà! She no stick!

Cheese in a Can—I take you now to Wrightstown, Wisconsin, just upstream of Kaukauna on the Fox River in the northeast corner of the Dairy State. Up to their elbows in cheese for generations, Badgers had long dreamed of a cheese spreadable enough to not break the cracker. Some progress, indeed, had been made at Kaukauna, with Kaukauna Klub high-viscosity cheddars, but it remained for a young Edwin Traisman at Nabisco to dare to dream of pressurizing an aerated Colby into Snack Mate, later Easy Cheese. The secret—pressurizing the can separately from the cheese, and making nano-bacon particles that wouldn't clog the nozzle. Incidentally, Traisman is the same food scientist who showed Ray Kroc how to freeze his fries so they would still fry up crisp!

Super Glue—It is not known if the inventor of Super Glue first used it to glue his fingers together, like so many of us since, but it was in 1942 that Harry Coover, while working for Eastman-Kodak in Rochester, NY, was working on making clear plastic gunsights for the war effort, only to be frustrated when their cyanoacrylate plastics kept sticking to everything. It wasn't until 1951 that Coover, looking for adhesives for fighter jet canopies, turned an earlier failure into success. After the public rollout of Super Glue in 1958, Coover lifted Garry Moore off the ground with a single drop for *I've Got a Secret*.

WD-40—Norm Larsen came up with WD-40 after thirty-nine failures to develop a compound that would displace water for missile applications, since you don't want your Atlas nosecone rusting. The general male public went crazy for it at and since its introduction in 1958, and is still finding uses for it unimagined by its creators—when applied to toilet seats, it prevents the snorting of cocaine. The notion that fish oil is the active ingredient is an urban legend; that ingredient would be Stoddard solvent, suspiciously like kerosene.

Botox—Botox may cure the golfing condition known as the Yips, adding to increasing arsenal of uses. It's come a long way from being the bacterium that causes botulism to the one that cures wrinkles—how was that leap of faith made? In 1820, a German physician Justinus Kerner first proposed using "sausage poison" to relieve nerve tremors. Its cosmetic use had to wait for the husband-and-wife dermatology team of Jean and Alistair Caruthers in Vancouver in 1990—on April 15, 2002, tax day, the USDA approved it for use on the resulting frown lines. When injected, botox binds selectively with nerve endings, inhibiting acetylcholine release and paralyzing the wrinkly muscle. About 200 bucks every 8 weeks once you get the habit.

The Segway—George W. Bush is famous for going ass over teakettle on one, they are banned on many sidewalks and most thoroughfares, but Dean Kamen envisioned his personal transporter as a boon to mankind who could use a little "electric personal assistive mobility." They would be good in a warehouse, or at the Pentagon. Its working title was Ginger, as in Ginger Rogers, but I don't see the resemblance. The hype before the Segway was unveiled in 2001 pretty much exceeded its acceptance by the public, whether leaning to the right or the left. Two computers, two tilt sensors, five gyroscopes, and two motors automate what one foot on and one foot propelling used to do on a scooter—and all for $6,000!

Viagra—Well, I just know what I hear, but it's supposed to work if you need that kind of thing, if you can get the timing down and someone undrugged willing to cooperate. Hard to believe there was a time before ED was diagnosed, but there you go. Just tired (or tired of?) is what we used to call it. Nicholas Terrett at Pfizer is supposed to have discovered the side effects of the blood pressure drug Sildenafil, but neither Pfizer nor Mrs. Terrett have been willing to confirm that. Ironically, increases the relaxation of muscles which increases blood flow to the affected areas. Side effects include blue lightning coming from your fingertips and separate rooms.

THE GOD PARTICLE

I don't claim to understand particle physics, but I do know a weak force when I have one, and, by elimination, a strong one when I see one: that would be physicist Peter Higgs, atheist and prophet of *The God Particle*. It was Higgs in Edinburgh who said "Let there be a Higgs boson to explain how all of the matter in the universe first put on weight, bypassing through a Higgs field of super dense but now extinct particles." Not to blaspheme, but cohort Leon Lederman, of Fermilab, said it ought to be called the goddamn particle, for how hard it has been to find. God may have had to have been involved, since the theory that something (mass) can come from nothing (cosmic symmetry) is nothing if not Creationist. Particle physics being the smackdown that it is (and don't kid yourself, Hawking is tough even from a seated position), Higgs's idea has been controversial since he first proposed it in the 1960s; he's had the Higgs Field all to himself, only in recent years gaining acolytes who have built the church—the Large Hadron Collider at CERN—on this boson. The Higgs boson is the only one in the Standard Model showroom (the extended family of photons, leptons, gluons, and quarks that everything consists of) that has yet to be shined up and parked on the floor.

It goes something like this: the Big Bang distributed the primeval symmetry with a sort of grain to it; particles that go with the grain—say, a photon—have no mass; particles that go against the grain (like Higgs himself) get pretty big, like the W and Z particles. To clarify for a moment the fact that I have no idea what I'm talking about, a boson, like my head, has a positive spin but, unlike my head, obeys the Bose-Einstein statistics, which is where I get off. The only boson thought to exist in the Standard Model (the Deluxe is extra) of physics is Higgs's or God's, and it is only a question of the 80-year-old Edinburghian living long enough to be vindicated when it shows up. For forty years he's been waiting for the Godot Particle. So far, no luck, either at Fermilab, where the buffalo roam in Batavia, Illinois, or at CERN in Geneva, but with the Large Hadron Collider just coming online, we may soon be able to confirm the very existence of the God Particle, and so begin the deification of Peter Ware Higgs.

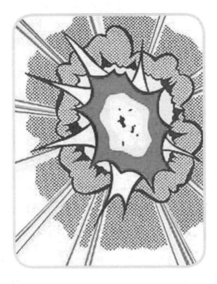

THE BIG BANG ERA

It's hard to picture a time before there was a Big Bang, but before Al Friedmann in 1922, most of us still thought that the stars were ornamental, just hung on the tree and left up all year. Friedmann, a brilliant Russian mathematician in the post-revolution honeymoon days, said that space and time were isotropic, where all points travel uniformly in all directions, fleeing a rather dramatic event, namely all matter conveniently condensed into a ball the size of a grapefruit exploding. Einstein at this time was saying the universe was static, so he was no Friedmann. Friedmann's calculations were reworked into the Big Bang by one of his upstart former students at Leningrad

U, George Gamow, who, along with Edward Teller (a man with no small interest in biggish bangs) gave the toddler some teeth. Before you knew it, atomic nuclei were streaming from ground zero like pea shot, colliding and recombining with other nuclei into a test version of matter, and still are, explaining the queasy feeling you sometimes get at 186,000 miles per second.

Here's where it gets hairy. First off, you need to accept the Cosmological Principle, or you're not going anywhere: how you look at the universe in no way depends on where you are, or who, or which way you happen to be looking. This makes for an edgeless universe originating from everywhere at once. If you're OK with that, then you need to chew on Planck Time—after Max, the father of quantum theory, which is the smallest and first unit of time and, by Planck One, the shortest epoch you're likely to see. The laws of physics, as amended, don't allow measuring the cosmos before the initial Planck; try and you're just wasting your time.

MOTHERS OF INVENTION

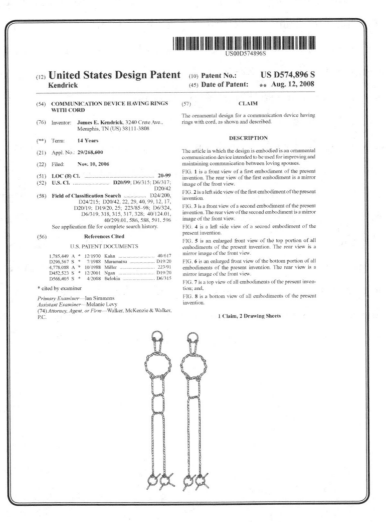

(12) **United States Design Patent**   (10) Patent No.:   **US D574,896 S**
Kendrick   (45) Date of Patent: ** Aug. 12, 2008

(54) **COMMUNICATION DEVICE HAVING RINGS WITH CORD**

(76) Inventor: **James E. Kendrick**, 3240 Crete Ave., Memphis, TN (US) 38111-3808

(**) Term: **14 Years**

(21) Appl. No.: **29/268,600**

(22) Filed: **Nov. 10, 2006**

(51) LOC (8) Cl. **20-99**
(52) U.S. Cl. **D20/99; D6/315; D6/317; D20/42**
(58) Field of Classification Search D24/200, D24/215; D20/42, 22, 29, 40, 99, 12, 17, D20/19; D19/20, 25; 223/85-98; D6/324, D6/319, 318, 315, 317, 328; 40/124.01, 40/299.01, 586, 588, 591, 596
See application file for complete search history.

(56)   **References Cited**
U.S. PATENT DOCUMENTS

1,785,449 A * 12/1930 Kahn 40/617
D296,567 S * 7/1988 Muramatsu D19/20
4,778,088 A * 10/1988 Miller 223/91
D452,523 S * 12/2001 Ngan D19/20
D566,405 S * 4/2008 Belokin D6/315

* cited by examiner

Primary Examiner—Ian Simmons
Assistant Examiner—Melanie Levy
(74) *Attorney, Agent, or Firm*—Walker, McKenzie & Walker, P.C.

(57)   CLAIM

The ornamental design for a communication device having rings with cord, as shown and described.

          DESCRIPTION

The article in which the design is embodied is an ornamental communication device intended to be used for improving and maintaining communication between loving spouses.
FIG. **1** is a front view of a first embodiment of the present invention. The rear view of the first embodiment is a mirror image of the front view.
FIG. **2** is a left side view of the first embodiment of the present invention.
FIG. **3** is a front view of a second embodiment of the present invention. The rear view of the second embodiment is a mirror image of the front view.
FIG. **4** is a left side view of a second embodiment of the present invention.
FIG. **5** is an enlarged front view of the top portion of all embodiments of the present invention. The rear view is a mirror image of the front view.
FIG. **6** is an enlarged front view of the bottom portion of all embodiments of the present invention. The rear view is a mirror image of the front view.
FIG. **7** is a top view of all embodiments of the present invention; and,
FIG. **8** is a bottom view of all embodiments of the present invention.

          1 Claim, 2 Drawing Sheets

THINGS WE DIDN'T KNOW WE NEEDED
SPOUSE COMMUNICATOR

WHAD'YA KNOW ABOUT
SCIENCE?
ROUND

1. A "fuzzball" is a character found in:

   (a) dryers

   (b) nano technology

   (c) string theory

2. Maybe not "more evolved," but who's evolved *more*, man or chimp?

3. You inadvertently condense all the water vapor around Venus—how deep an ocean have you gotten yourself into?

   (a) Lake Erie-ish

   (b) Bosporus-like

   (c) Miles wide but an inch deep

4. A chaperone protein:

   (a) tags along on protein dates

   (b) helps proteins with their folding

   (c) stands under the basketball hoop at protein dances

5. Women looking at a nude photograph of a male first check out the:

   (a) face

   (b) ring finger

   (c) context

6. According to a study in a yet undetermined discipline, researchers at the National Taiwan University discovered the soul to be housed in the:

   (a) prostate

   (b) pineal gland

   (c) adrenal gland

7. Do old stars ever come out of retirement to spawn new planets?

8. Can you teach an old ant new tricks? Or will they never change?

9. Among lark buntings, the big white wing patches were last "in":

   (a) after Labor Day, 1998

   (b) 2000, for spring

   (c) you saw a few in fall 2003, but not that many

ANTS and GERMS

10. Do fruit flies suffer from insomnia?

   (a) sometimes

   (b) never

   (c) no, but they keep the bananas up

☞ Univac, the first commercial computer, predicted in 1951, with just 1 percent of the vote in, that Eisenhower would win. Of course, everyone but Stevenson already knew that. Univac was Remington Rand's way of branching out from shavers and typewriters. Their first sale was to the Census Bureau, who may still be using it. Univac—Universal Automatic Computer—boasted 5,200 vacuum tubes dotting its 29,000-pound self with a 400-square-foot footprint, and a main memory of 1,000 words, about as many as a two-year-old.

WHAD'YA KNOW ABOUT SCIENCE? (ROUND 2 ANSWERS)

1. (c) You get fuzzballs with string theory, from having to come up with such fuzzy (complicated) space-times to account for strings in your black hole, or something like that. It's a little fuzzy to me.

2. Chimps. They have evolved further, although they had further to go. Chimps, in fact, are still evolving and may eventually be able to perpetrate securities fraud.

3. (c) You would cover Venus with an ocean 3 cm deep, only useful for water bugs and pond scum, but a start, nonetheless.

4. (b) Chaperones help with the folding…in this case of histones and DNA into nice, neat nucleosomes. If you're looking for one, you can probably find it in the ER, the endoplasmic reticulum. Bad ones help *E. coli* do its dirty work.

5. (c) Women always look at a guy's context first, assessing why and where the heck the dude is nude in the first place. Then they go straight to the you-know, don't kid yourself.

6. (b) Pineal gland, right where Descartes, who called it the "seat of the soul," left it. Long the mystery gland, the pineal dispenses melatonin, which regulates our wake/sleep patterns and whether we miss the change of seasons or not, should we ever get away from them. James Brown was really the Godfather of Pineal.

7. Yes, in fact, dying stars shed material thought to seed new planets, something that Stanley Kubrick predicted in *2001*. The red dwarf Mira-A, some 350 light years from us, ejaculates an Earth mass every 7 years, like Way Old Faithful.

8. Sure can. Ants are smart as a whip, learning quickly from trial and error and smelling when things just "ant" right. It is not for nothing they have been favorably compared to grasshoppers all these years. Ants have been observed cutting leaves into smaller shapes if they have a low ceiling to haul them through.

9. (a) In the fall of '98, white patches on the males' wings were all the rage among female lark buntings, themselves quite drab. Every mating season the female is free to consider different attributes; some years it's the curve of the beak or a well-turned talon.

10. (a) 10 percent of fruit flies suffer from chronic insomnia, unable to stop the buzzing in their heads, or the uneasy feeling there's a banana peel somewhere in the house. Fruit flies have the whole circadian melatonin thing just like we do, and, in fact, everything about them resembles us, which is pretty depressing.

EUREKA!

EUREKA!

A rchimedes may have discovered his famous principle in the bathtub, but didn't jump out and run naked through the streets of Athens shouting Eureka, even though he was entitled: it was that big a deal. Oh, not just whether the crown was gold or not, but for mathematics. Before he was killed in the siege of Syracuse in 211 BC (a defender ran him through after he told him not to step on his figures in the dust), Archimedes had discovered most of the basic mathematical principals. *On the Sphere and the Cylinder* was an elegant and very readable description of how to calculate the volume ($V = \frac{4}{3}\varpi r^3$) and surface ($S = 4\varpi r^2$) of a sphere. Archimedes was so proud of it he asked for a model of a sphere described in a cylinder to be perched on his sarcophagus (according to Cicero). He was a patient man, inscribing all those increasing polygons inside a circle until he came up with ϖ in a procedure known as Archimedes' method of exhaustion. *On Conoids and Spheroids* was good, but *On Spirals* only so-so, and many wrote him off until *Quadrature of the Parabola*. His *Method Concerning Mechanical Theorems* describes the method of his mathematics, many of which weren't fully appreciated until centuries after he had bitten the dust.

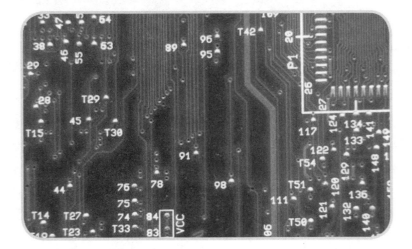

IN THE BEGINNING...

...were Noyce and Kilby, although not as a team (like Boyce and Hart); *Robert Noyce* of Texas Instruments came up with the "integrated" and *Jack Kilby* of Fairchild the "circuit," creating a life form, i.e. ours. Kilby's chrome-and-finned 1959 ICs had all of ten circuits on a 3mm chip; within ten years, chip functionality had increased a hundredfold, and at Intel ICs morphed into microprocessors and consumer electronics ensued. If I could pretend for a moment to understand the principles involved, a typical microelectronic circuit, many of which can now perch on your pinky should the need arise, consists of active devices—transistors and diodes—and passive devices—capacitors and resistors—nestled on a bed of silicon, that notorious semi-conductor. Current passes between them, or doesn't. At this point in the narrative we are in over my head with Boolean logic, where NOT, AND, and OR conspire with their truth tables to perform binary operations in subatomic algebra. I suspect that clock frequency is a factor and registers store preprogrammed instructions, but I couldn't swear to it. Today, millions of operations are performed by these circuits every second; we may reach the point where all possible operations will be performed every possible second and cause something big to happen, like a black hole or the opening of the seventh seal.

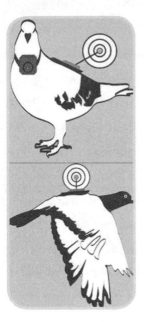

B.F. SKINNER'S FLEET

S hould ICBMs someday rush toward their targets by means of encapsulated pigeons pecking at discs, credit will go to B.F. Skinner, father of behaviorism and Lord of the Pigeons. True, Pavlov had his dogs and Watson his white rats and eleven-month-old boys, but Skinner could condition the lowliest of urban fowl into brilliant if entirely reflexive decision-makers. Skinner wrested psychology out of the hands of the theorists and put it squarely under the beaks of the *Columba livia, Columba leucocephala,* and *Columba fasciata.* He was the Birdman of Harvard. Behaviorism regards human—or any animal—behavior as just so many responses to stimuli; control the stimuli and you condition the human, as Skinner in fact did with his own daughter, weaning her in his Air Crib Baby Tender, a soundproof, germ-proof, air-conditioned box which only admitted daddy-approved stimuli, insuring an optimal infancy and many years of psychotherapy. In B.F.'s view, the Skinner Box begins at home. Nor did it end with infancy—Skinner's work continued with programmed learning via learning machines, where the student's correct answers are immediately reinforced with rewards. But, wait, there's more—Utopia, in fact, based on the social engineering concepts of behaviorism as portrayed in *Walden Two* and *Beyond Freedom and Dignity*, which makes the case that free will gets in the way of scientifically obtainable behaviors which, in the right hands, could produce a harmonious well-organized society without resort to messy genetic intervention. Skinner did not so much die in 1990 as stop responding to stimuli.

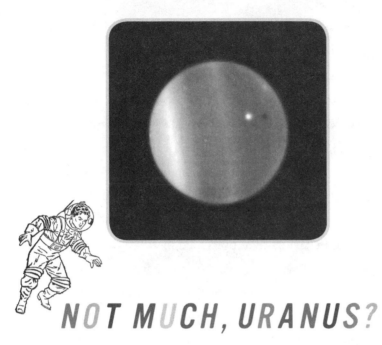

NOT MUCH, URANUS?

Uranus has for too long been eclipsed by its flashier neighbor, Saturn, and the big bully Jupiter, receiving only one flyby from *Voyager 2* in 1971, which found it cloud covered and with its axis very nearly on its equator. Often lumped together with Neptune, with which it seems to have a lot in common, Kuiper's (he of the asteroid belt) assertion that it has lost appreciable amounts of hydrogen and helium over the years has been borne out, and Uranus may not be the massive ball of gas it once was, but would still balance seven Earths. Its composition—variously called "mud," "ice," or "rock"—of frozen methane, hydrogen, and ammonia makes for a less than hospitable terrain; not even H.G. Wells proposed the existence of Uranians. Seasonal changes have been observed on Uranus by the Hubble Space Telescope, with basically two 40-year-long seasons, bad and worse, worse being 300°F below with massive methane-acetylene storms, at least giving its 84-year year a little variety. As they say on Uranus, if you don't like the weather, wait. Man will never set foot on Uranus, its surface being a hydrogen and helium sea, but the methane sunsets are said to be stunning. Also on the plus side add the brightest, if most flammable, clouds in the outer solar system, and rings around Uranus with a subtle beauty all their own. Latest count finds 22 moons; Titania and Oberon, the two largest, were discovered by the father of Uranus, Sir William Herschel, in 1781.

A MU ARAE HOME COMPANION

In our quest for an earthlike planet, we sometimes forget we already have one; maybe we should see if this one can sustain life. The latest candidate for a second home is about the size of Uranus with plenty of affordable, albeit methane, lake frontage. One could easily imagine a handy little *pied à Mu Arae c*, commutable in space-time—being only 50 light years away with a lot to recommend it—the sun is quite like ours, only Mu Arae-light is softer and more flattering. Any life form with problem skin can be grateful they're Mu Araen. On the downside, they're expecting 1160 degrees today, although it's a dry heat. Of three planets circling mama Mu Arae, one is too hot, one is too cold, and ours, Mu Arae c, is just about right, at least compared to what else is on the market. There's another property we can look at, a bit closer in, Giliese 581c, but it's not as nice unless it's ammonia ice-water you're looking for. Meanwhile, back on Mu Arae, the questions remain: is there life capable of understanding we're looking for it? Is the price firm or are they willing to haggle? Is life silicone-based or did they have them removed? Is there zoning? Do the locals look more like Michael Rennie or Kang and Kodos on the Simpsons? Do they want to serve mankind or *serve* mankind? Could we get in early if things heat up around here, just until we find something within our means?

MOTHERS OF INVENTION

(12) **United States Patent**	(10) Patent No.:	**US 7,410,358 B2**
Morehead	(45) Date of Patent:	Aug. 12, 2008

(54) **MANNEQUIN WITH REPLACEABLE HAIR PIECE**

(75) Inventor: **Shawn Morehead**, Knoxville, TN (US)

(73) Assignee: **Mane Attachments**, Knoxville, TN (US)

(*) Notice: Subject to any disclaimer, the term of this patent is extended or adjusted under 35 U.S.C. 154(b) by 322 days.

(21) Appl. No.: **11/277,623**

(22) Filed: **Mar. 28, 2006**

(65) **Prior Publication Data**

US 2007/0238388 A1   Oct. 11, 2007

(51) Int. Cl.
G09B 19/10   (2006.01)
(52) U.S. Cl. **434/94**
(58) Field of Classification Search 434/94, 434/99, 100, 267, 295, 296; 446/319, 321
See application file for complete search history.

(56) **References Cited**

U.S. PATENT DOCUMENTS

3,225,489 A	12/1965	Ryan	
3,279,122 A	10/1966	Blenner	
3,448,540 A *	6/1969	Macciante et al.	446/337
3,458,943 A *	8/1969	Trowbridge	434/94
3,808,736 A *	5/1974	Terzian et al.	446/296
3,843,031 A	10/1974	Oh et al.	
3,903,640 A	9/1975	Dunn	
4,070,790 A	1/1978	Strongin et al.	

4,403,962 A *	9/1983	La Vista	434/94
4,810,196 A	3/1989	Walker	
4,874,345 A	10/1989	Dirks	
5,041,050 A	8/1991	Ritchey et al.	
5,090,910 A *	2/1992	Narlo	434/82
5,498,189 A *	3/1996	Townsend	446/100
5,586,696 A	12/1996	Martinez	
6,109,921 A *	8/2000	Yau	434/100
6,217,407 B1	4/2001	Laursen	
6,527,618 B1 *	3/2003	Faunda et al.	446/394
2006/0008780 A1	1/2006	Pang	

* cited by examiner

Primary Examiner—Kurt Fernstrom
(74) *Attorney, Agent, or Firm*—Knox Patents; Thomas A. Kulaga

(57)   **ABSTRACT**

An apparatus having a support base and a removable hair portion for training personal appearance workers. In one embodiment, the releasable hair portion is the crown of a mannequin head and is detachably fixed to the support base of the mannequin head, which is adapted to be fixed to a work surface or mount. In another embodiment the releasable hair portion is the chin and surrounding area, which is detachably fixed to the support base of the mannequin head. The removable hair portion of the mannequin attaches to the support base of the mannequin head with a latching system that securely fixes the hair portion to the head. The latching system includes at least one fastening tab and a releasable clip that engages an opening in the support base. In another embodiment, a detent system is positioned between a fastening tab and the locking clip.

20 Claims, 5 Drawing Sheets

THINGS WE DIDN'T KNOW WE NEEDED

MANNEQUIN WITH HAIRPIECE

WHAD'YA KNOW ABOUT SCIENCE? ROUND 3

1. Do hugs raise or lower blood pressure?

2. Does the brain blink when the eye does?

3. Speaking of the (human) brain, it turns out to be ____ times larger than expected for a creature with our needs.

   (a) 1

   (b) 4

   (c) 7

4. Using nanotechnology, researchers at Clemson have perfected:

   (a) the self-making bed

   (b) self-cleaning clothes

   (c) the self-walking dog

5. What do you call a six-legged octopus?

6. We have ____ times more microbes than people cells in our bodies.

  (a) 10

  (b) 20

  (c) 50

7. Hard to believe they're related to the current residents, but the earliest primates around here tipped the scales at:

  (a) 180–185, tops

  (b) an ounce

  (c) ten pounds soaking wet

8. Thanks to advances in the teaching of science, today only 1 in ____ teenagers think the sun revolves around the Earth.

  (a) 5

  (b) 7

  (c) 10

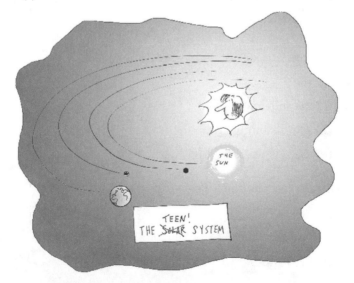

9. True or False: There is no medical reason why the average American husband in good health can't hear what his wife is saying.

10. What is the "second brain"?

    (a) the gut

    (b) the primitive forebrain

    (c) the you-know-what you-know-where

WHAD'YA KNOW ABOUT SCIENCE? (ROUND 3 ANSWERS)

1. Depends on the hugger (and the huggee), but at Chapel Hill they found hugging someone who is not in your department lowers the blood pressure and raises oxytocin—the hormone that mistakenly makes you think you care—levels.

2. University College in London found that parts of the brain switch off each time we blink, and that Prince Harry blinks 18 times a minute. These mini-blackouts are thought to be a soft reboot of the brain.

3. (c) 7 times. We really don't need much of a brain at all in our daily lives, certainly not 1300-plus cc's. Apes get by rather nicely on only 300 cc's, and squirrels can drive you nuts on 6. Estimates and individual needs vary as to how much of our brains we actually use, but let's just say there's a lot of room for growth should we utilize the little we do use not to destroy

ourselves. Evolutionarily speaking, we are in the Commodore 64 stage of brain development—most of the cranium is window dressing.

4. (b) The kids at Clemson (go Tigers!) have come up with a nano-particle polymer that can be manufactured right into clothing fibers to repel dirt and water and possibly even the person wearing it. The downside is that the fibers are all orange.

5. Henry. Well, the wags at Blackpool Sea Life Centre found the thing, so they get to name it. Technically, it's a hexapus.

6. (b) NPR, and they do consider all things, says 20 times more microbes than human cells in listeners like you. A hundred trillion of them I think they said—I was in the bathroom.

7. (b) An ounce. We may have, in fact, evolved from shrews. Some of us for sure. Estimates come from 55-million-year-old dwarf lemurs found in an Indian coal pit.

8. (a) 5. The stoner.

9. False. Every reason in the world, including the one they found at Sheffield University in England, that women's voices are more difficult for men to listen to than other men's because of the tone they take. The lack of a bass response Adam's apple in most women causes what can only be called a pitch problem to most men's ears.

10. (a) The gut, although you can't argue with (c), either. The enteric nervous system gives the colon a mind of its own, implicated in Irritable Bowel Syndrome. As the French say, whither the stomach, there the man. It's been well established that much of psychiatry is, in fact, digestion.

ELEMENTARY, MY
DEAR MENDELEYEV

I don't know if you've taken a look at the periodic table lately, but it's up quite a bit from the Earth, wind, fire, and phlegm of our day. With the latest, Ununoctium, all the way to 118, and the fat periodic lady hasn't sung yet. Most of the new ones seem to have been discovered at Livermore at Berkeley, which would account for Berkelium (97), Californium (98), Einsteinium (99), Lawrencium (103), Ununtrium (113), and Uuh, let's see, Ununhexium (116). Most of the new-fangled elements are unstable, short-lived, and don't really exist in life-as-we-know-it, but look really good on a resume. The last element worth a darn was Americium (95) which makes smoke detectors possible, albeit radioactive. The legendary Plutonium (94) has a whole lot of uses, unfortunately; with a half-life of 20,000 years, it is the antithesis of your fly-by-night Livermore particles. One kilogram of Pu can yield 22 million kilowatt hours of energy or the equivalent of 20 kilotons of TNT, *comme ci, comme ca*. Dmitri Mendeleyev quilted the first periodic tablecloth out of a meager 62 swatches in 1869. Hydrogen is the only element that behaves both as a metal and a non-metal, when it behaves at all. Most of the new elements have been made by bombarding Californium, and I mean like 10 billion *billion* times, into, like, *total* submission. The grail is the "island of stability" where exotic elements behave enough to have Nobel potential.

DARKEST ENERGY

Sounding more like an antebellum bodice ripper than a funda-mental force of nature, Dark Energy is the still-to-be-confirmed anti-gravity predicted by *Danny Dunn and the Anti-Gravity Machine* that pushes the pedal to the metal in the universe's expansion. This is a good thing, since, thanks to entropy, a cosmos that is not expanding is contracting; we could end up the grapefruit we started out as, awaiting another juicing.

Not to be confused with dark matter, the 99 percent of existence we can't seem to find, dark energy is the three-quarters of the uni-verse by weight (allowing for some settling) that must be there if everything really is expanding at the increasing velocity the red shift of the distant 1a supernovae suggest it is. The prior consensus, which everybody felt pretty good about, was that, while still having growing pains, the cosmos was slowing down somewhat, only natural at this time of life. Not everyone agrees that dark energy causes this counterintuitive speedup, but even Einstein couldn't wrap his head around it, calling his "cosmological constant," a repulsive force that slows things down to a crawl, his greatest blunder…and that includes not taking a shot at Marilyn Monroe. Quintessence is another candidate for big bully on the cosmic block, although it suffers from sounding too much like a veteran vacuum cleaner salesman's pitch: massive negative pressure to suck up even the most stubborn galaxies. The big wave to end all waves, quintessence is as long as existence itself, therefore impossible to store in a closet.

Dark Energy is highly viscous (10W-40 Quadrillion), not bright and not dense enough to interact with any other fundamental forces except gravity; the cost of having space—something's going to fill it.

HADDIE

A Pepeekeo, Hawaii, resident (and self-described Wikipedia science editor) sued in federal court to stop the Large Hadron Collider (the Large Hardon Collider, to critics) from firing up and creating a little black hole, or strangelet, that could puncture the Milky Way, sending oceans of nougat over the Big Island and beyond. The case was dismissed, and, sure enough, it did suck the Earth down the cosmic drain...........oh, all right, nothing happened. But you don't know that it couldn't have—"strangelets" have a Wiki entry. The boys at CERN, the European Organization for Nuclear Research, did have to lower their Geneva suburb to –456°F to get the big old collider, biggest since the one from the proto universe, to turn over. Some people once feared that splitting the atom would cause the unleashing of ping-pong balls from mousetraps all over the world, but it never happened. Walt Disney, fortunately, was able to get that genie back in the bottle. The 1,200 superconducting dipolar magnets (just like the ones you can get from Edmunds Scientific!) playing Pong with 600 million protons every second along a 17-mile oval does not seemed to have opened the seventh seal, the one that contains the Nobel prize.

There have been fundamental questions ever since there has been fundament, and Haddie, as she is affectionately known, hopes to answer a few: how much money can be spent on projects that aren't cash crops? Is it possible to work with the French? What the heck is a Higgs Boson, anyway, and wouldn't it be cool to go back to the first billionth of a second after the Big Bang? The price—10 billion, and that's in euros—small compared to the cost of the overall universe, particularly if there are 10 dimensions with each needing decor. Particle physicists have a very good GUT (Grand Unifying Theory) feeling about Haddie, and if they get even one simple elegant equation that explains everything micro to macro and, just maybe, has military applications, it will have been worth it. Even proving supersymmetry, the fundamental right of every particle to have a superparticle, would be super. If nothing else, Haddie will give grad students of Earth some really cool gear to futz with as she powers up with the unmistakable whir of reputations accelerating at nearly the speed of light.

BIG FLOPS

I've had my flops, but they were mostly in the Univac range; you know, a kiloflop at worst. Nowhere in the ballpark of the new-fangled defense department IBM hybrid Roadrunner that's gone petaflop, i.e., one quadrillion floating point operations per second. Now that's multitasking. It's a little hard to feel the pain of a quadrillion, but if you had a thousand million million aches, then you would. Stated more tidily, a petaflop is 10^{15}, 10^{24} Canadian (which here we think of as a whole yottaflop).

A simple calculator, and I number myself among them, can do 10 flops sitting down, but if you're going to destroy/redeem time/space in all ten dimensions, you're going to need some crunch. Back in the day in Chippewa Falls, WI, Seymour Cray went crazy with the brand new integrated circuit boards and got the Cray-1 to cruise at a not so whopping 80 megahertz, at the time of the Bicentennial more than enough for the modestly obliterative ambitions of Los Alamos. In the '80s Cray put four of them together for the Himself-2 and tweaked it up to a state-of-the-technology 800 megaflops, and the race was on. The success of Roadrunner now makes IBM twice as fast as IBM, and getting very close to simulating the real world in real time, and thus, winning. All this using a mere 20,000 chips and virtually no dip. As Seymour said, "If you were plowing a field, which would you rather use? Two strong oxen or 1,024 chickens?"

And the groundbreaking advance making this Golem possible? PlayStation 3 chips. No kidding. These guys are petagamers. When not miniaturizing nuclear payloads, decoding genes, or simulating climate change, they are the Resident Evil Metal Gear Solid Gods of War.

RED ROVER,
RED ROVER

The most exciting implication of the success of the Martian groundbreaking *Sojourner* mission is that now it is technologically possible for the Jet Propulsion Laboratory to turn over my garden from Pasadena, California, making this (Space Sticks and Velcro aside) the best trickle-down yet from the space program. Good stuff—the valiant little Rover lifting its mechanical leg over the hills and valleys of our desolate neighbor, and even picking up its own mess. Earth rovers should work this well.

Yet, for all its undeniable success, the *Pathfinder/Sojourner* mission has not been one to stir men's souls. If JFK had vowed to put an erector set on skates on the moon by the end of the sixties, it's safe to say the speech would not appear in his collected addresses. This was more the crazy dream of a guy you might see in the park with a metal detector and a little shovel stuck in his hind pocket, pulling a St. Christopher medal out of the soccer turf. The upside of the limited expectations of the program is that the little gizmo was not required to do a Wall-E and come up with something misquotable upon touching down.

What have we learned? Mars is a place where there used to be water, which is more than I can say for my basement. There may still be water, which I can say for my basement. It's been about 4 billion years since there was running water, and the landlord can't be reached. Mars has a lot of potholes, and no infrastructure to repair them. The temperature goes down to an Albertan 135 below, but climbs to a decent Upper Peninsula plus 27 during spring break. The seasons, highs and lows excepted, are much like Earth's, since the Mars tilt is close to ours, and not extreme like Uranus. The Olympus Mons is twice the Mons Mt. Everest is, and the Valles Marineris is a mega Grand Canyon without the park service. The polar caps are dry ice, so things keep indefinitely. Mars is not an optical illusion, but actually red and appears to be rusting, a disappointment for those of us who maintained the lawn furniture would hold up a lot better in an airless environment. Their rocks are very much like our rocks, which should please some and leave others just a little disappointed. At least we've learned from Lucille Ball, in "The Long, Long Trailer," not to bring them all home. The Ares Vallis plain looks remarkably like two desert lots my dad purchased after the war close to Roswell, New Mexico, where expatriate Martians, who could verify all this, may be housed.

MOTHERS OF INVENTION

(12) **United States Patent**
Brunning

(10) Patent No.: **US 7,410,074 B1**
(45) Date of Patent: **Aug. 12, 2008**

(54) **PAINT BUCKET**

(76) Inventor: **Robert Brunning**, 9207 Powderhorn Dr., Fountain Hills, AZ (US) 85268

(*) Notice: Subject to any disclaimer, the term of this patent is extended or adjusted under 35 U.S.C. 154(b) by 757 days.

(21) Appl. No.: **10/932,464**

(22) Filed: **Sep. 2, 2004**

(51) Int. Cl.
B05C 21/00 (2006.01)
B65D 25/00 (2006.01)

(52) U.S. Cl. 220/570; 220/696; 220/697; 220/633; 15/257.06

(58) Field of Classification Search 220/570, 220/752, 754, 771, 571, 571.1, 572, 639–654, 220/660–693, 481, 482, 477, 751, 480, 695, 220/697, 699; 15/257.05; 224/148.5; D32/53.1
See application file for complete search history.

(56) **References Cited**

U.S. PATENT DOCUMENTS

D202,134 S	8/1965	Bryan	
3,292,815 A	12/1966	Smith et al.	
3,493,988 A	2/1970	Tidwell	
3,829,926 A	8/1974	Salladay	
4,205,411 A *	6/1980	Cupp et al.	15/257.06
4,266,686 A *	5/1981	Carter	220/697
4,297,762 A	11/1981	Crysdale	
4,561,556 A *	12/1985	Bendix	220/697
D363,304 S	9/1989	Sabatino	
5,046,749 A	9/1991	Owens	
5,314,061 A *	5/1994	Bedrossian	206/229
5,341,969 A *	8/1994	Accardo et al.	222/465.1
D355,287 S	2/1995	Camp, Jr.	
5,400,916 A *	3/1995	Weber	220/495.02

5,810,196 A	9/1998	Lundy	
5,829,628 A *	11/1998	Loum	220/695
5,941,410 A *	8/1999	Mangano	220/735
5,966,772 A *	10/1999	Woodnorth et al.	15/230.11
6,062,389 A *	5/2000	Kent	206/518
6,105,816 A *	8/2000	Shea	220/697
6,176,389 B1 *	1/2001	de Laforcade	220/695
6,199,718 B1	3/2001	Ellis	
6,260,730 B1 *	7/2001	Fellman	220/495.02
D458,723 S	6/2002	Malvasio	D32/53.1
D477,702 S	7/2003	Kohn	
6,622,340 B2 *	9/2003	Rosa	15/257.06
7,191,913 B2 *	3/2007	Byrne	220/570
2002/0096525 A1 *	7/2002	Bertoldo et al.	220/544
2004/0195248 A1 *	10/2004	Garcia	220/570

* cited by examiner

Primary Examiner—Anthony D Stashick
Assistant Examiner—Ned A Walker
(74) *Attorney, Agent, or Firm*—Parsons & Goltry; Michael W. Goltry; Robert A. Parsons

(57) **ABSTRACT**

A paint bucket includes an upstanding continuous sidewall incorporating opposing sidewalls, and opposing front and rear walls. The rear wall has two first support panels each adjoining one of the opposing sidewalls, a central panel having a width and an upper end including an upper edge, and a lower concave end leading to an opposing lower edge adjoining a bottom wall of the paint bucket. A horizontal support panel, having a width equal to the width of the central panel, adjoins the upper edge of the rear wall and the upper edge of the central panel. Two second support panels each adjoin one of the first support panels, the central quadrilateral panel, and the horizontal support panel, and opposing openings are provided through the horizontal support panel each for accommodating therein a paint accessory.

22 Claims, 4 Drawing Sheets

THINGS WE DIDN'T KNOW WE NEEDED
UNKICKABLE BUCKET

WHAD'YA KNOW ABOUT
SCIENCE?
ROUND 4

1. Evolutionarily speaking, fish gills became:
   - (a) ears
   - (b) forearms
   - (c) eyelids

2. On this list of suspects, which is tearing the universe apart by turning gravity's attraction into repulsion?
   - (a) Miley Cyrus
   - (b) dark energy
   - (c) dark matter

3. Horace Epstein of the Lachen Institute, looking at a large family in Gobblers Knob, KY, found a DNA sequence on the X chromosome which he believes is the _____ gene.
   - (a) funny
   - (b) fat
   - (c) flamboyant

4. Using videos of University of Wisconsin Badgers caught in the acts of being themselves, researchers at Berkeley's Institute of Personality conclude there are ____ types of laughs.

    (a) 2

    (b) 6

    (c) 12

5. Thanks to advances at the University of Texas, lie detectors are now able to monitor the subjects':

    (a) redirected thoughts

    (b) stomach churns

    (c) nuance

6. According to the medical journal Lancet, the _____ ratio is the best predictor of heart problems.

    (a) waist-to-hip

    (b) waist-to-bottom

    (c) cheek-to-cheek

7. Do dogs see man as their best friend?

8. "Cosmetic neurology" is the new applied science of what?

9. The endangered Kauai wolf spider babies cling to their mother's back by:

   (a) static electricity

   (b) velcro

   (c) sheer willpower

10. Will rats trained in Japanese be able to pick up German?

WHAD'YA KNOW ABOUT SCIENCE? (ROUND 4 ANSWERS)

1. (a) Ears, or at least so they say up in Uppsala University in Sweden. While still in the primordial pool, the bony structure of the gills of the *Panderichthys*, a carp forefather, began to transition into hammer, anvil, and stirrup.

2. (b) Dark energy, which could make up 70 percent of the energy in the universe…who knows, it's dark. Can't see it. Quintessence is the going word, for a type of dark energy whose characteristics account for the expansion of the cosmos. That's all I know.

3. (a) Horace found the funny gene by exposing subjects to episodes of *Seinfeld* and C-Span and not telling them which was which.

4. (c) 12 kinds of laughs, at least among Badgers: dominant, submissive, obligatory, forced, tittering, aggressive, passive, imperceptible, explosive, mocking, tentative, and belly.

5. (b) Stomach churns; it will now be easy to tell if your gastroenterologist is lying.

6. (a) Waist-to-hip; should be a ratio less than one, 0.9 for men and 0.8 for women.

7. No. A Penn State study found that dogs are very fond of their man but best friend has to be another dog. It's the same as with kids.

8. Cosmetic neurology is the exciting new field of brain enhancements—botox for the brain, smart drugs such as HT-0712, which is a, whad'ya call it, memory enhancer. The next step up from think drinks.

9. (b) Velcro, or what would be velcro if the name weren't trademarked. The comb-like teeth on baby's claws hooks into mommy's back hairs.

10. No. They tried speaking German to Japanese rats at the University of Barcelona, and the *nezumis* just stood there.

GREGOR, PASS THE PEAS!

Before Birdseye there was Mendel, the father of pea genetics, and the only father of anything who was also an Augustinian brother. Gregor Mendel, of Heinzendorf, in what is now the Czech Republic, proved that science and religion could get along, and that one out of four pea plants, brothers, bulls, or rotifers will be dominant, one looks like the mother, one the father, and one nobody can pin down. His study of variation in peas (*Pisum sativum*, sugar snap) while he probably should have been doing his vespers, resulted in Mendel's Laws of Inheritance, which might be summarized as you can pick your friends (and your friend's nose) but you can't pick your relatives. Published in 1866 as the little noticed "Experiments in Plant Hybridization" (in a very nice illuminated scroll), Mendel said that each parent passed on traits, not just *her* side, and that every trait has two versions, only one of which is passed along, and that by chance. All the traits that do slip through are independent of one another, making it unlikely you'll receive both your father's blue eyes and his recessive hairline, but, trust me, it does happen. At this point I'd like to take back what I said about science and religion being good bedfellows, since, after Mendel's death in 1884, the abbott burned all his notes and data, because only God can make a pea. Mendel wasn't credited for his brilliant science until the genotype boys began to dominate in the early twentieth century, the foremost being Hugo de Vries, who was able to replicate Mendel's results without an abbot looking over his shoulder. The three-to-one distribution of traits in the second filial generation has been disputed as being a little too tidy, but it has held up to this observer's eye in the four Feldman boys.

AS THE TYPE IS CAST

There are two types of people in the world: those who believe there are two types of people in the world and those who don't. But even among the type who believe there are, there is little agreement as to which two. Hippocrates spoke of the *phthisic*—tall, thin, and tubercular—and the *apoplectic*—short, fat, and stroke-prone. Pyramus spoke of those he liked and those he didn't. The poet Coleridge believed that babies were born either Aristotelians or Platonists, depending on whether they were "insies" or "outsies," while Nietzsche saw men as either Apollonian—moderate and orderly conservatives prone to opium use—or Nietzschean—mad supermen better than everybody else.

Sir Francis Galton divided humans into the verbalizers and the visualizers, while the Canadian physician Sir William Osler visualized them as either "larks" or "owls" and probably lived to regret verbalizing it. Jung separated the collectively conscious into introverted Hamlets and extroverted Napoleons, leaving little room for those who want to conquer the world one minute and think about it the next.

One of the more insightful attempts to classify humankind was actually a three parter dreamed up by the Roman Celsus with his *in vino veritas* types: the "aggressive," who fights when drunk; the "sociable," who dances and sings when drunk; and the "sentimental," who cries. Celsus believed that, when sober, men were pretty much an undifferentiated mass.

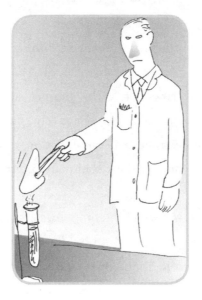

LIGHT A MATCH!

I t's hard to tell where the sense of smell ends and the sense of well-being begins. My mother could smell gas in the kitchen all the way from Boston Store downtown, and take the bus back *on the same transfer* to turn it off. There's a sense of smell. She used to sniff each of us on the way out the door to school each morning; in those days nobody thought anything of it. Dogs do much the same thing, although they're a little less obvious about it. This will sound weird, but one of the things I tried hard to remember about my father was his smell, nothing overwhelming, mind you, just the eau de Dave Feldman that said Dad was in the house. I flatter myself to think

I've had some of eau de dad rub off on me, but it's grossly underappreciated amidst three females with zero odor tolerance—unless it sells for good money, they don't want to smell it. It doesn't make a lot of sense to me—we have five senses, slightly more in Canada, why strap your nose behind your back? A thousand odor receptors are crouched and waiting day and night in the soil of a cilia forest for the waves of discreet and not-so-discreet exuding molecules—why not stop and smell, you noses!

Europeans have been smelling one another for millennia; the Franks the Visigoths, the Ostrogoths the Jutes, all catching the unmistakable whiff of the Huns passing through. The Greeks were unafraid to smell—Hippocrates never said give me a whiff of that guy's armpit and I'll move the world, but he might have, back in the day when physicians carried a nose around their necks instead of a stethoscope. Smell is cultural: nobody smells at table like a Frenchman, who, perhaps not paradoxically, has the worst personal hygiene on the continent, but it doesn't bother him. Louis XIV, it is said, "stank like a carcass," and his carcass smelled like Louis XIV. To be fair, during "The Great Stink," the English smelled no better than the French, and only ventured out with a "promenade," a small perfumed child, clutched to the bosom. The Andaman Islanders in the Bay of Bengal are perhaps the most olfactory of all peoples, seeking favor with and appeasing the gods with tobacco smoke and root and bark incense, and even have a calendar with the year divided into smells. Smells often do not translate well—nobody likes the stinky king of fruits, the durian, except the Indonesians, while one of the few odors an American likes—gunpowder and gasoline aside—vanilla, leaves most Japanese cold. For all its virtues, Japanese culture totally missed out on Tollhouse cookies. Americans will put up with a little incense for religious reasons, but go into aroma shock in a Shinto temple with thirteenth-century ventilation. The Japanese are aroma-centric; aroma ducts often are built into offices and factories to release just the right amounts of lemon, jasmine, and eucalyptus to increase data inputting efficiency by 30 percent.

Pheromones, the Joan Collins of chemicals, are airborne and subjective to say the least. Humans have the sex ones, not so much the territorial, alarm, and food trail ones. The first pheromone was discovered in silkworms in 1959. Bombykol hit like a bombshell on the battlefield of smell science; until then, mostly armpits and volunteer noses making the world safe for Secret. Releaser pheromones, the long-distance champs, can have aphids drumming little legs on thoraxes from miles away; in humans, they account for what is known as *sexy hot*. Sexual pheromones indicate a willingness to consider offers of genetic contribution from a sow in estrus or a gypsy moth in a mulberry bush...the rest is up to you. Bees have their Nasonov gland, and mammals Jacobson's organ, so named because the vomeronasal gland sounds disgusting. Jacobson's is the nose's brain, nestled twixt nose and mouth, calling them like it smells them. Much of what we taste, in fact, is what Jacobson's smells and gets no credit for. Human women can synchronize their menstrual cycles through pheromones, but so far it is not a trial sport in the Olympics.

UP THE LAZY GENOME

I've been meaning to look into this laziness gene. Eh, I'll get to it when I get to it. Thought it might be covered if it's a pre-existing genetic condition. J. Timothy Lightfoot, kinesiologist and no slouch himself over at UNC–Charlotte, says we may have an out when accused of this particular deadly sin, being predisposed to lethargy and all. I knew it was none of my doing, because I would never do it. If your father was lethargic, it makes you wonder how he ever got around to being your father. And so will you. Amazing Grandpa ever left the old country at all. It's not all cut and dried, but Professor Lightfoot found a huge difference between active and inactive mice on the wheel; I mean like 8 miles a day (comparable to a man running 50) to 0.3 miles a day (comparable to a man getting up from the Barcalounger at halftime to make more chips and dip). Turns out this sports fan didn't choose to be lazy, it chose him. Same for cleaning out the gutters and putting the garage door back on the track. If he were dyslexic, he'd be home free. Conversely, the energetic all-do-wells who make the rest of us look bad, training for the Iron Man when they're not putting a koi pond in the backyard, deserve no credit, and any comparisons and contrasts are specious. They got a nice set of neurotransmitters is all, while the rest of us are serotonin (and other fluids) deprived from the get-go. We didn't go at the get-go, because we didn't get. Interestingly, Lightfoot also found that the females were lighter of foot among mice, running 20 percent farther and 30 percent faster than the males, so it's no wonder their human counterparts think we're sloughing off. That's gender bias, friends, rearing its twitchy nose.

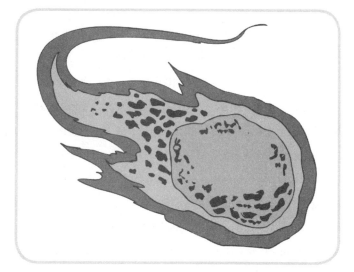

KILLER ASTEROID
HURLS TOWARD EARTH!

According to NASA scientists, obliteration by a killer asteroid is pretty much a sure thing unless we do something, and quick. And they're not just saying that because NASA has suffered so many setbacks and funding cuts that the billions needed to produce and man the tracking telescopes and asteroid diverting rockets would provide them with the major boondoggle that space travel once promised. Not at all. The Apollo asteroid belt alone bowls over a hundred massive extraterrestrial balls right down our alley annually, a good percentage of which would be undeterred by our atmosphere. Worse, according to NASA's David Morrison, 99 percent of *NEOs*, near-Earth objects, half a kilometer and larger have still not been mapped; they could be anywhere.

In March 1989, an asteroid a half-mile across skipped within four hundred thousand miles of Earth; had it been a hundred thousand miles across, it would have come within a half-mile of Earth. In 1908, an asteroid airburst flattened 800 square miles of Tunguska, Siberia, with a force equal to a ten-megaton nuclear bomb, although still not large enough for the Russians to report it. Rasputin correctly thought it auspicious. NASA reassures us that it would have to be a million tons of TNT to give us any real problems; e.g., extinction, irreversible climate change, shroud. The thermometer on the Spaceguard study is stuck at orange, but that may just be to keep up with Homeland Security (which, for some reason, finds destruction from space outside its mandate). What they don't tell you is that asteroids with five- to ten-meter diameters burn up in the Earth's upper atmosphere once a year, with as much force as the bomb which wiped out Hiroshima. According to the Palermo Technical Impact Hazard Scale, near-Earth asteroid (29075) 1950 DA , nicknamed Jim Morrison (for "This Is the End"), has the highest probability of impacting the Earth, sometime around spring break, 2880—so make your travel plans accordingly.

If further lack of reassurance is needed, look no further than the German schoolboy who corrected NASA's calculations on the possibility of the asteroid Apophis striking the Earth in 2036 with devastating effect at a mere 450 to 1, not 45,000 to 1.

ERAS AND ERRATA

YEARS AGO	ERA	PERIOD	ACTIVITY	DOMINANT
Tuesday–2 million	Oyozoic	Turdtiary	Decomposition of dinosaurs into useful hydrocarbons; wacky mammals with big hair.	Kudzu, brand-new sequoias and bilbaos; not-as-cute giant guinea pigs.
2–67 million	Vayozoic	Sedentary	Chilly, even bundled up, gum erosion, must chew carefully, don't get up too quick.	Mammals resembling upright opossums who wear hats.
67–140 million	Mess O'Zoic	Vivacious	Fabulous variety of sauropods, theropods, every kind of pods; diplodocus pretty cocky.	Flightless birds; legless snakes; frogs the size of a St. Bernard; mosquitoes like seagulls.

YEARS AGO	ERA	PERIOD	ACTIVITY	DOMINANT
140–208 million	Big Mess O'Zoic	Upper Jurassic	Trial-and-error mating among hybrids; rodents the size of elephants, elephants no bigger than mice; piles of dead pre-sonar bats.	T-Shmex, sexually ambiguous dinosaur who tries to find self.
208–250 million	Hopeless Mess O'Zoic	Wiseassic	Discontinued prototypes; limited-time-only species, ambitious fish.	Talking carp; common ancestor of dog and man, capable of walking self.
250–290 million	Slowozoic	Notmuch-assic	Collision of continents: Africa abuts South America; Kenosha rams Racine; Maine has to be pulled from Labrador.	Cats land on feet; sloths wait it out; cephalopods oblivious.

YEARS AGO	ERA	PERIOD	ACTIVITY	DOMINANT
290–570 million	Slow-o-ozoic	Fergetta-boutic	Fools' paradise of symbiotic, if weird look-ing, plants and animals of surprising complexity with-out the usual complications.	Fairies; sprites; things that go bump in the night; Earthbound angels await-ing theological developments; bed bugs.
570 million–oh, 3.8 billion	Proto-plasmic	Teenypodic	One-celled organisms form unions; bacteria not looked down upon; hosts few, far between.	Paramecia do backstroke in primordial soup; viruses vie with germs.

UNITED STATES PATENT OFFICE

ABRAHAM LINCOLN, OF SPRINGFIELD, ILLINOIS.

BUOYING VESSELS OVER SHOALS.

Specification forming part of Letters Patent No. 6,469, dated May 22, 1849; application filed March 10, 1849.

To all whom it may concern:

Be it known that I, Abraham Lincoln, of Springfield, in the County of Sangamon, in the State of Illinois, have invented a new and improved manner of combining adjustable buoyant air chambers with a steamboat or other vessel for the purpose of enabling their draught of water to be readily lessened to enable them to pass over bars, or through shallow water, without discharging their cargoes ; and I do hereby declare the following to be a full, clear, and exact description thereof, reference being had to the accompanying drawings making a part of this specification. Similar letters indicate like parts in all the figures.

The buoyant chambers A, A, which I employ, are constructed in such a manner that they can be expanded so as to hold a large volume of air when required for use, and can be contracted, into a very small space and safely secured as soon as their services can be dispensed with.

Fig. 1, is a side elevation of a vessel with the buoyant chambers combined therewith, expanded ;

Fig. 2, is a transverse section of the same with the buoyant chambers contracted.

Fig. 3, is a longitudinal vertical section through the centre of one of the buoyant chambers, and the box B, for receiving it when contracted, which is secured to the lower guard of the vessel.

The top *g*, and bottom *h*, of each buoyant chamber, is composed of plank or metal, of suitable strength and stiffness, and the flexible sides and ends of the chambers, are composed of india-rubber cloth, or other suitable water-proof cloth, securely united to the edges and ends of the top and bottom of the chambers.

The sides of the chambers may be stayed and supported centrally by a frame *k*, as shown in Fig. 3, or as many stays may be combined with them as may be necessary to give them the requisite fullness and strength when expanded.

The buoyant chambers are suspended and operated as follows : A suitable number of vertical shafts or spars D, D, are combined with each of the chambers, as represented in Figs. 2 and 3, to wit : The shafts work freely in apertures formed in the upper sides of the chambers, and their lower ends are permanently secured to the under sides of the chambers : The vertical shafts or spars (D,D,) pass up through the top of the boxes B, B, on the lower guards of the vessel, and then through its upper guards, or some other suitable support, to keep them in a vertical position.

The vertical shafts (D, D,) are connected to the main shaft C, which passes longitudinally through the centre of the vessel—just below its upper deck—by endless ropes *f, f*, as represented in Fig. 2: The said ropes, *f, f*, being wound several times around the main shaft C, then passing outwards over sheaves or rollers attached to the upper deck or guards of the vessel, from which they descend along the inner sides of the vertical shafts or spars D, D, to sheaves or rollers connected to the boxes B, B, and thence rise to the main shaft (C,) again.

The ropes *f, f*, are connected to the vertical shafts at *i, i*, as shown in Figs. 1 and 2. It will therefore be perceived, that by turning the main shaft C, in one direction, the buoyant chambers will be expanded into the position shown in Fig. 1; and by turning the shaft in an opposite direction, the chambers will be contracted into the position shown in Fig. 2.

In Fig. 3, *e, e*, are check ropes, made fast to the tops of the boxes B, B, and to the upper sides of the buoyant chambers ; which ropes catch and retain the upper sides of the chambers when their lower sides are forced down, and cause the chambers to be expanded to their full capacity. By varying the length of the check ropes, the depth of immersion of the buoyant chambers can be governed. A suitable number of openings *m, m*, are formed in the upper sides of the buoyant chambers, for the admission and emission of air when the chambers are expanded and contracted.

The ropes *f, f*, that connect the main shaft C, with the shafts or spars D, D, (rising from

THINGS WE DIDN'T KNOW WE NEEDED
HONEST ABE'S BOAT BUOY

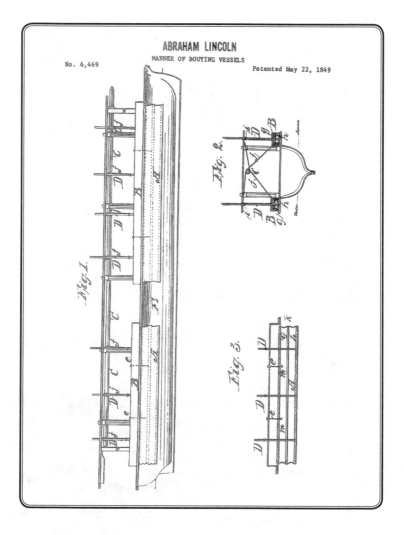

1. Your breath is ____ percent water.
    (a) 99
    (b) 99.77
    (c) 99.9

2. Having a friend at your side makes an impending hill seem:
    (a) insurmountable
    (b) 5 percent less steep
    (c) 10–15 percent less steep than it is

3. Doctors recommend _____ for the old arthritis.

    (a) 5 glasses of wine a day
    (b) 5 glasses of wine a week
    (c) you can't drink enough

4. Which of the following may work like Viagra...if you know what I mean?

    (a) mango

    (b) passion fruit

    (c) watermelon

5. There is some evidence that male breasts, or Travoltas, are on the upswing due to estrogen mimics in what?

6. When they weren't flying, Pterosaurs used their wings for:

    (a) legs

    (b) arms

    (c) camp stools

7. Your daughter's "not fair" reaction is chemically dictated by:

    (a) estrogen

    (b) endorphins

    (c) serotonin

8. The Milky Way is a(n):

    (a) duopus

    (b) quadropus

    (c) octopus

9. Do fruit flies stay more active if there are young fruit flies around?

FRUIT FLY

10. The solar system is:

    (a) dented, and thus damaged goods

    (b) leaking cosmic gas

    (c) humming ever so low

WHAD'YA KNOW ABOUT SCIENCE? (ROUND 5 ANSWERS)

1. (a) 99 percent water and 1 percent you, including some 200 compounds such as DNA, proteins, and fats. You can have fat breath.

2. (c) 10–15 percent less steep; if you climb every mountain, have a friend with you. It won't turn them into molehills, but psychologically it helps, according to the Englishmen who went up a hill but came down a mountain at the University of Plymouth in the UK.

3. (b) 5 glasses of wine a week, more if you got it really bad—get someone to pull the corks for you. The Karolinska Inskatute in Sweden found that a nice Cabernet before bed can lower the risk of arthritis 50 percent. Plus, other studies find you get all kinds of good flavonoids! Lift your glasses!

4. (c) Start with one watermelon and increase dosage as needed.

5. Water bottles. Bisphenol-A (BPA) in plastic fools the body into thinking it's drinking from a female, according to a study at Cardiff University in Wales.

6. (a) Legs; silly to let a 10-meter span go to waste. The Pterosaurs stalked their prey awing on land using their wings as walkers while they got their stubby little legs going.

7. (c) The neurotransmitter serotonin spends most of its time regulating aggression, but low levels can produce a feeling of being treated unfairly, at least if you're a female going to UCLA.

8. Surpringly, (a) just two arms on our home galaxy, the other two being pseudopods.

9. You bet. Chun-Fang Wu at Iowa found that *drosophilia melanogaster*, the elder, demonstrated youthful vigor when in the presence of young ones, arguing favorably for extended fruit fly families.

10. (a) Dented, although "damaged goods" is an editorial comment. Scientists tell us it's all poked in on one end, "like a giant hand" is pushing it. What does that tell you, scientists?

WHAD'YA KNOW

ABOUT

ODDS AND ENDS?

SELF-HELP FOR THE
SELF-HELPLESS

Σαε Ολδ Σαε Ολδ; ηατχηα Γοννα ο?

L et me cut to the chase: we all have a purpose. Well, maybe
not all. And maybe not the *purpose* you would have proposed,
but a purpose, from the Middle English *purpose* and the French
purposer: to intend, propose, to get around to it. No two *purposes*
are alike...otherwise they're nothing like snowflakes. Botanically
speaking, the flowering of human consciousness produces a fruit;
the pit being your *soul*, the pulp the *ego*, the skin the *id*, and the
puree your *purpose*.

One's *purpose* exists in the *now* and *then*, and, then, only *here* and
there. It is possible to misplace your *purpose*, but not on *purpose*.

Purpose is a noun, but increasingly is being verbed—*to purpose*—and used as a gerund, *purposing*, joining the company of *being*, *becoming*, *kvetching*, *hyperventilating*, *extra-vehiculating*. Life *is* purposing, and I can't italicize that enough, all about assigning motive to one's actions, one's thinking, one's spouse. With purposing comes meaninging, giving meaning to what would otherwise seem mere reflexes or tics. Meaningness, if you will, may at first seem to be a meaningless pop philosophy attempt at a buzz word, but ask not for whom the Eckart Tolles, it tolls for thee. We can be meaning to get something done, be well-meaning, even be mean-spirited, or apply the golden mean: it's all the same to life.

What is the key? The key is the device that opens the lock. Usually Schlage, for some reason. *Mindful mindlessness*, if I haven't mentioned it, is the key to the door of your many-chambered nautilus, the seat of all mixed metaphors. One must unlock the door to come in, or it's breaking and entering. Mindful mindlessness is the technique which allows you to proceed as if you actually were thinking about what you were doing. *Mindful*—full of mind—*Mindlessness*—that which you don't mind, i.e., the quality of. *Effortless effort* was never easier. Certainly more so than the perplexing *everyday suchness* of the '70s, which thirty years later still makes no sense. What to do? Nothing. A CPA runs off with a receptionist half his age, what can you do? It's best not to get involved, and above all don't say anything to Bessie. Might as well broadcast it. The best action is often no action at all; the best inaction always is. There is power in "now," but "then" is money in the bank—and money is power.

MY LOVE AFFAIR WITH THE BEATLES

That I love you more than any other guy.
I know that it was you cause
I looked up to see your face.
Although your mind's opaque.
I saw the light. I saw the light.
I could tell the world
A thing or two about our love.
Say the word.
The things you do

About the good things that we can have
Even though you're giving me
The same old lie.
If we close our eyes.
and I believe her.
I got no time for trivialities.
I'm the one who wants you.
He promises the earth to me

The world is treating me bad.
I'm not going to make it—
I'm not that kind of man.
I could turn away
And you won't see me
This could only happen to me.
All I do is hang my head and moan.

That I'm not trying to pretend.
Meaningless.
I will say the only words
That you understand.
Oww...Oww. Owww.
I think of love
As something new.
Half of what I say

Director Paul Berry and friend,
UW-Madison Herbarium

IT'S TWUE! IT'S TWUE!

W hat's huge and smelly and looks like a giant penis? No wonder *Amorphophallus* (*that's where the phallus comes in*) *titanum*, the corpse flower, draws crowds. The stench may be overwhelming, but it's nice to view an attraction and not have the smell of rotting flesh be your own. When this Audrey Jr. opens, it's special, or so the thousands filing past to pay their respects at the University of Wisconsin herbarium think. Giant flies and a Super Beetle were attracted, too, on this particular morning, normally a bit early even for old Up and Arum. Back in Indonesia they are known to sleep in. In Jakarta it is said that when the corpse flower blooms it is time to move on.

Titan Arum, at this very rare moment in June 2007, was fully erect in the Ag greenhouse at the University of Wisconsin, which would stay open all night—who could sleep? Besides, the smell is stronger at nightfall, and it takes a heady whiff to attract hordes of tourists, graduate students, and flower club ladies looking for a walk on the wild side. The process of blooming is intense and only lasts a few days, but boy oh boy, is it worth it. At full glory, when the flower looks like Penis on the Half-Shell, Titan Arum extends itself to a full 10 feet, maroon head unfurling 3 or 4 feet across. Before you know it, say 72 hours, it's over. Both of UW's Titan Arums bloomed in June 2005, but it's hard to predict when one or the other or both will again; they don't seem to be aware one of one another, and cross-pollination is strictly discouraged by their guardians, since who wants fruit that size? A cultivated Titan Arum (and some of them are, you know) will bloom only 3 or 4 times in its 40-year lifetime, and never leaves the house. UW botanists must be doing a corpse flower mating dance for theirs, however, since their Titan Arums burst forth 4 times in 5 years. Something in the humus?

OVER-THE-TOP PLANT RUNNERS-UP

2nd Place—*Rafflesia arnoldii*: giant parasitic Rafflesia, found in the Philippines, has the largest bloom in the world, four feet of it— and that's all. No stem, leaves, roots, nothing. It bites the vine that feeds it. Resembles the propeller of the Titanic with barnacles. Sometimes called the corpse flower, for its attractive ambiance, but we know it's not.

3rd Place—*Dracunculus vulgaris*: and it is, too, if a plant can be vulgar. Not just the mighty black appendage against the purple flower, but an aroma that makes you long for vomit. You can call it Voodoo Lily, but that don't change a thing. If you need one, try Oregon, California, Tennessee, or Puerto Rico. Vulgaris gets around.

4th Place—*Wollemia nobilis*: thought extinct, and not particularly missed, this former fossil tree has bark that looks like a convention of dung beetles on a pillar of elephant doo, and will have you wondering about what Mother Nature is on. Aside from that disturbing core, it's a rather nice conifer found only in New South Wales, where it's affectionately known as the Wollemi pine, although it is not a pine. They've been growing there since the Cretaceous, which is about 90 million years.

HAIL, KHAZARIA!

My first reaction, I have to admit, was relief. Gentiles have no way of knowing what a burden being Jewish can be—having to be good in school whether you're academically inclined or not, needing to bag one of the Jewish Trinity: a degree in medicine, law, and/or accounting. Stopped for no gain at contact sports because your mother owned the line of scrimmage. Having an alibi always at the ready for the night of the crucifixion. Pretending to like halvah. Being circumcised no matter what the current thinking is. It's not easy being Greenberg.

All that changed in an instant with a swab of my oldest brother Clayton's cheek, which he has a lot of. Clayton, born in 1936 (do the math), is at the point of his life—the end, I guess you'd call it (though may he live to be a hundred and twenty and now be just middle-aged)—where he feels the need to get his genome in order. Clayton has always believed himself a descendent of Hrólf Kraki of the *Ulfheðnar*, wolf-clad warriors who used to go berserk on the bear-clad Berserkers of old Iceland, somehow misplaced with Dave and Gerry Feldman of Milwaukee, Wisconsin. That's just Clayton. But the haplogroup doesn't fall too far from the family tree, and, turns out, neither the Norse yggdrasil he was expecting, or the Yew of an adopted Ashkenazi clan on 58th Street. The results, in a moment, but first a disclaimer: DNA analysis can only prove what you're not, not what you are, and there's quite bit more of what not than are.

Cutting to the haploid chase, not only is there no Feldman tribe shortlisted among the original twelve, our mitochondrial DNA, dear old R1b1c, has never set strand on the Holy Land, having uncoiled in another mythical place entirely: the north Caucasus Kingdom of Khazaria. Some background: around 838 AD, King Bulan of Khazaria decided to play a parlor game with the state religion, at the time Turkic shamanism was worshipping a not-altogether-satisfying snow-white goose. King Bulan had the idea of having a Muslim, a Christian, and a Jew not go into a bar, but, rather, join him in the royal antechamber and pitch him their religions, with the best spiel becoming the official religion of Khazaria. While the Muslim and Christian portrayed various restrictive moral strictures with no re-ward in this lifetime, the Jew offered wholesale and was awarded the franchise. Within a generation, Khazaria retooled itself as a Jewish Homeland for gentiles and blue-eyed Jews (with no correction) were *de rigueur*.

So we, Clayton included, are Aryans, and at best converts, which mother always said were the worst. Mom, herself, was a Kahn, easily an Ellis Island mishearing of "Khazarian." The Kahns must have been in dry cleaning all the way from Timis to East Gary, Indiana. Dad was born in Kiev, historically the northernmost reaches of the Khazarian Motherland into the Rus. The Cossacks would be chagrined to know all those years they were actually terrorizing fellow Caucasians (not that we expect an apology any time soon). We're more Aryan than Hitler. Put that in your Riefenstahl and Leni it. It's a shock to the system (all this aggravation for nothing) but not all bad: Michael Chabon, in *Gentlemen of the Road*, portrays the Khazarians as Jews with swords, and very successful at statecraft even with taking Saturdays off. Plus, no chance of Tay-Sachs. Still, it's going to take a while to adjust, with no known ethnic dishes, traditions, or dances. "Wandering Caucasians" does not have the same panache as our former descriptive, and, if we Khazars are chosen, nobody remembers for what.

THANKS FOR THE MEMOS:
PEG O' MY FART

To: Therapy Staff

From: Ellen

I first want to say how much I love and appreciate each of you. If I didn't love you, it would be hard to say the following; but because I do, I must, even though it is difficult.

It has come to my attention that one or more of you is regularly passing gas in the inner office.

Please stop it! This is not a joke! That is a small area; it has poor ventilation, and it causes problems for those working in there.

Peg did not bring this to my attention. They do not know of this memo, and I prefer it not be discussed with them. It you want (or need) to discuss this with me (especially if it is your problem), I will do so. (Gas or flatulence indicates GI problems; you may want to discuss this with your doctor.)

Thanks for helping me air this out.

WHAD'YA KNOW ABOUT
ODDS AND ENDS?
ROUND 1

1. Look straight into his/her eyes and smile if you want to:

    (a) be considered attractive

    (b) lie

    (c) pick his/her pocket

2. If it's protein you're after, should you go with the oatmeal or the ale?

3. Whose coffee "has no flaws"?

    (a) Dunkin Donuts

    (b) McDonald's

    (c) Starbucks

4. Match the fragrance with the celebrity:

    (a) Glow   (1) Donald Trump

    (b) Curious   (2) Jennifer Lopez

    (c) The Fragrance   (3) Britney Spears

5. By fiat, a C-cup holds ____ fluid ounces.
   (a) 13
   (b) 21
   (c) 27

6. If trading for a Presbyterian pastor, you'd have to give up a Baptist senior pastor and:
   (a) $11,000
   (b) $23,000
   (c) a Buick Le Sabre and an organist to be named later

7. Match the predominant aging fear with the nationality:
   (a) German   (1) Weight gain
   (b) Swedish   (2) Memory loss
   (c) Dutch   (3) Flagging sexuality

8. In the time it takes to say your name, the national debt has grown:
   (a) $47.50
   (b) $20,108
   (c) $33,333.34

9. High-resolution imaging has discovered the Mona Lisa's
   (a) Adam's apple
   (b) eyebrows
   (c) slight moustache

10. The *Guinness Book* record for microbe longevity is _____ years.

    (a) 50,000

    (b) 100,000

    (c) 163,007

☞ Researchers at the University of Bristol in the UK have been treating rat depression with the Mycobacterium microbe, with good results.

☞ Straight hair actually tangles more than curly hair, since the greater the angle of intersection, the more likely hairs will knot.

☞ The oldest sheet music yet discovered was a little ditty the Ugorits, who lived in what is now Syria, inscribed around 1400 BC.

☞ According to the bee census, there are 19,200 species of bee.

☞ Reincarnation time for aluminum cans is 3 months.

☞ In sales rank, it's (1) the Bible, (2) *Gone with the Wind*, and (3) *The Lord of the Rings*.

WHAD'YA KNOW ABOUT ODDS AND ENDS? (ROUND 1 ANSWERS)

1. (a) Be considered attractive, or so says Aberdeen University in the UK, where facial body language has been studied to within an inch of your nose. This also works to sell term life insurance.

2. Ale, and it goes down a lot quicker, too. Turns out Guinness is a meal in a glass with 18.6 grams of dark effervescent protein per pint.

3. (b) Mickey D's, the only flaw being when it lands in your crotch after hitting the car window at the drive-through, but, hey, that's actionable. *Consumer Reports* rates them over Dunkin Donuts and Starbucks, which it chastised as "burnt and bitter."

4. (a)-(2); (b)-(3); (c)-(1). OK, Trump is obviously Curious...no, that's Britney (after Hairless went nowhere); The Donald is The Fragrance, like there could be no others; and JLo's the Glow (of motherhood?). Liz Taylor's still got the White Diamonds, although she doesn't take them out much anymore.

5. (b) 21 ounces by general agreement, and there's one meeting I'm sorry I missed. A holds 8 oz., B holds 13 oz., and, the big boys, D holds a full 27 ounces if you give full measure.

6. (a) Presbyterian pastors are pricey, but a good Baptist senior pastor and $11K should do it, maybe a vicar to be named later.

7. (a)-(2); (b)-(3); (c)-(1). With Swedes it's sex, with Germans it's memory, and with the Dutch it's weight gain, even on the verge of losing pretty much all of it.

8. (c) $33,333.43, if you're Alvin Berg; $66,666.86 if you're Maya Golden-Krasner. Too bad they ran out of money to keep the National Debt Clock going.

9. (b) Her eyebrows; genteel women would pluck them in those days, but the Mona's lack of same probably occurred after some over-zealous cleaning by a curator who is no longer with the Louvre.

10. (b) Some controversy here—UC–Berkeley claims to have found living 100,000-year-old bacteria under 3 kilometers of snow in the Antarctic, but Raul Cano has revived some 30-million-year-old bacteria from the gut of a very old bee. Not sure if you can count all those dormant years or not.

BEST MOVIE MOMENTS

1. **"They're coming!"** from *Invasion of the Body Snatchers* (1956): Kevin McCarthy's frantic exhortations on the Santa Monica freeway (where traffic is inexplicably moving), warning that the pods are already in Orange County and the replicants are already in place in Studio City. Commonplace now, but crazed professionals weaving through rushing traffic stood out in 1956. Dr. Miles J. Bennell was Jeremiah of the '50s and the last physician on Earth making house calls.

2. **The omelet** in *Big Night* (1996): After preparing a feast that would choke Babette for no-show Louis Prima, Stanley Tucci

(Secondo) lovingly folds himself into an omelet in the kitchen. Didn't shower after *Psycho*; made a lot of omelets after *Big Night*—none approaching Secondo's. The man *was* the omelet.

3. Speaking of **Psycho**, not so much the shower scene but **the car sinking** in that handy swamp out back, stopping—cut to Norman chewing his fingernails—then sinking again to the uncharted depths for the sluice pond. God knows what else was already lining the bottom; Mom's boyfriend's Buick for sure. Special mention goes to Janet Leigh for being Janet Leigh. She and Lee Remick, and the young (circa *The Apartment*) Shirley MacLaine—they don't make them like that anymore. You can't beat Janet Leigh in a big white Playtex in a crummy hotel in Juarez in *A Touch of Evil*, that flashlight picking her out from across the way!

4. Paddy Chayefsky's **Network**, which gives us the divinely or demonically inspired TV news anchor, Howard Beale, is famous for the Beale rant, "I'm mad as hell, and I'm not going to take this anymore!" parroted by New Yorkers through their open windows across all five boroughs. But Chayefsky also presages reality television with the network's willingness to go to any extreme to attract ratings:

> HOWARD BEALE and MAX SCHUMACHER, two TV newsmen
>
> INT. A BAR—3:00 A.M. Any bar. Mostly empty. MAX and HOWARD in a booth, so sodden drunk they are sober—

Howard: I'm going to kill myself—

Max: Oh, shit, Howard—

Howard: I'm going to blow my brains out right on the air, right in the middle of the seven o'clock news.

Max: You'll get a hell of a rating, I'll tell you that, a fifty share easy—

Howard: You think so?

Max: We could make a series out of it. *Suicide of the Week.* Hell, why limit ourselves? *Execution of the Week—the Madame Defarge Show!* Every Sunday night, bring your knitting and watch somebody get guillotined, hung, electrocuted, gassed. For a logo, we'll have some brute with a black hood over his head. Think of the spin-offs—*Rape of the Week—*

Howard: (beginning to get caught up in the idea) *Terrorist of the Week?*

Max: Beautiful!

Howard: How about *Coliseum '74?* Every week we throw some Christians to the lions!—

Max: Fantastic! *The Death Hour!* I love it! Suicides, assassinations, mad bombers, Mafia hitmen, murder in the barbershop, human sacrifices in witches' covens, automobile smashups. *The Death Hour!* A great Sunday night show for the whole family. We'll wipe fucking Disney right off the air.

5. *The Thing from Another World* (1951): A lot to like here, from the surprisingly creditable Groucho-lackey George Fenneman as a scientist, to the nice touch of the electric blanket on the block of ice encasing the murderous vegetarian alien, and, jeeze, the whole opening sequence where in true Air Force fashion they blow the flying saucer to smithereens trying to remove it from the Arctic ice. A few heat bombs go a long way. For me it will always be the little flat of baby carrots breathing in and out that the naïve botanist has managed to start under grow lights. Baby carrots—with lungs!

6. In *Mr. Blandings Builds His Dream House*, Mrs. Blandings (the wonderful Myrna Loy) gives color instructions to the painters, as written by Norman Frank and Melvin Panama:

    Muriel: Now I want the living room to be a soft green. (*Pedelford nods*) Not quite as bluish as a robin's egg, but yet not as yellow as daffodil buds.

    Pedelford: Mm.

    Muriel: (*handing him a sample*) The best sample I could get is a little too yellow, but don't let whoever mixes it go to the other extreme and get it too blue. It should just be sort of a grayish yellow green.

    Pedelford: (*making a note*) Mm-hmm.

    (*They turn to the dining room.*)

    Muriel: Now the dining room I'd like yellow. Not just yellow, a very gay yellow.

Pedelford: Mm-hmm.

Muriel: Something bright and sunshiny. (*sudden inspiration*) I tell you, Mr. Pedelford, if you'll just send one of your workmen to the A&P for a pound of their best butter and match it exactly, you can't go wrong.

Pedelford: (*making a note*) Mm.

Muriel: This is the paper we're going to use here in the foyer. (*Hands sample to him*) It's flowered but I don't want the ceiling to match any of the colors of the flowers. There are some little dots in the background, and it's these dots I want you to match. Not the little greenish dots near the hollyhock leaf, but the little bluish dot between the rosebud and the delphinium blossom. Is that clear?

(*Pedelford looks carefully at the sample, then*)

Pedelford: (*making note*) Mm-hmm.

Muriel: The kitchen's to be white. Not a cold, antiseptic hospital white—a little warmer but not to suggest any other color but white.

Pedelford: (*note*) Mm.

Muriel: Now for the powder room, I want you to match this thread. (*hands him thread*) You can see it's practically an apple red. Somewhere between a healthy Winesap and an unripened Jonathan.

Pedelford: (*making note*) Mm.

(*There is a crash from the kitchen*)

Muriel: Will you excuse me?

(*Muriel hastily exits toward the kitchen. Pedelford turns to his assistant.*)

Pedelford: Got it, Charlie?

Charlie: (*deadpan; indicating rooms with his thumb*) Green, yellow, blue, white, red.

Pedelford: Check.

7. *No Country for Old Men* (2007) wins for best use of pneumatic devices to advance plot under the steady hand of Chigurh, who apparently worked in a stockyard at one time. Any number of door knobs are blown out, although maybe the Coens go to that once too often. The cattle-killing device held to the head of a hapless motorist is a real headturner, showing the versatility of his little portable setup. I'll stick with the door-knobs. A shout-out to Cormac McCarthy for advances in pneumatics.

8. De Niro's finger in a teenage Juliette Lewis's mouth was the scariest of the many scary things Max Cady did to the Bowden

Family in the *Cape Fear* (1992) remake; although, when you think about it, it pales next to the thought of Juliette with Woody Allen. Robert Mitchum, as depraved as his character was, never thought to do that to Lori Martin in the original (1961), although he became the poster boy for insolence for all time.

9. The rotting fish in *Blood Simple* (1984): oh yeah, there was a dead guy slumped on the desk as well, but it was that nice string of crappies rotting there that got to you. The guy deserved it (sending a hit man after his wife) but the fish, well, they were just used as a graphic element. Dan Hedaya's hand out of shallow grave and W. Emmet Walsh dying under a dripping sink in this one too.

10. Too obvious, but Jack Nicholson's Robert Dupea order at the diner in *Five Easy Pieces*:

> **Dupea:** I'd like a plain omelet, no potatoes, tomatoes instead, a cuppa coffee, and wheat toast.
>
> **Waitress:** No substitutions.
>
> **Dupea:** What do you mean? You don't have any tomatoes?
>
> **Waitress:** Only what's on the menu. You can have a #2, plain omelet, comes with cottage fries and rolls.
>
> **Dupea:** I know what it comes with but it's not what I want.
>
> **Waitress:** I'll come back when you make up your mind.
>
> **Dupea:** Wait a minute, I have made up my mind. I'd like an plain omelet, no potatoes on the plate, a cuppa coffee, and a side order of wheat toast.

Waitress: I'm sorry, we don't have any side orders of toast. It's a muffin or a coffee roll.

Dupea: What do you mean you don't make side orders of toast. You make sandwiches, don't you?

Waitress: Would you like to talk to the manager?

Dupea: You've got bread and a toaster of some kind?

Waitress: I don't make the rules.

Dupea: Okay, I'll make it as easy for you as I can. I'd like an omelet plain and a chicken salad sandwich on wheat toast, no mayonnaise, no butter, no lettuce. And a cup of coffee.

Waitress: A #2, chicken sal sand. Hold the butter, the lettuce, the mayonnaise, and a cup of coffee. Anything else?

Dupea: Yeah, now all you have to do is hold the chicken, bring me the toast, give me a check for the chicken salad sandwich, and you haven't broken any rules.

Waitress: You want me to hold the chicken, huh?

Dupea: I want you to hold it between your knees.

EXTRAS–READ
ALL ABOUT 'EM!

James Gleason, whose Brooklyn accent and side of the mouth delivery made him one of the most widely used supporting actors in Hollywood films, from *Forty Naughty Girls* to *Murder on a Bridle Path*; also the newspaper editor behind *Meet John Doe*.

Harold Huber, NYU grad born Huberman in the Bronx, became the slicked-back heavy of undetermined ethnicity in Charlie Chan movies and the stool pigeon in *The Thin Man*.

Richard Loo, who, despite being Chinese, played every sadistic Japanese commanding officer known to Hollywood. That was him in *God Is My Co-Pilot*.

Frank McHugh, who did it all with his almost-leading-man good looks, from lead to sidekick to comic relief, starting with *The Dawn Patrol* through *The Front Page*, *Ever Since Eve*, *On Your Toes*, *Going My Way*, and as the monkey man in *Mighty Joe Young*.

Mike Mazurki, the ex wrestler whose chiseled bad looks and slur made him a natural for Moose Malloy in *Murder, My Sweet*, where he full-nelsoned Dick Powell.

Beryl Mercer, every son's mother, who in *All Quiet on the Western Front* cautioned Lew Ayres not against bullets but against "all the no-good women out there." As Ma Powers in *The Public Enemy*,

she opened the door to have her gangster son, a gagged and trussed James Cagney, fall in.

Mantan "feets, do your stuff" Moreland, Charlie Chan's chauffer, *King of the Zombies*, vaudeville master of the "incomplete sentence" routine seen in the Chan movies.

Barbara Nichols, that kind of woman in *That Kind of Woman*, as well as *Naked and the Dead*, *Pal Joey*, and *Sweet Smell of Success*.

Alan Mowbray, the butler's butler who mastered his masters in *Topper* and scores of other comedies and dramas; helped found the Screen Actors Guild and was the devil in the Hal Roach propaganda film *The Devil with Hitler*. Played assassin Val Parnell in *The Man Who Knew Too Much*.

Maria Ouspenskaya, who, as the gypsy Maleva, clued Lon Chaney in to the downside of werewolf bites in *The Wolf Man*, learned the Stanislavski Method from Stanislavski at the Moscow Art Theater.

Franklin Pangborn, ubiquitous and hilarious desk clerk, undisputed master of the pince nez (were they glued on?), and the only man who ever tried to get Ginger Rogers out of a hotel room. That was him in *The Bank Dick* and *Never Give a Sucker an Even Break*.

THANKS FOR THE MEMOS:
NOT IF I SEE YOU FIRST

Subject: Farewell

Dear Coworkers and Managers,

As many of you probably know, today is my last day. But before I leave, I wanted to take this opportunity to let you know what a great and distinct pleasure it has been to type "Today is my last day."

For nearly as long as I've worked here, I've hoped that I might one day leave this company. And now that this dream has become a reality, please know that I could not have reached this goal without your unending lack of support. Words cannot express my gratitude for the words of gratitude you did not express.

I would especially like to thank all of my managers both past and present. In an age where miscommunication is all too common, you consistently impressed and inspired me with the sheer magnitude of your misinformation, ignorance, and intolerance for true talent. It takes a strong man to admit his mistake—it takes a stronger man to attribute his mistake to me.

Over the past seven years, you have taught me more than I could ever ask for and, in most cases, ever did ask for. I have been fortunate enough to work with some absolutely interchangeable supervisors on a wide variety of seemingly identical projects—an invaluable lesson in overcoming daily tedium in overcoming daily tedium in overcoming daily tedium.

Your demands were high and your patience short, but I take great solace knowing that my work, as stated in my annual review, "meets expectation." That is the type of praise that sends a man home happy after a 10-hour day, smiling his way through half a bottle of meets expectation scotch with a meets expectation cigar.

And to most of my peers: even though we barely acknowledged each other within these office walls, I hope that in the future, should we pass on the street, you will regard me the same way as I regard you: sans eye contact.

WHAD'YA KNOW ABOUT ODDS AND ENDS? ROUND 2

1. The National Association of Uniform Manufacturers has voted which state troopers the best dressed?
   - (a) Pennsylvania
   - (b) Washington
   - (c) Ohio

2. Among car colors, _____ is the new silver.
   - (a) white
   - (b) black
   - (c) silver

3. True or False: The more wine costs, the better it tastes.

4. What is ultrasonically welded from 3 pieces of nylon and lycra and has 10 percent less drag than its predecessor?

5. The official and proper medical symbol is:
   - (a) snake on a staff
   - (b) 2 snakes on a staff, with wings
   - (c) the urine sample

6. In perhaps the 2,001st of its 2,000 uses, WD-40 is being sprayed on the public toilet seats of England—why?

7. According to *Bon Appétit*, is it gauche to bang your knife against the water glass if you have a few things you'd like to say at the table?

8. According to Amir Aczel (in *Chance*), to maximize the odds of finding the perfect mate, you should date ____ of the available candidates and marry the best of that sampling.

    (a) 37 percent

    (b) 51 percent

    (c) all

9. Which takes more steps to walk off: a cheeseburger, or a doughnut and a garden salad with fat-free dressing?

10. Adam's first wife was:

    (a) Dolores

    (b) Estelle

    (c) Lillith

WHAD'YA KNOW ABOUT ODDS AND ENDS? (ROUND 2 ANSWERS)

1. (b) Hands down, Washington State Troopers; it's the bow tie.

2. (a) White is the new silver, black is the new white, and Buick maroon is still Buick maroon.

3. *Mais oui.* The California Institute of Technology overpriced some pedestrian cabernet and people lapped—lapped—it up.

4. The Speedo Laser Racer swimsuit, which made such a splash at the Beijing Olympics. The suits, soon to be available to the general public, provide excellent protection against belly flops.

5. (a) Snake on a staff; do not confuse the official medical symbol, the rod of Asclepius, with the Caduceus, or rod of Hermes, the flying snaked staff the messenger god used to clear his path. In fact, I would check the seal on your internist's diploma right now.

6. Well, there was that guy glued to the toilet at Target, but in England they've found if you WD the seat and the tank top, the cocaine just congeals.

7. No; since 1922, Emily Post has been banging her water glass to add a few words about what is and what isn't proper conduct at affairs of this sort. It should be done lightly, and with a smile,

and only if you're expected to get up and say something, and never by the help.

8. (a) Simply date 37 percent of all those willing to go out with you and one of them, mathematically, will rise to the top. For stubborn cases, you may have to go 56–57 percent. If you've dated all of them, you've gone too far.

9. The doughnut and garden salad, an interesting culinary choice, takes a mere 7,910 steps to walk off; the quarter-pounder cheeseburger, 7,590. Either way, it's nearly four miles, and time for supper.

10. (c) Lillith; he and Estelle just dated for a while. Lillith is the mystery woman of the Bible, seen by some as Adam's first wife and others as a screech-owl she demon of the night, if there's any difference there. Just kidding, dear.

BACK PAIN? KILL HER

I UNREAD MESSAGE

I hope they don't outlaw spam any time soon since (1) then only outlaws will spam and (2) who else bothers to write any more, especially offering to give my pecker legendary status. I'm touched somebody cares. If there aren't already, there should be Spammies for outstanding, above and beyond the call junk mail. I have some nominations—in the "re:" category...

    re: avertive parsimony ywca catheter

    re: Alexis foppish bylaw declarative

    re: newscast vegetate potboil

re: Amadeus crosswort goad

re: Billy, the orgy.

re: Boyd, but Cardiff bernardo bleeker vernal Moslem

re: pete amphibious venturi

re: hallelujah spangle acknowledge

re: nikko emil businessman criminal

William Burroughs would have been hard pressed to cut and paste some of this stuff, which must have come out of a PC that scuttles on insect legs, but is it literature? Kind of a literary mis-sampling, perhaps, like the body of this missive for eDrugs wrong out of Dickens:

to move a box, I answered. Wot box said the long-legged young man. I told him mine, which was down that street there, and which I wanted him to take to the Dover coach office for sixpence. Done with you for a tanner said the long legged young man and directly

They tend to leave you hanging like that, but then, so did the serialized Dickens. I assumed he moved the box, and I'm guessing he got the tanner. A spammer in Russia, looking for entree to the English-speaking market, is going to grab whatever's at hand, and chances are it's Dickens. You can bet the estate won't get a tanner for its being troubled.

Estelle Jackson and Brinna Murphy, in their respective messages "Re: Brian May vandal" and "after Michelson or secure," paint an attractive picture of the Golden Apple Gas stock offering at $1.10, projected to hit $3.75 in 12 to 18 days ("This is ready to Rock!") using none other than Uriah Heep to close the deal:

> Youre a devilish amiable looking fellow Gibbs just what you used to be having to take care of the most wonderful woman in the world restored the sunshine to his face be wanted on some business by Uriah said Sally yes and the sense of being unfit for days in London if I like it either on my way down into Suffolk or in coming back in a word in a close condone A waiter showed me into the dickey automaton and so did Mrs Strong They sang together and played duets together and we had quite a very obdurate butcher as he stood scraping the great block in the shop and moreover

"Dickey automaton" may not be strictly *David Copperfield*, but you've got to admire "the sophism citric of despicable realm," whatever the source, whatever it means. With backing like this, how bad can the stock be?

I just received a prospectus for Hoodia—the life-changing appetite suppressant as seen on Oprah—from no less than Count Leo Tolstoy, which made the unusual pitch of the travails of Anna, a train accident, and whether to contact the husband or boyfriend. Mme. Bovary wrote and stopped just as quickly, but it was all about foot surgery. These days I've noticed an upsurge in erectile-dysfunction drugs using Samuel Beckett; *Waiting for Levitra* might seem counter-intuitive, but, maybe not:

410

Good. Now I can begin to suck. Watch me closely. I take a stone from the right pocket of my greatcoat, suck it, stop sucking it, put it in the left pocket of my greatcoat, the one empty (of stones). I take a second stone from the right pocket of my greatcoat, suck it put it in the left pocket of my greatcoat. And so on until the right pocket of my greatcoat is empty (apart from its usual and casual contents) and the six stones I have just sucked, one after the other, are all in the left pocket of my greatcoat. Pausing then, and concentrating, so as not to make a balls of it, I transfer to the right pocket of my greatcoat, in which there are no stones left, the five stones in the right pocket of my trousers, which I replace by the five stones in the left pocket of my trousers, which I replace by

...the "erection pack"? Ten Cialis and ten Viagra and a bottle of water from Your Canadian Pharmacy, all for $129.95 (US). They've got the Hoodia, too, I notice, and the same Human Growth Hormone they say Barry Bonds used. Beats sucking stones.

PHOBOPHOBIA ITSELF

Iknow what FDR was getting at, but the fact is if you fear fear itself, that's a lot. Pretty much fills your dance card of fear. At the very least, you're a candidate for IBS (not a cable network, it turns out, but irritable bowel syndrome), at which point you have nothing to fear but not finding a bathroom itself. Generalized panic disorder—anxiety attacks—that's the easy-to-get ticket to that rewarding sense of siege that we've come to expect from modern living. Mine is the occasional performance anxiety, but if you performed like I do you'd have it, too.

Some anxiety makes sense; if you didn't have it, there'd be something else wrong with you. Eating from street vendors, for example.

Dancing at a salsa club. Peeing off a moving boat in sight of the dockside diners. Speaking French to a Frenchman. The whole wide world of environmental anxieties, like agoraphobia—the fear of everything that's not you—and syngenesophobia—the fear of everyone related. With work, it's possible to have both mysophobia—fear of getting dirty—and ablutophobia—fear of bathing—simultaneously. So common is claustrophobia now, a person feels hemmed in.

Not all phobias are problems; some, like otterphobia—fear of otters—or parthenophobia—fear of virgins—will probably never come to the fore. On the other hand, anthropophobia—the being uncomfortable around your genus—will keep you home on a Friday night, where, hopefully, you won't contract clinophobia—fear of your bed. Having said that, let us not forget that the autophobe has nothing to fear but fear himself, the didaskaleinophobe, nothing to fear but school itself, the batrachophobe, nothing to fear but frogs themselves, and the politicophobe has nothing to fear but FDR himself.

CROP CIRCLE
OUTLOOK: JUNE

The crop circle in the shape of a Guernsey in three-quarters profile discovered near New Holstein, WI, is actually the work of local farmer and environmental artist John Schmudlap, who says he was just trying to get in on the corn-maze craze. So the tower was not to hone in alien spacecraft, but to look for city folk not used to being lost in the corn. Flattened wheat not that far from Sioux City, Iowa, on closer observation was found to have a herd of Herefords on top of it. All appeared to be local. Art students from Drake took responsibility for the Audi logo in the oats near Keokuk. Still unexplained is what force or cataclysm mowed down the Goldenrod in the vacant lot in New Berlin, WI; what those big concrete circles you see are when flying over the nation's midsection, more to the west; and who or what took a roll in the hay near the sign for Intercourse, PA, off highway 30. Come to think of it, it was closer to bird-in-hand.

FLAT EARTH
V. HOLLOW EARTH

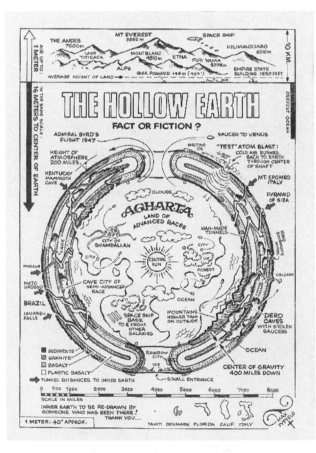

Flat Earth	Hollow Earth
Explains flat tax.	Explains big hole at south pole.
Why don't things roll off?	Why don't things fall in?
Unlikely, since promoted by English wanker.	Nobody has anything to gain from it.
OK, but no turtle.	Means Earth has an asshole.
Why's everybody else round?	...filled with nougat?
Flop over = rotation?	Float away like a balloon?
Pictures from space parallax or something?	Can I see an X-ray?
Why would it be?	Seriously, why would it be?
What did Magellan sail around?	What did Jules Verne journey to the center of?
Explains why things "fall flat."	Accounts for hollow feeling.
What's up with the moon?	Does Uranus have a hole?

THE WISDOM OF SOLOMON, OR SAY ANYTHING

Behold, thou art fair, my love; behold, thou art fair; thou hast doves' eyes within thy locks[1]: thy hair is as a flock of goats[2], that appear from mount Gilead.

Thy teeth are like a flock of sheep that are even shorn[3], which came up from the washing[4]; whereof every one bear twins, and none is barren among them[5].

Thy lips are like a thread of scarlet[6], and thy speech is comely[7]: thy temples are like a piece of a pomegranate[8] within thy locks.

Thy neck is like the tower of David builded for an armory[9], whereon there hang a thousand bucklers, all shields of mighty men[10].

Thy two breasts are like two young roes that are twins, which feed among the lilies[11].

Until the day break, and the shadows flee away, I will get me to the mountain of myrrh, and to the hill of frankincense[12].

Thou art all fair, my love; there is no spot in thee[13].

Come with me from Lebanon, my spouse, with me from Lebanon[14]: look from the top of Amana, from the top of Shenir and Hermon[15], from the lions' dens, from the mountains of the leopards.

Thou hast ravished my heart, my sister, my spouse[16]; thou hast ravished my heart with one of thine eyes[17], with one chain of thy neck.

How fair is thy love, my sister, my spouse![18] how much better is thy love than wine![19] and the smell of thine ointments than all spices![20]

Thy lips, O my spouse, drop as the honeycomb: honey and milk are under thy tongue; and the smell of thy garments is like the smell of Lebanon[21].

A garden enclosed is my sister, my spouse; a spring shut up, a fountain sealed[22].

Thy plants are an orchard of pomegranates, with pleasant fruits; camphor, with spikenard[23], Spikenard and saffron; calamus and cinnamon, with all trees of frankincense; myrrh and aloes, with all the chief spices.[24] A fountain of gardens, a well of living waters, and streams from Lebanon[25].

Awake, O north wind; and come, thou south; blow upon my garden, that the spices thereof may flow out. Let my beloved come into his garden, and eat his pleasant fruits[26].

---

1   Pigeon eyes peeking out from bangs. I'm just saying.
2   How did she take that, I wonder?
3   So far so good.
4   Clean—and white—and—fuzzy?
5   Let's pray this is a mixed metaphor. If her teeth each bear twins something is dreadfully wrong a good 5,000 years before oral surgery could help.
6   Thin?
7   Voice important because you're going to be hearing a lot of it
8   Dove eyes in a *pomegranate*.
9   Do you mean to say this; swan-like, sure, but like an armory tower? How do you top that?
10 Neck big enough for a thousand guys to hang their bucklers on. What every woman loves to hear.
11 OK . . .
12 Well get thee, already.
13 For thou art pomegranate not apple.
14 Lebanon. Knew there was a catch
15 Mt. Heron, with Syrians on top.
16 At least as worrisome as "My Darling, My Hamburger."
17 Not that thou art one-eyed.
18 Again with that.
19 And cheaper!
20 Takes care of herself—good selling point.
21 Kiss a hive you're going to get stung.
22 If she is your sister, your spouse let's hope her fountain is sealed up.
23 Actual orchards? Metaphorical ones?
24 If the good nard, worth a pretty shekel. Calamus an aphrodisiac Solomon stored in drums.
25 Yes, but how much under water?
26 She went for it!—with pleasant fruit relish!

THANKS FOR THE MEMOS:
BUT WHERE ARE THE POP TARTS?

Betsy, in the roll-top desk, in a pop tarts box, are
a TON of "Crucifixion" nails—should you need
them for next Sunday's service.

—Andi

WHAD'YA KNOW ABOUT
ODDS AND ENDS?
ROUND 3

1. A Japanese engineer's difficulty understanding a technician's southern accent resulted in:

   (a) IM

   (b) the fax machine

   (c) the breathalyzer

2. Do you swim faster in water or goo—or is it a wash?

3. Lucy, the biggest diamond in the cosmos, is a crystallized star weighing in at:

   (a) 10 trillion carats

   (b) 10 trillion trillion carats

   (c) 10 billion trillion trillion carats, after cutting and polishing

4. In Aramaic, what does "Spreet mets'aayaa deelaak huu" mean?

   (a) I blame the Romans

   (b) Everlasting love of the Savior

   (c) Thine is the medium Sprite

5. Are you better off being licked by your dog or cat?

6. Of the hundreds of colors lures come in, how many can a bass see?
   (a) 0
   (b) 2
   (c) 1

7. Can you eat the stickers on fruit?

8. What is the trick behind Houdini's "Metamorphosis"?

9. The Order of the Elephant—Bengali or Danish?

10. In car-salesman lingo, what's the "Monroney"?

WHAD'YA KNOW ABOUT ODDS AND ENDS? (ROUND 3 ANSWERS)

1. (b) The fax machine; invented by Shintaro "Sam" Asano, who as a project engineer with Japanese citizenship at NASA was not allowed on the launch site and was forced to devise a graphic means of communications with his cohort from Tuscaloosa.

2. It's a wash. Ed Cussler at the University of Minnesota tried all kinds of goo, up to and including Jello, but was surprised to find that it didn't seem to make much difference.

3. (c) 10 billion trillion trillion carats, and only a hundred bucks holds it for you. The catch is, you'll have to pick it up...in Centaurus, about 50 light years from Earth. And then you have to think about the setting.

4. (c) Thine is the medium Sprite, according to a reporter from the *Manchester Guardian*, who heard it used on the set of Mel Gibson's *The Passion of the Christ* by Jesus trying to stay in character.

5. "Better off" is subjective, but if it's bacteria you're worried about, choose the cat-licker. Fifth-grader Lacey Lafromboise of Albequerque in her science fair project, using her pets and

the Minot State University labs, found her two dogs had twice the bacteria in their drool as her two cats. Lauren Palmer, in her California State science fair project, found that the worst animals to swap spit with are humans, having 250 bacteria colonies on their agar plate as compared to 100 for poochey.

6. (b) 2; a bass can see red and green, but not Red Green.

7. Yes, but are you really that lazy? Granted, they are kind of hard to get off. By U.S. government mandate, however, they must be edible...if not tasty.

8. It's all in the trunks, not Houdini's but the big ones on stage; the Outagamie Museum of Appleton, WI, Houdini's hometown, said a trap door on the trunk allowed the handcuffed-in-a-sack magician to tumble out and into a second trunk while freeing himself in 3 seconds. As easy as that.

9. The Danish Order of the Elephant, as established by King Christian V in 1693, honors Danish royalty, other heads of state, and assorted bigwigs. When an Elephant Knight dies, they have to give the sash back. Queen Elizabeth is an Elephant, and so is Nelson Mandela.

10. A Monroney, after legendary salesman Mike Monroney, of Oklahoma, is that short piece of fiction known as the sticker, and you would be the stickee. Bird-dog is a referral kickback; gasser, a guy who acts like he has the money to buy but doesn't; hammer, to exert pressure on the buyer to close, and after that, roll 'em.

THE TEN SERVING SUGGESTIONS

WHAT WITH THE TEN COMMANDMENTS BEING SO CONTROVERSIAL...

1. Do not do unto others—people sue.

2. Respect thy elders, for they is you.

3. Walk a mile in your neighbor's moccasins, but not literally.

4. It is better to have loved and lost. Far.

5. "Follow your nose" has no deeper meaning.

6. Archimedes didn't own a lever.

7. God plays Go Fish with the Universe.

8. The longest journey begins with a Canadair commuter jet.

9. On the other hand...no feet, no need for shoes.

10. After postmodern, what?

Statement of Taxes

For Year 1941

No. *977*   Ward *1*

Total Valuation $ *910/100*

PITTSTON, PA.
AUG 16
3:30 PM
1941

ONE CENT

Mills		THIS SIDE OF CARD IS FOR ADDRESS
4.0 State	$	
5.2 County	$ *4* *73*	*Thos Yachna*
3 Poor	$ *3* *03*	
18 Borough	$ *18* *18*	
46 School	$ *41* *86*	*313 Bennett*
School Per Capita	$ *2* *50*	
TOTAL	*70* *30*	DURYEA, PA.

Pay promptly and Save 5 per cent

BRING THIS CARD WITH YOU

☞ Read Other Side

HAVE THERE
ALWAYS BEEN TAXES?

While, historically, the line between taxation and outright
extortion is fuzzy, it's not taxing credulity to say that
whether the best of times or the worst of times, they have always
been taxing times. Some Biblical historians believe that Moses
come down from Sinai with a set of tax tables. Egyptian tomb
reliefs provide little tax relief, depicting Eternal Revenue officials
accurately as adder-headed jackals driving taxpaying herds into
the maws of vulture-headed treasury officials. A haiku dating to

the Chou Dynasty in China pays tribute to the overlord and his t
ax collectors:

Big rat
Big rat
Do not gobble our millet.

Taxation probably began in the cradle of civilization and will undoubtedly follow it to the grave. Ancient kings—who claimed to be
gods on leave—intercepted offerings made to the main office before
they were burnt and of no use to anyone. In return, the subjugated
were provided with all the benefits of the modern state: incessant
warfare, a rigid class system, human sacrifice to sweeten the pot, and
public buildings. In Mesopotamia, Egypt, Sumer, India, and China,
taxes were collected in kind—in fact, in all kinds: horns, feathers,
jewels, grain, oxen, flax, jetsam, daughters, precious metals, fish, oil,
sheep, produce, and bric-a-brac. The Caesars were justly famous for
being rendered unto, while the provincials were merely rendered.
Jesus coaxed a publican, Zacchaeus, out of a sycamore in Jericho,
resulting in the miracle of the penitent tax collector, although it did
not end the practice.

DEDUCT THIS

I'm not sure if you can deduct the cost of the *Kiplinger Report*—not ones to toot their own horn, they haven't said, but Kiplinger knows deductions, and recently shared some you may not have thought up that worked for somebody else. For example, if you feed feral cats on your farm or junkyard, to help control other feral critters, you can deduct the kibble. Feed the rats directly, you can take nothing. The food I provide my dog, Sugar, pricey and scientific a diet though it may be, is not deductible because he has no job description, or duties *per se* unless it's bunny patrol. However, should he have to relocate to look for work, I can deduct the entire cost of moving Sugar and his pet puggle, Tina, to Saskatoon. Moreover, if I attend a convention of Labrador owners on Baffin Island, it will be deductible as long as it's not pleasure, which shouldn't be hard to prove. Somebody high up in the tax code has even thoughtfully allowed an earmark for Caribbean meetings but, me, I just like the sound of Baffin Island.

Less useful is the body oil deduction a bodybuilder can take, as a tool of the trade. I glisten, it's for naught. Steroids, a major expense for body builders and, if you believe the reports, other athletes as well, are not deductible, although the legal expense they incur is. Surgical augmentations are not necessarily tit-for-tat deductions, although the Kiplinger boys are unashamedly titillated by Chesty Love, exotic performer, who made a convincing case to an IRS auditor that if 56-FFs aren't deductible, nothing is. While the IRS does not rule out deductibility for male enhancement, so far no one has stood up and claimed it. Stomach stapling is allowable on a gut to gut basis, and Lasik surgery only if you do look better without glasses. A nose job disguised as sinus surgery fools no one.

Kiplinger reports that beer given away may be deductible, providing you can establish that business was discussed while buying a round for the house, and not merely the result of being a good drunk. Meals are deductible if an agenda, schematic, or flow chart on a napkin or tablecloth can be produced. Home entertainers can put in a swimming pool and take it as a medical expense under a wide variety of available conditions—check your local listings for conditions near you. Medical marijuana—even the good shit—is not deductible as a medical expense, although it can lead to stronger and more deductible medical conditions. If you have clients, and the word is loosely defined, and meet them on the lawn, you can deduct Lawnboy, the mosquito trap, and the grill, and save the receipts for any seeds that blow into your yard. Alaskans who need something to offset the annual state stipend should buy and fly a Cessna to keep an eye on your condo rental outside Denali, and write it all off. Babysitters, yes, if you're leaving the kids with a sitter not to go out to party, but to make the world a better place—and are prepared to prove it, once you have.

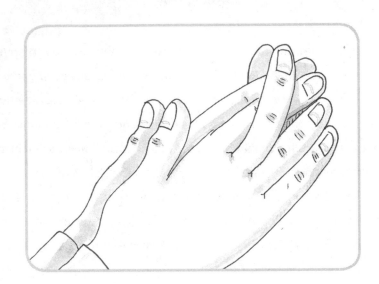

THIS I BELIEVE

Like Mom used to say, you've got to have a little something here, tap-tap. I thought she meant gas, a little being a good thing because it proved you were eating. Now I know she meant belief, like in Maxwell House Coffee or Hanes Support Hose. That it depends on which waitress you get at Heinemann's as to how big your slice of pie is, because some of them are Jew-haters. You know, beliefs. Tap-tap, here. I've given it some thought, Mom, and

This (is what) I Believe:

Please join me in singing the opening coda: "I believe for every drop of rain that falls, someone gets wet." Thank you, you may be seated. Let us or leave us give thanks that each drop does not beget a flower, because we'd be up to our asses in blooms, many, if not most, of which could easily pass for weeds. Then you'd have "I believe for every drop of rain that falls, a wee-ed grows," which, meter problem aside, is more like it. I think it's important for everyone to have a belief, no matter how absurd or unlikely it may be, and I believe it's crucial they keep it to themselves, cozy and secure in the bosom of unassailability. Amen. Individual beliefs and farts, you know, everybody kind of likes their own. What to believe, what to believe? Laws of Nature, too easy, except for string theory, which I'm afraid might turn out to be right, in all ten dimensions. I'm having a lot of problems with three, I don't need aggravation from a barnacle reality on the hull of this one: scrape it off! Other realities are not in the purview of my health insurance which, once you get past the national debt deductible, only scantily covers a tiny list of rare conditions, nothing pre-existing like a parallel universe. Belief in God: yes, definitely, pending a sign, hopefully in universal graphics, archetype stick men illustrating something unmistakable. No angels, no pins, no saviors will call. That religion is best which religiosifies least. Man has free will, for all the good it does him, is my belief. You can't worry about the judgment of others, even if it is final. I believe in a God with a great sense of humor, like a big Dalai Lama, or a Salvador Dali Lama, you know, flaming giraffes to comically illustrate some point or another. I no longer resent being here for His amusement, and, in fact, I say: Look at this! As for political beliefs, you bet, I glom one of the shooting stars of beliefs, flashing through across the election cycle while the polls are still open in California, like young Elvis portentously saw in Flaming Star. *Politician* may not be a dirty word, but it's not a nice one. I nearly went into political science until I saw that the degree was awarded by a witch doctor. I guess if there's one belief you have to have in your wardrobe for mix 'n' match, it's the Golden Rule, although it suffers from having let Golden Books impinge on its trademark like it would impinge on theirs. The Golden Rule is something you can't argue with, unlike, say Hammurabi's Code: a man's house falls on your head, your house should fall on a man's head, or the time-honored Vendetta or blood-libel. Nowhere does it say, "Blood-libel unto others the way you would have them blood-libel unto you," yet. "Do unto and get the hell out," the current reconstruction, is not nearly as golden as the original. No one's going to needlepoint the Brass Rule.

BUDDY HOLY

THE D-LIST

It may have been a dream, but I saw Sonny Bono, in one of those furry linings he used to wear, skiing down Ricola mountain, right between the guys blowing the Alpine horns. Bad taste, especially for a throat lozenge, but not impossible ever since Fred Astaire broke the plaster ceiling by dancing over it with the Dirt Devil in lieu of Ginger Rogers, becoming the first dead celebrity to strike commercial pay dirt. Duke Wayne, Gandhi, Lou Gehrig, Bogart, Cagney, Gene Kelly, Einstein, Elvis, and Martin Luther King Jr. soon followed, and suddenly it was *Dawn of the Dead* on Madison Avenue. Louis Armstrong was blowing again before he was even cold, Pearl Bailey's feet hurt posthumously, and, more recently, Kurt Cobain sat on a cloud, an angel in Doc Martens, along with less-likely candidates Sid Vicious, Joey Ramone, and Joe Strummer. Well, Joey Ramone, maybe. Clayton Moore, the Lone Ranger, surprisingly, remains untapped for Range Rover, but they will not let poor Orville Redenbacher or his pal from the Motion Picture and Television Retirement Home Col. Sanders rest in peace, they who gave their all in life for the dubious causes of popcorn and fried chicken. The Rat Pack still ring-a-ding-a-dings, with Sammy Davis Jr. playing Applebee's, which swings like the Sands.

Forest Lawn is rocking: Elvis, whose stock had dipped if not plunged at the time of his death, bounced back to the top of the charts at 49 million dollars last year, just ahead of give rest-in-peace a chance John Lennon at 44 million, whose estate benefited from the Beatles' settlements with EMI and the other Apple, followed by the perennial good if dead man, Charles Schulz, apparently buried with his Speedball, at 35 million, mostly from the playlet they force middle school drama students to do. Bullets for newcomers Tupac Shakur, Steve McQueen, and James Brown, coming soon to a Diet Coke, athletic shoe, or family restaurant near you.

Forbes's Top 13 Dead Celebrities

1. Elvis Presley

2. John Lennon

3. Charles Schulz

4. George Harrison

5. Albert Einstein

6. Andy Warhol

7. Dr. Seuss (Theodore Geisel)

8. Tupac Shakur

9. Marilyn Monroe

10. Steve McQueen

11. James Brown

12. Bob Marley

13. James Dean

AND THE JELLY-FACED
WOMEN ALL SNEEZE

It would be impossible to convey to my girls, able to effortlessly download and savor Disturbed's "Down With the Sickness," the impact of Bill Fritch slipping me "Bringing It All Back Home" in Miss Stern's speech class—white-shirted, black-framed, be-dickied, black Sta-Pressed pants with black penny loafers and white socks me. After playing it over and over behind closed doors in my room, I came out dressed the same, but I was changed, my adolescent angst and generalized anger against all the hypocrisy of the world given a voice, and one not much better than mine, also fine-tuned in mafter training. Dylan was the anti-Anka, and Mrs. Brown and her lovely daughter could just scratch their heads, while the big girls did cry.

Much of it was obscure and still made sense. A.J. Weberman may have been the official garbologist, but I was a lyric diver in the great bin of Dylan. Implications are always in flux: Dylan is like paint that never dries. I tend to believe in the *literal* Dylan, that there is a place where insurance men strap heart attack machines across the shoulders of the insured. And then the kerosene. That's always been my experience with insurance men. I've been stuck inside Mobile and had the Memphis blues—you would, too. In "All Along the Watchtower," which I'm pretty sure was a movie with Tyrone Power, plowmen dig his Earth—soybeans, probably, around here—without knowing what any of it is worth. Not their job, just hired on to Maggie's Farm, where her husband puts his cigars out in their faces just for kicks. Dylan says, "She wears an Egyptian ring," she wears an Egyptian ring, simple as that. "For Christmas buy her a drum," she wants one, even if she ends up leaning that picture of you in your wheelchair up against it, a pretty passive-aggressive thing to do. Why "don't" the pump work?—"the vandals took the handles." You don't need Doppler radar to know which way the wind blows. Objectivist— sometimes things are just things. "His bedroom window is made out of sticks." Craftsman School. "Hypnotist collector" is tougher, but, after all, there are people who collect anything—that's the point. I could tell you what it means but I just don't know how.

Not that there isn't meaning beyond the literal, portents, even— "Masters of War" came out 40 years before the video game, banks today do give out road maps of the soul, and Highway 61 is nothing if not the Information Highway, where, with a click, you can find "forty red white and blue shoe strings / And a thousand telephones that don't ring." You see sailors in beauty parlors. All the time. Old girlfriends? Some *are* mathematicians, some are carpenter's wives. Dylan is about lyrical imagery: making love with the new boyfriend with the garage door open, she put her hand in his chalk, cut to "Shakespeare in the alley with his pointy shoes and his bells"… Dylan the modern Shakespeare, dressed as the Fool, who, in the Bard, is the wise one (just like the geek in Mr. Jones). The French girl is down with that. "Gypsy Davy with his fantastic collection of stamps." Striking. Bending down to tie his shoe in front of the top-less dancer—click. It's a photo. Priceless. Imagine Toulouse Lautrec padding up to a Can-Can girl in full Can. The groundbreaking "Idiot Wind," the first in-your-face-Twain doing something about the weather, while it "blows like a circle around (his) skull / from the Grand Coulee Dam to the Capital." As a kid in Milwaukee, I won-dered around which landmarks our Idiot Wind might blow—From Gimbels downtown to Red Star Yeast? Yes, for me. To this day I'm not just hungry, "I'm hungry like a man in drag."

THANKS FOR THE MEMOS: INITIATE IT EVEYTIME

I have a couple of issues that I need to address with all of you with some of you more than others. I will say this one more time and if I see it happen again you will be eliminated from bonus for the month. First of all, I know some of you are not morning people, if your not I don't care! When you walk into this office (MY OFFICE) you are all to be on top of things, energetic, and enthusiastic.

WHEN YOU WALK INTO MY OFFICE IN THE MORNING, YOU ARE REQUIRED TO SAY GOOD MORNING, YOU ARE TO BE ENERGETIC AND POSITIVE. I SHOULD BE ABLE TO SENSE IT AND MOST IMPORTANTLY, THE CUSTOMER NEEDS TO SENSE IT. CUSTOMERS ARE TO FEEL WELCOME AND DELITED TO BE HERE.

I HAVE NOTICE OVER THE PAST MONTH THAT FOR THE FIRST HOUR OR TWO CUSTOMERS WALK IN,,,,,,AND EACH ONE OF YOU HESITATE YOUR "GOOD MORNING" TO CUSTOMERS IS WEAK (I HAVE NOTICED SOME OF YOU NOT EVEN SAY THAT TO A CUTOMER, OR SAY HELLO) THAT IS UNACCEPTABLE. THIS WILL NOT HAPPEN AGAIN.

I WILL REPEAT MYSELF, IF YOU ARE NOT A MORNING PERSON, I DON'T CARE. THIS IS MY OFFICE WITH MY RULES AND THIS A REQUIREMENT. YOU ARE TO WALK INTO THIS OFFICE WITH A GREETING OF "GOOD MORNING" TO YOUR STAFF, TEAM, MANAGEMENT AND ALL CUSTOMERS, YOU ARE NOT TO WAIT FOR SOMEONE TO SAY IT YOU, YOU ARE TO INITIATE IT EVEYTIME!!!!!!!!!!!!!!!!!

Maybe some of you are not used to doing this, and maybe some of you don't like to do this I DO NOT CARE!!! IT IS MANDATORY!

I HAVE REPEATED MYSELF WAY TO MANY TIMES ABOUT THIS, AND I AM TIRED OF IT. AT THIS POINT AND TIME, IF YOU DO NOT FOLLOW THIS RULE IT IS AN AUTOMATIC ELIMINATION OF BONUS FOR THE MONTH NO QUESTIONS ASKED, NO SECOND CHANCE!!!!!!!!!!!!!!!!! ONE LAST THING, SOME OF YOU HAVE GONE OUT OF YOUR WAY TO DO THINGS FOR OTHERS. LIKE GETTING COFFEE, ETC IF SOMEONE GOES OUT OF THERE WAY FOR YOU SAY "THANK YOU" TO THAT PERSON LEARN TO RESPECT EACH OTHER.

I WANT AN EMAIL FROM EACH OF YOU THAT YOU HAVE READ THE ABOVE EMAIL AND UNDERSTAND IT.

Frank Danzig

GLOBAL MUTUAL FIDELITY FIELD REPRESENTATIVE

1. Carcinogenic polycyclic aromatic hydrocarbons are most likely to hit you at:
   (a) Howard Johnson's
   (b) rush hour
   (c) Mass

2. Has Jack Daniel's dropped from 86 to 80 proof, or is that an urban legend?

3. If you're giving somebody the whole *megillah*, what are you giving them?

4. If you're opposed to veal, _____ is supposed to taste a lot like it.
   (a) baby wasp
   (b) sea slug
   (c) lion

5. For total carnage, the Family Media Guide to Horror Film Death recommends:

    (a) *Halloween* 1–12

    (b) *Texas Chainsaw Massacre 2*

    (c) *Freddy vs. Jason*

6. True or False: Bolo ties were originally used to bring down game in South America.

7. Out on the links, "the yips" are:

    (a) loud, boorish golfers doing *Caddyshack* takes

    (b) the jerks

    (c) golfers who swing and miss

8. Which is the prunes wrapped in bacon, grilled, and served on buttered toast: devils on horseback or angels on horseback?

9. Mom should have warned you about:

    (a) shopping cart handles

    (b) straps on buses

    (c) toilet handles

10. In curling, what is the hack?

    (a) the foothold you push off of

    (b) that stoney thing with the handle

    (c) the broom

WHAD'YA KNOW ABOUT ODDS AND ENDS? (ROUND 4 ANSWERS)

1. (c) Mass; you will breathe in 20 times more of the aromatic carcinogens from incense than you will on the Interstate getting there.

2. It's an unfounded rumor started by Jim Beam.

3. The whole varnished truth, over-elaborated and belabored. From the Yiddish.

4. (c) Lion; in a blind taste test, diners frequently confused lion for veal. Lion may be the only thing that doesn't taste like chicken.

5. (c) With 167 impalings in 1 hour and 36 minutes, you can't beat *Freddy vs. Jason*, although many will try.

6. False; you're thinking of *boleadoros*, leather thongs that can take a monkey out of a tree.

7. (b) Jerks, or hand tremors, especially while penciling in your score.

8. Get it straight—prunes wrapped in bacon, *devils on horseback*, oysters wrapped in bacon, angels on horseback (shuck first).

9. (a) There's nothing more germ-infested that they've been able to find than shopping cart handles, unless it's those little seats

babies' butts have been all over. For those who want the details: 1,100 colony-forming units of bacteria per 10 sq cm.

10. (a) The rubber foothold you push off with when you slide the stone through the house towards the biter in an attempt to make an anti-freeze and not go off the broom.

THE COLLECTOR

Cat whiskers. Envelope linings. Bricks. Kentucky Fried Chicken bones. You name it, somebody saves it. Proof is Philadelphia's Mutter Museum Chevalier Jackson Collection of things swallowed and removed, which has several surprises I don't want to spoil for you, and its collection of celebrity body parts—Grover Cleveland's tumor and the thorax of John Wilkes Booth—is second to none. Not everything would occur to everybody: my friend Jeff's collection of individual frames where nothing happens in the comic strip "Nancy" is a good example; not to mention, please, a friend's grandpa in Montana who put his urine up in quart jars. Vibrators you can see how you might accumulate, but hog oilers? Things giraffe, pineapple, or pig. Metered postmarks. Small animal teeth and bones. Gallstones. Clouds. I don't know, that's what she said. Cumulus, mostly. The Chicago World's Fair of 1893, in miniature. Famous hair. Bar codes. Wrappers of anything, surprisingly collectible since they're usually thrown away.

Tim from Toledo collects broken drumsticks of famous drummers, including one from Rick Allen, Def Leopard's one-armed drummer, almost but not quite in the same league as Cynthia Plaster Caster's molds of rock musician's manliness, from Bowie to Gene Simmons (in that order). Souvenir boulders, just like Lucy in *The Long, Long Trailer*. William Davis King (the patron saint of collectors) craves "put postage here's," every known variety of tuna label, and freebies from the Akron-Canton airport. A perennial are potato chips resembling Charles de Gaulle, or somebody, sadly, now with no Johnny Carson to show an interest. Cereal box and Cracker Jack toys and detergent giveaways. Milk bottles, beer bottles, amphoras—any kind of bottle. Patent medicine. Lint. Bullets. Racially offensive Japanese products, like Darkie toothpaste. Fallout shelter candy. Found photographs. Dental appliances. Hardware fittings, washers, nuts and bolts...anything that might come in handy but doesn't. Used nails—justify that. Dirt from around the world. The Liberace Museum in Las Vegas, in toto, and the Helendale, California Exotic World's collection of famous g-strings. The nooses, gas chamber supplies, and high voltage seating of the Colorado Territorial Museum in Cañon City.

The Cup Museum in Sister Bay, WI, with its styrofoam cup signed by Henry Kissinger. A waitress from a well known diner in St. Paul, MN, claims to have a good deal of the balled-up and thrown-under-the-table napkins of Garrison Keillor. Bowling Green's Kentucky Museum has a collection of "feather crowns," the ring of feathers found inside the pillow of the deceased, particularly those it took a while to discover. Napoleon's penis, a true one-of-a-kind, going through probate even as we speak, from the estate of urologist John Lattimer of Columbia University. His daughter doesn't think she'll keep it—I guess she's not a saver.

THAT OLD
RETURN-HOME PAIN

Nostalgia is the inescapable consequence of having a past, no matter how inconsequential. Although it has come to mean a longing for things or times past, the word has Greek roots: *nostos*, "a return home," and *algos*, "pain," which may refer to the pain of either being away from or returning home. Back in the day, a decent interval was observed before waxing nostalgic, but today, thanks to the pace of life and TiVo, it's common to experience instant nostalgia, or so I fondly remember just thinking. This hit home the other day when I overheard a kid wistfully recalling the early work of Miley Cyrus. I visit the past but try to not overstay my welcome, and never take the bait of a Summer of Love reference (for me the Summer of Self-love) or Woodstock, which I thought at the time was a lot of trouble to go through for a Sha Na Na concert.

Nevertheless, there is a nightstand *cum* time capsule which lies in the same soil as our conjugal bed. Every so often I dump the contents out of one or the other and wallow in wholesale sentimental associations. Among my souvenirs, you'd find: a pen my uncle Abe gave me, inscribed "Stolen from A. Bass"; a tortoiseshell barrette of unknown origin; my John Lennon wire rims; a quarter flattened on the railroad tracks along St. Paul St.; my late cat Arthur's front tooth, knocked out in a brawl; Dad's cat's-eye tie clip; a buffalo nickel; a key to an apartment whose locks have long since been changed; a Mount St. Helens postcard; an aluminum medallion from a bus station machine stamped MIKE FELDMAN, AGE 9; a Polaroid of my ex-wife's ex Appaloosa; a rawhide chew from my friend and confidant Rocky; the business card of Juan de la Torres of Santa Fe ("You always have a friend, odd jobs, gutters, and down-spouts"); a tiny Cracker Jack magic slate; my only toddler picture, in which I appear to be an unhappy little teapot and you can see the shadow of Dad's fedora on the front lawn; a packet of pansy seeds packed fresh for 1976; a silver pocket watch, broken, of the type once worn by nuns; my National Merit Certificate from high school with the Roto Rooter number in Mom's pencil; a New York subway token; a rusting McGovern button; a newspaper article taped to an index card, dated 12/31/51 by my father, describing the removal of the foot of two-year-old Michael Feldman from the basement sewer with a new device caller the "Foot Extractor" ("Michael didn't even cry"); a bar chip from the Crystal Corner, good for one large drink; a standing room media pass to any Cubs game in 1984; a letter from a collection agency in mint condition; lyrics to a song entitled "Anyone but You" on the back of a Union Cab check stub; an unwound cassette of Ram Dass; a little boy who pees but doesn't anymore; a souvenir button from Grandma Prisbrey's Bottle Village in the Simi Valley; and a fortune from a Chinese restaurant: "You will save anything."

TYPE SMITTEN

Ideally, you could come up with something *Brazil*-like, a Remington Noiseless that with each muted slap sent an impulse to Office 2007 for further consideration. You can get a program that makes your keyboard clack, but without the spin of the roller and smell of the ribbon it fools no one. The typewriter was invented in my hometown of Milwaukee (Christopher Sholes, 1867), which might account for my loyalty, although I don't feel the same way about Pabst Blue Ribbon or Harnischfeger

cranes. There is something about hunting and pecking on an Underwood Champion or a Royal De Luxe that
makes you choose your letters carefully and your
words economically, as if the type were being set
with hot lead and you didn't want any mistakes flung
in your literal lap top. My first school themes were
hammered out on Dad's ancient L.C. Smith (from back
in the day before he met Corona), she of the basket
shift and the prancing horses tattoo. A stately
old gal, although her "e" and "h" were cratered
and had to be taken on faith, exclamations marks
(as in "…a book everyone who likes to laugh should
read!") were period-backspace-small "l," and the
type itself was elite, making it tough to fill up
one required typewritten page with as few words as
possible, even fudging at 2½ spacing. When I won
the daily double at Arlington my first year in college, I put the 90-dollar payout into an Olivetti
Primavera portable, the model that turned out to
be Inverno for the once highly regard Turinos,
all extruded plastic with characters that tangled
like those in a spaghetti western. Certainly wasn't
Tennessee Williams's Olivetti Studio 44 Named
Desire, nor Dylan's Lexicon 80 with the answer,
my friend, "Blowin' in the Wind." I still suffer
from the romantic delusion that if I had Dashiell

Hammett's Royal De Luxe, I could write "Return of the Maltese Falcon," or, on Hemingway's Corona 3 perched on the bar at the Cafe de Medicis, peck out "The Sun Also Sets" between rounds.

I actually saw Faulkner's Underwood Standard on the desk at Rowan Oak, in the little bedroom his wife didn't enter, which had plot outlines right on the walls. It was all I could do not to pack it up and attempt to resurrect the Snopes tribe. The docent said school kids always ask where the monitor is. Jack Kerouac used the same model to run all 120 feet of "On the Road" into, a man literally on a roll, and, according to Ginsberg, fastest of the beat typists, at 120 wpm. Manual snob that I am, I assumed no great art had ever been written on an IBM Selectric until reading that Ralph Ellison wrote "Invisible Man" on his, while Hunter S. Thompson fired repeated rounds from one into "Fear and Loathing." William S. Burroughs never wrote on a Burroughs Standard, preferring to pawn a succession of Remingtons to fill his prescription needs. His, by the way, were not the anatomically incorrect hybrid bug machines of the Cronenberg "Naked Lunch," but could have been.

Issac Bashevis Singer believed his Yiddishe tricked-out Underwood Universal was possessed with a dybbuk, a mischievous demon that completed stories it liked and defeated those it didn't. The first author of renown ever to own or attempt to use a typewriter was Mark Twain, who purchased a Hammond in 1873 for the princely sum of 125 dollars, after being seduced by a young woman who could turn out 57 words in a minute, even though they turned out to be the same 57 words each time she did it. Twain writes, by hand, of his early experience as a typist:

At home I played with the toy, repeated and repeated and repeated "The Boy stood on the Burning Deck," until I could turn that boy's adventure out at a rate of twelve words a minute; then I resumed the pen, for business, and only worked the machine to astonish inquiring visitors. They carried off many reams of the boy and his burning deck.

☞ Ayn Rand, née Alisha Rosenbaum, used the last name of her Remington Rand.

☞ Stephen King's wife, Tabby, claims he married her for her Olivetti portable.

☞ Like Twain, Robert Louis Stevenson had a Hammond machine, but used it only for invoices.

☞ Hemingway wrote, "A typewriter writes the way people talk."

☞ John Updike said his Olivetti and he were "growing old and erratic together," and didn't think he'd bother to fix either.

FELDMAN'S BEST FRIEND

Ididn't have my first dog until I was 21 and married, too old for a dog and too young for a wife. We couldn't have major mammals when I was a kid because Clayton and Howie had a collie before I was born which came to an untimely end beneath an ice truck. This ban held even though the odds on a pet being crushed by an ice truck were greatly reduced and in fact nearly zero by the time I came along in all that post-war euphoria. The biggest thing we had was a guinea pig, Tony, which Arthur rescued from a research lab he was spending the summer in as a youth-inizer. Other than Tony, there were just the ladybugs that came in under the window I pathetically tried threading leashes to, and the usual ill-advised assortment of painted turtles from vacations, goldfish from fairs, and a salamander Arthur found while fishing who quickly went AWOL, turning up months later mummified under his slipper in the closet.

But a boy needs a dog. I'm not sure about girls; mine seem pretty oblivious of theirs; Nora, while she's made a wonderful doggy memory book of Sugar photos and drawings, won't go so far as to walk him, and Ellie mistakenly thought the thing she needed to love was a Puggle named Tina. She has subsequently been wrong about a quarterback and a hockey forward. It's a shame because a dog helps train you. If you don't get a dog by a certain age, let's say 11, you will never know how to scratch anyone behind their ear to give them pleasure or get accustomed to having your commands ignored, and you certainly will never know unconditional love. I can't remember the last time a female bounded up wagging her hinder in unmitigated joy as I cracked the door, unless it was on my way out. Cat lovers say this need for acceptance from something that will lick anything makes dog people insecure codependents, but Sugar and I just lift our legs to that. While I would only sniff a butt under the most carefully controlled conditions or lick my genitalia if I could, there is something about the dog that speaks to the man. I enjoy peeing in the backyard under the stars with my dog; it's just unfortunate that the neighbors put in a picture window on that side of the house. I relate to the way he looks around self-consciously when taking a squat because I do, too, under those conditions. I might also eat until I vomit, although I would not, then, have seconds.

Perhaps I got too attached to my first dog, Rocky. I loved the way he had what looked like the outline of his head, ears up, in white on his gold chest, like an emblem. He was completely untrained, and I respected that. When we lived in the country, there was nothing he liked better than a good severed cow leg, which I found touching, even though I had to drive one farm down further each morning to throw it back in the culvert. He could retrieve a cow leg from within a two-mile radius; I'm sure with a little practice he could've brought home some better cuts. I think I may have confused myself with Rocky at times; OK for a kid, but not so good when you're thirty. When you live alone with a dog for a while differences seem to disappear, the only one remaining that one of us enjoyed rolling on a carp, and one pooped and the other picked it up. He was high-strung and a barker, but I've lived with a lot worse since. Rocky and I had ten wonderful years right up until he chased a rabbit across the path of a Blazer and, having lost a step or two by then, failed to clear its grill. (The driver came out yelling, "Is he all right? It's only a light truck!")

Sugar, of course, can never be my first dog, and that makes a difference, but I can see that many of the traits I thought were uniquely Rocky—turning the head askance, for example, to feign understanding; very nearly being able to form the word "Out!" with lips that don't work that way; resting his head in my lap like I was the Buddha—all being, in fact, dog traits; the same ones that made man such a successfully domesticated species. While Rocky was a mutt, Sugar has a pedigree, putting him one up on me, but he doesn't flaunt it. He comes from hunting stock, his sire being Bodacious Black Gunstock: if I ever want to shoot ducks, he would be entirely in favor of it, since, so far, they have proven extremely difficult to swim out to and nab unwounded. Nothing incites him like a duck, unless it's a Pekinese. Hates small dogs. In fact, he's not much of a dog lover in general, considering himself to be more furry Feldman and less yellow lab. At first, I confess, I felt funny walking him because he looked like a gentile's dog, not a Jewish Shepard like Rocky, but now that his whines and mine are pretty much indistinguishable I feel he fits right in. I talk to Sugar, and confide in him, but nothing I don't want repeated; it's not the emotional dependence I had with Rocky or with the first wife, for that matter, but maybe that's just inevitable.

FAMOUS AND
NOT-SO LAST WORDS

When I was a kid, I thought if I didn't talk too much I could save some words so as not to run out mid-sentence while mortally wounded in the dust of Main Street, held up by a buddy, unable to finish my ultimate sentence. I'm talking last words, the final RIPoste you have coming and should utter when the time comes if you happen to go up in spontaneous human combustion in front of American Idol Rewind. Smoking slippers and red-hot titanium frames may not be how you'd like to be remembered. It's a good idea to rehearse your last words so you don't blow the line when it can't be fixed in the mix. Pope Alexander VI, for example, probably didn't intend "Wait a minute!" to be his last words; even in Latin, *exspecto a minute* is not memorable. You *exspecto* more from the Holy See. John Paul II at least said, "Amen." Gregory mentioned something about his nephew, but it was hushed up.

Humphrey Bogart had the best last words, "I should have switched from scotch to martinis," although Lou Costello's, "That was the best ice-cream soda I ever tasted," is a close second. Food does come up at these moments, and drink—Ulysses S. Grant called for "Water!", Admiral Nelson for "Drink, drink, fan, fan, rub, rub…," and just before a tableside assassination, Mexican revolutionary Alvaro Obregon ordered "mas totopos" (more chips)! Margaret Mitchell complained about the orange juice ("It tastes bad") and Keynes, always Keynesian, concluded, world economics aside, "I should have drunk more champagne." Asked by his wife if she should bake him some potatoes, Dutch poet Gerrit Achterberg uttered the poetic, "Yes, but not too many," and fell over dead, waiting. Tallulah Bankhead's "Codeine; bourbon" was characteristic. Hal Linden said Jack Soo, from *Barney Miller*, complained, "It must have been the coffee," while dying.

Some bon morts are inexplicable, like Boris Karloff saying, "Walter Pidgeon." *Walter Pidgeon* is the last thing you'd expect Boris Karloff to say, and, turns out, it was. Dutch Shultz, while never eloquent, was never less so than at the end: "Hey, Jimmie! The chimney sweeps. Talk to the sword. French Canadian Bean Soup." After all that time at Walden he had to think about it, you'd think Henry David Thoreau would have come up with something better than

"Moose. Indian." George Bernard Shaw, always at the ready, must have had "Dying is easy, comedy is hard" in his breast pocket for decades. The Red Baron said, simply, "Kaputt," while Ethan Allen, told the angels were waiting for him, reportedly said, "Let 'em wait!" In the middle of yet another "Tiptoe through the Tulips," Tiny Tim finally said, "No I won't!" and hit the sawdust. Lope de Vega, the playwright, closed act three with "Dante makes me sick."

Marie Antoinette may or may not have suggested cake as an alternative to bread, but nothing became her more than, having stepped on the executioner's toe, saying, "Pardon me, sir, I didn't do it on purpose" ...more than he could say. Abimelech, one of the Hebrew judges in Judges, crushed by a millstone dropped by a woman from a higher court, pleaded, "Draw your sword and kill me, so they can't say, 'A woman killed him.'" Sinatra said something stupid to Nancy before wing-a-ding winging it: "I'm loosey." It may have been the hemlock talking, but Socrates said to Crito, "We ought to offer a cock to Asclepius." Stan Laurel said, "I wish I was skiing." Never known for knowing when to get off, Jolson did in the end, saying, "I'm going, I'm going." Groucho, naturally, has the last word: "Die, my dear? Why that's the last thing I'll do!"

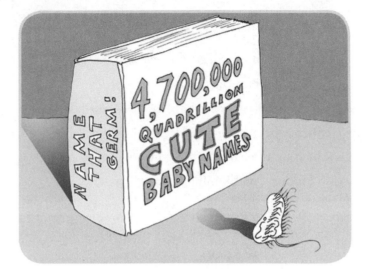

A DAY IN THE LIFE

In one day…

- …the Earth travels 1,609,000 miles
- …19 percent of all communications from the recently deceased will occur
- …a fruit fly can fly 6½ miles
- …carbon monoxide levels in the blood return to normal after quitting smoking
- …you must be arraigned for a crime committed in Massachusetts
- …you will cover 16,405,000 miles if traveling at 1 percent of the speed of light.

...a baby blue whale will gain 200 pounds

...the parasitic roundworm *Ascaris* lays 200,000 eggs

...you lose 7,000 brain cells

...you will say 7,000 words if female, 2,000 words if male

...you will lose between 40 and 100 hairs

...you will go to the bathroom 6 times

...you will lose about 14 million skin flakes

...you will laugh 300 times if you're 6 years old, 15 times if you're 40

...you will sweat 1 to 3 pints

...you will inhale 4,000 gallons of air

...you will service 26 hens 46 times, if you're a rooster

...and you'll produce 4,700,000 quadrillion offspring if you're a bacterium under ideal conditions.

THANKS FOR THE MEMOS:
WOW

To: All store managers

There must be 50 ways to say "You're Great!"

If you're looking for a new way to recognize the people you work with, try these phrases on for size.

way to go * super * outstanding * excellent * great * good work * neat * well done * remarkable * I knew you could do it * I'm proud of you * fantastic * superstar * looking good * bravo * hurray for you * beautiful * now you're flying * you're catching on * you've got it * you're special * you're incredible * hot dog * dynamite * you're unique * nothing can stop you now * good for you * you're a winner * remarkable job * beautiful work * you figured it out * terrific * magnificent * marvelous * what a victory * I admire you * spectacular * great idea * you've discovered something big * you figured it out * you're important * phenomenal * you're my hero * great success * super work * how creative * hip-hip-hooray * what a good listener * you're fun * you tried hard * you care * you mean a lot to me * you belong * I value your opinion * you've got a friend * I trust you * you make me laugh * you brighten my day * I respect you * I couldn't have done it without you * I like working with you * you just made my day

* WOW

1. In dance, a bun head with banana feet would be what?

2. What does a funambulist do for a living?
   (a) Walk tightropes
   (b) Swallow swords
   (c) Drive spikes into
       his or her nose

3. Dogs prefer:
   (a) hip-hop
   (b) country/western
   (c) eastern European balalaika music

4. Is the toilet seat cover the boon to womankind it pretends to be?

5. Al Qaeda operatives planning vacations need to ask their supervisors ____ weeks in advance.
   (a) 10
   (b) 36
   (c) are you kidding?

6. The Pink Zebra, Cherokee Purple, Wilgenberg, and Black Prince are all:

    (a) squashes

    (b) zinnias

    (c) tomatoes

7. Between a rock and a pebble is a:

    (a) hard place

    (b) cobble

    (c) pebbock

8. Do those fake owls do any good?

9. Do trees cause pollution?

10. Of the 30 million airline bags that go missing in a given year, how many are still on the loose?

    (a) 29 million

    (b) 200,000

    (c) just mine

☞ A left-handed snail is most likely to survive a crab attack.

☞ If you want to strike out a toddler, throw him a changeup.

☞ Scotch tape got its name after a customer accused 3M of being stingy with the adhesive.

> ☞ There are 5 Labradors for every shih tzu.
>
> ☞ The brand most mentioned in rap hits is Mercedes-Benz.
>
> ☞ The University of Pennsylvania found that people who bowl with strangers are the happiest bowlers.

WHAD'YA KNOW ABOUT ODDS AND ENDS? (ROUND 5 ANSWERS)

1. That would be a ballet dancer with high arches.

2. (a) A pretentious tightrope walker; from the Latin *funambulist*, a tightrope walker.

3. (b) Why Cottonelle would have any interest in the listening habits of dogs, I don't know, but their research shows dogs break down 18 percent country, 16 percent easy listening, 14 percent oldies, rock and pop 12 percent each, and only Snoop Dogg listens to hip-hop.

4. It most certainly is not, if paper, which placed on a wet toilet seat, ferries bacteria twixt toilet and tushies. I don't know about the endless plastic ones at airports, but they never work anyway.

5. (a) An al Qaeda terrorist must let his branch manager know at least 10 weeks in advance if he/she plans to take some time off.

6. (c) Tomatoes, the heirloom types you can pass on to your kids in lieu of an estate.

7. (b) Cobble; if you can't pick it up, it's a boulder. Rocks, when expensive, are ornamental. Pea-sized gravel is best for a driveway.

8. Well, for company, yes, but to scare off pests from your garden one expert said, "An Elvis doll would be as effective."

9. Ronald Reagan was right, trees cause pollution. The more trees you plant, the more CO_2 they inspire, and, whad'ya know, global warming. Don't yell at me, yell at Carnegie and Stanford.

10. (b) Amazingly, only 200,000 bags end up for sale at the Unclaimed Baggage Center in Scottsboro, Alabama, where Salvador Dali left his prints.

THANKS FOR THE MEMOS: LET'S NOT DO THE DEED DAMAGE TO OTHERS

안 내 문 (Notification)

♠ 제 목 : 주민 여러분께 당부드립니다.

♠ Subjet : Management office asks residents not to do.

▣. 남(이웃)에게 피해를 끼치는 행위를 하지맙시다.
  Let's not do the deed damage to others(neighbors).
  1. 저녁 9시 이후에는 소음을 내는 행위를 하지맙시다.
  After 9 PM, please try not to make a noise.
  2. 집안을 수리 할시는 주간에 하시기 바랍니다.
Activities that make noise should be done during the daytime.

▣. 현관문을 발로 차거나 라인계단을 뛰지 맙시다.
  Let's not kick porch door and run in stairs.

▣. 애완견의 대 소변을 철저하게 처리합시다.
  Make sure to pick up feces left by your pet.

▣. 불장난을 하지맙시다.(소화기 장난금지)
  (소화기는 화재 발생시에만 사용합니다.)
  Let's not do the playing with fire
  (the small arms uses at a fire extinguisher o'clock)

2007년 01 89

Life Apt management office

472

BONUS THANKS FOR THE MEMOS: RULES FOR PET BREEDING

가축사육 입주자 준수사항

■ 승강기, 화단, 옥상, 어린이 놀이터등에 가축(개)들의 배설물 방치 및 가축(개) 알레르기, 진드기, 기생충, 털갈이 등으로 위생상, 미관상 당아파트의 입주자들에게 많은 민원이 발생되고 있습니다.
현재 가축(개)을 사육하고 있는 세대에서는 단지내 산책, 화단출입, 놀이터 출입, 승강기 탑승을 절대 금지하여 주시고 가축들의 이동시에는 반드시 애관견 가방과 개줄을 이용하시 바랍니다

Rules for Pet-Breeding

■ Civil applications are frequented from tenants of this apartment complex due to issues related to hygienic as well as aesthetic aspect, such as pet excretion left unattended in elevator, flower bed, rooftop and children's playgroung, allergic conditions caused by animals, ticks, parasites and hair shedding, etc.
For pet-breeding households, it is requested to refrain from taking a walk around the complex, riding on elevator and entering flower bed as well as playground and to use pet-carrier(dog lead)when traveling with your pet.

MIKIPEDIA ENTRY

Michael Feldman

From Mikipedia, the free encyclopedia

For the Canadian politician, see Mike Feldman

Michael Feldman, the popular media icon and witty aphorist, is the host of *Michael Feldman's Whad'Ya Know?*, a radio program distributed by Public Radio International heard on maybe a gazillion stations in virtually every English and Latinate-based speaking nation, and in Farsi. His humor has been likened to that of Twain, Thurber, S.J. Perelman, and Cato (the Elder), being a homespun yet sophisticated amalgam of insightful satire and a wide-ranging cross-cultural intellectualism sometimes known as the Milwaukee School, for his hometown, where his alma mater has been named Washington High School in his honor. Self-effacing to the point of hardly ever referring to himself by name, Feldman has raised a generation of radio listeners who think of him as Uncle Feldman. A handsome man, Feldman had his choice of many women, selecting the one or two he did purely for genetic reasons, producing two flourishing female offspring who worship their father. In over twenty years hosting and producing *Whad'Ya Know?*, Feldman has never once abandoned his show to pursue an exchange student overseas. Winner of too many awards to mention, including the Madison (WI) Kiwanis Speaker Appreciation trophy, the Peabody Duck Walker honor, and the Neenah (WI) Foundry Personalized Manhole Cover, Feldman has more keys to more cities than you can shake a stick at (his youngest, in fact, teethed on the key to Omaha). Beloved is not too strong a word to describe the esteem Michael Feldman is held in by his adoring audience, many of whom credit him with bringing them together as couples and encouraging them to have families of their own. His charismatic, youthful appearance, often compared to a young Dick Clark, surprises some who come to the live show in Madison (WI) causing many to wonder why he's not in television, which Feldman dismisses as "Radio you have to look at." Feldman has contributed many aphorisms to the language, including the famous "Whad'Ya Know?—Not Much, You?" call and response, "listeners who are sticklers for truth should get their own shows," "sit on your hands and let someone else have a chance for a change," and many others, including the repeated use of "actually" to mean "really." Widely respected and feared among radio professionals, the "Host with the Most" has been added to the collection of the Museum of Broadcasting in New York (NY) and received the ceremonial coffee cup from the Chicago (IL) Broadcast Museum. A genius grant is rumored to be just around the corner. Michael Feldman has either written or read 7 or more highly acclaimed books, including *War and Peace, Madame Bovary,* and *Something I Said?: Innuendo and Out the Other.*

External links

- Biography at the notmuch.com website
- Profile at About.com
- Listed as Alive on deadoraliveinfo.com

This United States biographical article related to radio is a stub. You can help Mikipedia by expanding it.
Retrieved from "http://en.mikipedia.org/mikiMichael_Feldman"

Categories: 1949 births | Living people | American public radio personalities | American radio personalities | American humorists | Jewish American writers | Public Radio International | People from Madison, Wisconsin | People from Milwaukee | University of Wisconsin-Madison alumni | Wisconsin Public Radio | United States radio people stubs

ACKNOWLEDGMENTS

Thanks to everybody past and present on *Whad'Ya Know?* especially my cohorts, the Three J's: Jim Packard, John Thulin, and Jeff Hammon, and, of course, brother Clyde Stubblefield, the Funky Drummer, who travels with us but mostly stays in his room with the TV turned up and a bucket of wings. Not to forget my man, in the English sense, Lyle Anderson, who writes the prize copy that makes the young girls cry, and drives us around at a nice, steady pace. My researchers who try to make me sound like I know what I'm talking about, Diana Cook, whose drop is the front porch swing, and Kelley Osborne. Thanks to Nora Feldman, coincidentally my daughter, for the photo work and her brilliant essay on texting. lol. Esteemed *New Yorker* cartoonist Michael Shaw, who gladly gave up one of his "Feldman" attempts, making him now a *Whad'Ya Know?* cartoonist. And above all, John Frederick Sieger, musician, artist, man about town, probably even a raconteur for all I know, for his brilliant collaboration—man, you're the tooniest!